GW00391233

BUSINESS SUCCESS

A WAY OF THINKING ABOUT STRATEGY, CRITICAL SUPPLY CHAIN ASSETS AND OPERATIONAL BEST PRACTICE

by

Andrew Cox

EARLSGATE PRESS

Published by Earlsgate Press.

© Andrew Cox, 1997

First published: May 1997

British Library Cataloguing in Publication Data.

A catalogue record of this book is available from the British Library.

ISBN 1-873439-76-8

Printed in Great Britain by Bookcraft, Midsomer Norton, Bath, Somerset.

For Angela, Adam and Tom

CONTENTS

LIST OF FIGURES

PREFACE

1

Thinking Appropriately and Living with Uncertainty

This book is about business success. In it I seek to explain my own views about why it is that some companies and some people achieve sustainable success and others fail. I start from the premise that if you can explain success then you can also explain failure, and vice a versa. I also maintain that any explanation of business success and failure will only be valid if it can also explain individual, as well as corporate and national, success and failure.

My thesis is based on a very simple argument about the causes of corporate and individual success and failure. This argument is stated at the outset as a point of reference to which the reader may return as and when necessary. The thesis is as follows:

> *The dominant thinking in all of the current business management and economics literature is that sustainable business and individual success is about competing successfully against others in markets. My thesis is that this thinking is only partially correct.*

Next I argue that:

> **The control of relatively scarce material resources is the major factor in ensuring sustainable business success.**

From this position it follows that:

> **Owning, controlling and leveraging those resources which cannot easily be imitated in supply chains is the key to success. These resources, which allocate value in supply chains, are referred to as critical supply chain assets.**

In the discussion which follows, the concept of the *supply chain* refers to the complex networks of business relationships which exist between individuals and companies, for the production of goods and services to an end consumer. The idea of a supply chain is a metaphor which summarises a complex reality of inter-connected contractual relationships, both formal and informal, between individuals and companies. A contested market exists when more than one individual or company competes to provide particular supply chain products or services.

It follows from the above that, even if a company is currently a leading player within a particular supply chain, this is not an indicator of *sustainable* success. Indeed it could be that current success is only a temporary phenomenon and that failure will occur in the future. This comes about because of the inability by a firm to control the *critical assets* in a supply chain, as a relative monopolist, and because of management's lack of appreciation of their tenuous current position. Many companies in the past have seen their current positions of temporary supply chain dominance eroded without fully understanding why. The hope is that this book may help to clarify why this happens.

This is the starting point from which, as the reader will discover, a sustained critique of all of the dominant explanations of success and failure in current business management thinking is built. This is not to argue that everything that has been written in business management to date is wrong. That would be an inappropriate argument because many writers have successfully pointed to actions which have contributed to business success and failure through the ages. Rather it is to argue that most current writers, even when they point to evidence of actions which lead to success or failure, do not know when the actions they highlight will be appropriate for others to emulate and when they will not.

The key here is the concept of *appropriateness*. The test of a competent person in business (and in life) has to be seen in terms of their ability to know when certain actions are appropriate or not under given circumstances. All too often people are looking for an answer when they should be looking for *a way of thinking*. I say this because it is this realisation which has had a profound effect on my own life.

I write this preface as the Professor of Strategy and Procurement Management in the Business School at the University of Birmingham in England. But I have only been in this role since September 1994. For two years before that I was Professor and Head of the Department of Political Science and International Studies at the same University and, before that, the Director of the Centre for the Study of Political Economy at the University of Hull. I did not, therefore, start out with the ambition or the hope of writing anything about effective business management.

When I started my academic career almost twenty years ago I was more interested in the relationship between government and the people in different countries. I was particularly interested in **the concept of power**: why some people had it and some did not. I was also keen to discover if there were prescriptions one could make about how to organise political systems to ensure a more equitable distribution of the material wealth in any society.

I soon learned as a student and as a young academic that my own ideas about what was the most appropriate thing to do were naive and biased. My prescriptions were based on subjective views of what I wanted to see happen, rather than on any proper understanding and analysis of what could be achieved.

I also came to realise that there was very little certainty about what would happen in the future. Furthermore, I noted that although many academics could explain what had happened in the past I realised that they constantly argued about the causes of these past events. As a result, it seemed to me that there was little chance of ever arriving at a satisfactory *answer* to what causes things to happen politically.

Fortunately a former colleague of mine—the late political philosopher Bob Berki—once said to me: *"The only thing you have to learn at University is that you have to live with uncertainty. After that its just about how you cope with the knowledge that there are no certainties."*

This was for me an important statement because eventually I came to link this insight to the realisation that there is no single *answer* to anything. If the world is contingent—which means that things change constantly—and there is uncertainty about how things will change in the future then it is unlikely that the *answer* we believe to be true for success today will necessarily be true for tomorrow. But does that mean we are in a hopeless state of uncertainty where everything and anything might be appropriate to the achievement of success?

I believe the answer to this question to be a categorical no. I cannot speak for others. There are some who believe that, because the world is contingent, then all views are equally valid. I do not agree with this view nor with the view that because it is difficult, if not impossible to predict the future, that we may as well give up hope and do anything we like. My years of study and enquiry about history and political economy have taught me one thing above all others and that is that:

> **Certain things do not change even if the technological circumstances within which we experience them do.**

The *certain things* I have in mind here are the human condition, with its struggle by individuals to appropriate for themselves the material and spiritual things of life in an environment of absolute and relative scarcity. This, as I gradually came to realise, is what the study of power is ultimately all about.

The important question is not, therefore, which political system is best, because all political systems do the same thing. All such systems are simply mechanisms by which an individual, or groups of individuals, organise the allocation of scarcity within given territorial areas. This being so the more important question must surely be which of the different types of political system available to us is the most appropriate to achieve any desired given outcome at any moment in time?

This view of who should have political power and how it should be used to allocate scarcity is based on *a way of thinking*. It is based on the realisation that we should not focus on the immediacy of things politically but should understand from *first principles* the generic properties of the human condition and the logical way in which human beings can organise themselves to allocate material scarcity. By starting here we begin to understand that:

> **There are, in fact, only a limited number of ways of organising the allocation of scarcity and that they are unlikely to be newly invented by us today.**

Not surprisingly, I realised I had come to an understanding first proposed by Aristotle many centuries ago. "My" idea was very similar to the great philosopher. It was just that I took some time to put it into my own context.

Aristotle had, in the period before Christ, already provided a framework for all of the possible 'ideal-typical' forms of political rule that human beings are capable of creating. Basically, he concluded that it is possible to have government by one person, by a few people or by everyone. These three forms of rule—monism, oligarchy and democracy—were seen to be the only forms of government possible. However, Aristotle recognised that each type of rule could have relatively benign or pernicious consequences for particular groups of citizens governed under them.

What conclusions can one draw from this 'ideal-typical' thinking? First, if we start from *first principles* we are unlikely to come up with new ways of organising the ways in which human beings allocate absolute and relative scarcity. Human beings have been struggling with the same problems since the dawn of time and we are unlikely to arrive at a new way of managing this allocative problem. Second, if there are only a limited number of ways in which allocative scarcity can be organised politically, the key question must not be what new ways of organising are there. The key question ought to be, of those which are possible, which is the most appropriate for any desired outcome under the circumstances in which we find ourselves.

When I first came to these conclusions, it was a profound realisation as far as I was concerned, and left me profoundly disillusioned with the study of political power. The problem was that I had discovered *the answer*. The answer was that one type of political system was not necessarily better than any other. There is no 'best' political system. Rather, all political systems have particular properties but some systems are likely to be more appropriate for the achievement of given outcomes than others under different circumstances. The test of adequacy is not, therefore, one of perfection but always of the relative appropriateness of the form of political rule under given circumstances.

Having come to this conclusion I had decided in the late 1980s to undertake a second career to my original academic one, but this time in University administration. The reason for this was self-evident. Having arrived at *the answer*—that the world is contingent politically—there seemed little point in pursuing an academic research career because there was little else for me to discover. Then a second formative experience confronted me—just as I had begun to develop an administrative career.

In the spring of 1992 I attended a conference in Paris at the Palais de Congress on the Champs Elysees. The theme of the conference was about ways of improving public and private sector management, and whether lessons could be learnt from either current public or private sector approaches. I was giving a paper, with a research assistant, on the inappropriateness of the new experiment in hived-off agencies in UK central government. The conference changed my career path in ways I could not have known in advance.

Two eminent American scholars had been invited by the French hosts to give keynote speeches. One of the most famous American marketing professors in the contemporary world represented the private sector perspective and, an American political philosopher, was to provide the keynote address from a public sector perspective. What ensued radically changed the course of my intellectual life. The keynote address became a fiercely contested debate between two academics with completely different *ways of thinking* about what is appropriate for the achievement of effective management.

The marketing professor's view was clear and unequivocal. He argued that although we cannot be certain about what to do, the most appropriate thing to do was to test out empirically every 'fad' (newly fashionable idea about business success) from wherever it came. By this means, he contended, we would eventually arrive at an understanding of what is the most appropriate way of doing things. The political philosopher fundamentally and vigorously disagreed with this proposition. On the contrary, he argued, that we must work out logically, by deductive reasoning, what theoretically causes business success. Only in this way, he argued, would we come to understand which operational practices will be the most appropriate in achieving success under given circumstances.

The difference in these two approaches is quite clear. On the one hand, an *empiricist* argument was presented. This holds that the way to know what to do to achieve business success is through the copying, or through the adaptation, of the practices which others have developed in their own circumstances. The aim being to test whether these are appropriate in similar, or the same circumstances. This benchmarking approach is the dominant *way of thinking* (or methodology) within current approaches to success in the business management literature.

The philosopher's view was very different however, and more like the approach adopted by Aristotle. This speaker argued for the development of a *first principles* approach to success in business management. Implicitly he called for the *rational and deductive* categorisation of all of the 'ideal-typical' ways there are of organising the allocation of scarcity. It occured to me then that, if this could be done, it would be possible for individuals and companies to understand how they can maximise the appropriation and accumulation of material value for themselves under different but constantly changing circumstances.

This debate was the turning point, as far as I was concerned, in my career path. I realised then, and have been further convinced by subsequent reading and research, that what Aristotle had created deductively for political philosophy nobody has really begun to address in the field of business management. There simply is no proper categorisation in the literature of the 'ideal-typical' forms through which individuals and companies can appropriate and accumulate value for themselves. More importantly, perhaps, there has been no proper categorisation either of the dynamic factors which shape and transform the unique supply chains which have been created to deliver goods and services to end consumers.

This volume is a first attempt to begin to address this gap but it does not simply take only one side of the argument presented above as the most appropriate *way of thinking* about business success. On the contrary, while I certainly favour the starting point of rational and deductive reasoning, one cannot reject totally out of hand the empiricist approach. In what follows I will argue forcefully against the empiricist *way of thinking*, but I will also argue that the rational and deductive view is limited in at least one important respect.

It is only possible, in my view, to properly understand business success if one is able to link a theory of causality (which has been developed by rational and deductive logic) with a method of systematic empirical testing. This is not to argue that testing 'fads' is therefore appropriate; it is merely to recognise that logically derived theories must also be capable of empirical verification in the real world. In what follows I will argue, however, that the current preference amongst academics and practitioners for 'fad' and benchmarking approaches is an inappropriate way to think about business success and failure.

I believe it is important for the reader to understand this background because it informs much of what is to follow. This small volume was conceived very much as a *work in progress* rather than as a completed argument. It merely begins the process of trying to establish that an 'ideal-typical' categorisation of business success and failure under dynamic supply chain (rather than market) conditions is possible and appropriate. Much work will be needed to complete what is being started here because the task has never been properly attempted before. Despite the mass of literature dedicated to supply chains, it seems to me that there is no real understanding of supply chains in business. Furthermore, one can argue that no research has been undertaken which systematically tests out theoretical propositions about how companies and individuals appropriate material wealth (value) for themselves from their involvement in these chains.

Consequently, this volume will have served its purpose if it provides a robust starting place for what may follow. If it stimulates honest debate and constructive, rather than defensive and destructive, criticism then it will also have achieved what was intended. I am certain many people will disagree with much of what is said because the ideas in this volume challenge many of the current views about business management.

This is part of its purpose. That is to open a debate which, in my view, is essential to the development of business thinking. A debate which starts from the concept that under changing circumstances it is possible, using the *way of thinking* outlined here, to understand theoretically and from *first principles* which things are important and which are not under changing circumstances. If this proves to be possible, it will allow the most able and the most informed individuals and companies to sustain their ability to appropriate material scarcity on a continual basis in the future. The outcome of such a debate, and the passage of time, will endorse or otherwise the thesis which is presented in this volume.

One final and pleasant task remains. I could not have achieved what little I have without the help of innumerable people. If I do not mention everyone who has assisted me here this is only because space does not allow and I have been forced to be selective. Much of what I have been able to achieve academically in recent years has been made possible by Jackie Potter, whose support in all things at Birmingham has been well beyond the call of duty. Only I know how much I owe her. It is a pleasure to thank her publicly.

Much of what is written here would also not have been possible without the support and encouragement of Professor Colin Rickwood, the Head of the Birmingham Business School. I also owe a special thanks to all of the team at the Centre for Strategy and Procurement Management in Birmingham. Thanks are due to Christopher Bouverie-Brine, for giving me the space and the practical opportunity to test out these ideas 18 months ago, and for his fund of practical comments and insights related to the arguments in this volume. A special thanks is also due to Lisa Harris, Paul Ireland, Chris Lonsdale, Ian Thompson and Michael Townsend for taking forward the research which has begun to test out these ideas empirically. A particular debt is also owed to Joe Sanderson and Glyn Watson for their research assistance over many years and for their detailed and valuable comments on earlier drafts of this volume. Thanks also to Michele for her diligent typesetting.

Outside the 'Birmingham mafia' I would like to thank Robin Cammish for all of his encouragement in helping me to make the transition from the political economy to the business world, and

Professor Richard Lamming for his tremendous friendship and intellectual support in all things in this transition period. A special debt is owed to Jon Hughes for providing the opportunity for me to test some of these ideas in a consulting environment, and for his unstinting, but friendly, critical appraisal of all of my arguments. I would also like to thank Javier Urioste for his helpful comments and for the vision he and his colleagues showed in allowing an iconoclast to discuss and debate these issues in the operational environment of a major multinational company.

Finally can I thank Professor David Farmer, whose encouragement, constructive criticism, fund of common-sense and belief in what I am trying to do in this volume, has been one of the most pleasant and rewarding aspects of the gestation process by which it has finally reached a wider public.

Angela, Adam and Tom know how important they have been in allowing me the time and space to complete this, I thank them yet again for granting it to me and dedicate the book to them.

Any sins of commission or omission are obviously mine alone.

Andrew Cox
Stratford-upon-Avon
March 1997

SECTION A

INTRODUCTION

2

Ignorance, Knowledge and Understanding

This book is about business success and failure. It is also about *ways of thinking* about how individuals and companies achieve sustainable success.

> *Sustainable success is defined as the ability by individuals or companies to maximise their capacity to appropriate and accumulate material wealth for themselves in an environment of absolute and relative material scarcity.*

It will be obvious that this definition of success can also be applied just as readily to nation-states. Countries seek to achieve sustainable national success by having within their boundaries individuals and companies that have the capacity to accumulate and appropriate material wealth from a global environment of absolute and relative material scarcity.

A word of caution is however necessary at the outset. This is not another *academic or consultants cookbook*. The arguments presented in this volume are simple enough. However, in order to be able to apply them effectively in a business environment, they necessitate considerable thought.

Yet, since the potential rewards for this effort are so great that effort will be well rewarded. No apology is made for this, although the author recognises that readers with different levels of experience and knowledge may read it.

In order to assist readers in this task every effort has been made to present the ideas in as clear a manner as possible. Although some of the ideas presented here are complex, and may challenge received wisdom and understanding, the author believes that if the reader starts at the beginning, and thinks carefully about the logical steps in the argument, then everything will become clear.

This means that if the reader has decided to skip the preface to this book then he or she may have made a mistake. The preface of this book explains what the author is trying to achieve and why. If the reader wants to really understand why this book has been written, and what the goals of the author are, then they are advised to read the preface before going any further.

> ***Please read the preface now if you have not already done so***

On Ignorance

The reason why it is important that the preface is read is because there is a tendency for busy people to skip the most important things. This is as true for books as it is for life in general. A large part of the argument in this book is about **appropriateness**, or people doing those things which have a high certainty of delivering valued outcomes.

If the book is about appropriateness it must also, logically, be about people failing to do what is appropriate. A substantial part of the argument in this book is that individuals and companies fail because they do not do the obvious and recognise the important things which are in front of them. The reason for this is that they are ignorant.

Ignorance means two things:

First, that people do not know what is the appropriate thing to do to achieve valued outcomes under different circumstances.

Second, that people do not have an appropriate way of thinking which will allow them to see, or to understand, what actually confronts them.

Ignorance, as defined here, is not therefore used in a derogatory way. It does not mean boorish and uncouth behaviour, nor does it mean stupidity, it means a lack of enlightenment.

Did you skip the preface? If you did then you took inappropriate action. All books are partial; they only deal with certain things. It is therefore imperative that the potential reader tries to understand as quickly as possible what the author is not covering, and why.

If you did read the preface then you are obviously doing something that is appropriate to the task in hand, but you may not know why. If you did not read the preface it is clear that, in the present context you did not know what was appropriate. However, you do now.

Hopefully, in reading the preface several things will have become clear:

- First, if you want to find out quickly why this book was written, and what its central arguments are, then it is best to read the preface first and not to read the text in a random fashion. This is an important learning experience in the context of this book because it is certain that if you do not start at the beginning you will not understand what is being said at the end. This simple example is crucial to the argument in this book and leads to:

The First Principle of Business Success.

> *Starting from 'first principles' is one of the keys to business success.*

- Second, the author believes that most of the currently dominant thinking in business management and economics is partial and based on *inappropriate ways of thinking*. This is not to argue that all of current thinking is wrong in its analysis of business success, but that the author believes that current analysis starts from the wrong place and with a lack of theoretical rigour. This leads to:

The Second Principle of Business Success.

If you focus on inappropriate things you will not be successful.

- Third, the author believes that the human condition does not change. It is, and has always been, about the struggle by individuals to create opportunities to appropriate and accumulate material wealth for themselves under conditions of relative and, in some cases, absolute scarcity. A further principle flows from this insight:

The Third Principle of Business Success:

It is highly unlikely that we will be able to invent new ways of achieving business success.

- Fourth, if the human condition does not change then there must be invariant and generic ways which people have used, and continue to use, to accumulate and appropriate material wealth for themselves out of scarcity. There will clearly be a range of approaches which individuals and companies can take but the argument developed in this book is linked to:

The Fourth Principle of Business Success.

> *The most appropriate strategy under all circumstances is to leverage those critical supply chain assets which can be owned or controlled.*

- Fifth, even though the human condition does not change the technological and regulatory circumstances under which it is experienced do. This is a very important fact. If technological and regulatory circumstances change then it is likely that the value of the current resources in society, and the valuable or *critical assets* within supply chains, will also change. Individuals and companies must therefore develop ways of adapting to change. This leads to:

The Fifth Principle of Business Success.

> *It is critically important to monitor the impact of technological and regulatory change on current supply chain assets and resources.*

- Sixth, it follows that sustainable business success is ultimately about developing an understanding of the impact of technological and regulatory change on the existing value of things. Only by doing this, it can be argued, is it possible to develop strategies and operational practices which allow individuals and companies to take ownership and control of those things in supply chains which are critical to the appropriation and accumulation of value. This leads to:

The Sixth Principle of Business Success.

It is more appropriate to develop ways of thinking about the criticality of assets in supply chains than to develop knowledge of products, services or markets.

The problem with this short summary of the arguments developed in this volume is that the reader may now *know* a large part of what the author has concluded, but he or she does not necessarily *understand* how the author has arrived at these conclusions, or why. In other words, the reader is not yet aware of the *way of thinking* which has allowed the author to arrive at the conclusion that certain actions are more appropriate than others to achieve business success. The reader is not properly enlightened because he or she has knowledge but not necessarily understanding.

It is a central tenet of the views expressed in this book that individuals should recognise their own ignorance and lack of enlightenment. This is because only by so doing is it possible for anybody to develop the knowledge and understanding about which things are appropriate, under given circumstances, to achieve valued outcomes. The fundamental problem is, however, that one of the most difficult things for individuals to acknowledge is their own ignorance.

When confronted with their own lack of awareness, or evidence that what they believe to be true is not so, people have a tendency to act irrationally. A rational person, when confronted by his or her own ignorance, or a gap between what they think is true and what is true, should accept the facts and change his or her opinions. Unfortunately the majority of people appear, in the author's experience at least, to do the opposite. They either refuse to believe what is before them, deny the facts or try to find alternative explanations or evidence in order to protect the original opinions which they have always held.

Those seeking solutions to why the management of change is so difficult to achieve need to look no further. Managing change is difficult for two primary reasons:

> *People do not really understand how to achieve business success, because they do not know which actions are most appropriate to achieve particular valued outcomes now, or in the future.*

and;

> *People resist innovation, because they are comfortable with those behaviours which have always allowed them to achieve valued outcomes in the past, and do not understand why change is now appropriate.*

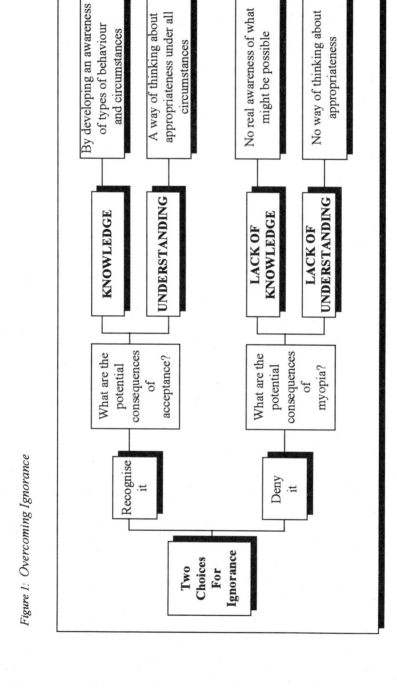

Figure 1: Overcoming Ignorance

If one wishes to manage change in any circumstances it is necessary to employ people who have open minds, and the capacity to recognise their own ignorance, or educate those who do not to develop this *way of thinking*. It also helps, of course, if senior managers themselves are prepared to recognise that they too are unenlightened. If senior managers could do this then they might be able to recognise that what was done in detail in the past might not have been the most appropriate way of doing things, and even if it was, it may not be the most appropriate thing to do in the future as circumstances change.

The recognition of ignorance is the easiest thing to do for an educated person because the more one knows and understands the more one realises there is to know and understand. No individual who is ever born will fully understand and know all there is to know so why do people find it so difficult to say "I don't know?". If people could only recognise, what Figure 1 demonstrates, that their own knowledge and understanding is limited, and keep an open mind, then they would more quickly learn what is appropriate under given circumstances.

There is a further problem, too. It is not just that people are unprepared to accept their own lack of understanding; they are also unprepared to recognise that knowledge is not really valuable in its own right. Knowledge is only valuable if a person understands when any particular piece of information can be used to achieve a specific desired outcome.

On Knowledge

Most people in the business community are interested in *best practice*. They are also interested in *world class* operational practices. There is also an industry of consultants and academics who peddle knowledge of *global best practice* and encourage the *benchmarking* of one's current practices against those of other companies. This view of business improvement and success is perhaps the dominant *way of thinking* in modern business management.

> ***One major argument of this volume is that normally benchmarking is an inappropriate way of thinking about business success. This is because it often leads to the adoption of 'fads' which fail.***

When the author says this to practitioners he normally experiences tremendous scepticism and sometimes a great deal of opposition and hostility from the audience. The reason for this is because people do not understand what the author means. Those who challenge this argument do not ask why or how the speaker has arrived at this conclusion but seek, first, to refute the thesis on the grounds that they have personally copied or adapted a certain company's practices and it has led to business success and improvement. If the author disagrees and points out that the basis of *sustainable business success* is not about copying or adapting, but about owning and controlling assets so that others cannot imitate or replicate them, the practitioner usually responds by saying that this is fine but he or she needs to have operational answers today about what should be done.

What is happening here is a dialogue of the deaf, as Figure 2 demonstrates. There is clearly a failure of minds to meet. The author is attempting to explain to the audience his *way of thinking* about causality in business success. The practitioner, on the other hand, is concerned to prove that his or her personal experience is the most appropriate way of doing things. The practitioner is concerned to reinforce his or her own belief that what he or she is doing is appropriate. This is because their working lives are dominated by the need to meet short-term

Figure 2 : Types of Benchmarking

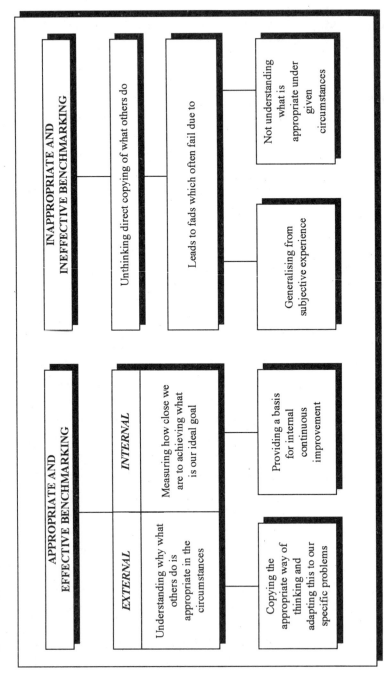

APPROPRIATE AND EFFECTIVE BENCHMARKING

EXTERNAL

Understanding why what others do is appropriate in the circumstances

Copying the appropriate way of thinking and adapting this to our specific problems

INTERNAL

Measuring how close we are to achieving what is our ideal goal

Providing a basis for internal continuous improvement

INAPPROPRIATE AND INEFFECTIVE BENCHMARKING

Unthinking direct copying of what others do

Leads to fads which often fail due to

Generalising from subjective experience

Not understanding what is appropriate under given circumstances

operational targets. Whilst achieving these targets is in one way appropriate, it may not be in the context of the arguments presented in this volume.

There is an old saying that a little knowledge can be a dangerous thing. Never was a truer statement made of practitioners at all levels of business management. Managers do not have the luxury of time to think systematically about what they are doing and whether or not it is appropriate; what they have are deadlines and a need to achieve short-term targets. In achieving these targets those who succeed will be, by definition, those who, for whatever reason, are doing something which is in some way appropriate.

The problem is, however, that even if what is being done now does lead to some success it is not always obvious whether this or some other—not currently known—practice might be even more appropriate, and capable of generating even higher levels of success than existing operational practices. Furthermore, even if what practitioners are doing under one circumstance may be wholly appropriate it is not necessarily the case that the same practices will always be appropriate for other individuals or companies under all other circumstances.

Consider for a moment the use of the Just-in-Time (JIT) approach. Japanese car assemblers, such as Toyota, use this approach in their production assembly processes. A large number of manufacturing companies around the world, both within and outside the car industry, are copying and adapting the JIT principle as a way of improving their business processes. It would surely be silly for someone to argue that this may not be the most appropriate way for *all* companies in the car sector, or in manufacturing globally, to organise their production and supply relationship practices. The author does not, however, think that this is, necessarily, the most appropriate thing for all manufacturing companies to do.

The reason most people copy JIT practices is because they reason that, if JIT is what Toyota and other Japanese car assemblers do, then, because they have demonstrably been successful in world markets, it is obvious that the adoption of JIT leads to business success. It can be argued, however, that JIT is not necessarily the most appropriate way to manage manufacturing assembly and supply relationships under all circumstances. This argument can be developed on purely theoretical grounds and is not dependent, necessarily, on the observance of other companies' practices.

The argument here is simple enough. Toyota must have had specific reasons why it originally developed JIT. The reasons may have had very little to do with the company deciding that it should create the ideal way to manage production and assembly processes. Perhaps the most important reasons were the shortage and cost of land in Japan and the fact that, historically, Toyota already had—by chance—suppliers in close proximity and a relationship power structure which allowed it to be able to control what its most important suppliers were doing. This relationship structure is based on the creation of *a hierarchy of structured dominance* and was historically built into the zaibatsu structure of Japanese society and economy. *In these circumstances* JIT was a logical and eminently sensible thing for Toyota to do.

It was this powerful set of mutually reinforcing factors which, once put together with other factors, like design and specification excellence, disciplined and relatively cheap labour and a low currency, allowed Toyota and other Japanese car manufacturers to achieve a competitive advantage over others in the world market. JIT was arguably only one factor in this success but, for some benchmarking inclined academics, consultants and practitioners it has become the most important reason for success. Unfortunately, even though the (potentially fortuitous?) discovery of a more efficient way of managing production, through assembly and collaborative supply chain control, rather than through vertical integration and arms-length supplier contempt, may have contributed to success the circumstances which generated this are contingent. Those things which contributed to success in the past may not necessarily be the most appropriate things to do to achieve success in the future.

This can be understood easily enough if we think of the difficulties Toyota now faces after the recognition by others of what it has been doing. The problem that Toyota has had to grapple with is that other people copy what it has done. Today, because a sufficient number of car assemblers have done so, and have been able to achieve similar operational benefits, Toyota faces severe competition. This, as Michael Porter has recently recognised, leads to the erosion of profitability as people compete aggressively, and undermines business success in the long-term. (Porter, 1996) Toyota can only sustain its business success, therefore, if it can ultimately find something which others cannot copy or imitate, or if it can create barriers to entry through scale economies based on volume production.

There is another problem with this assumption that copying can lead to success, which can be referred to as the *tyranny of experience*. What this means is that practitioners have knowledge of particular practices and, when they move from one supply chain and market structure to another, they believe that because things worked in one environment they will always work in others.

It has already been argued that copying within the same supply chain and market is no certain route to sustainable success. It follows, therefore, that trying to introduce and copy those practices which were appropriate in one supply chain in a totally different one is highly unlikely to be a recipe for success. The reason for this is that supply chains have unique properties which require specific and appropriate treatment if sustainable business success is to be achieved in them.

The message here is clear. It is possible to have all of the knowledge in the world about what is and has been done in the past, and to know descriptively all of the practices of a particular company. The problem is, however, that copying these practices does not guarantee that success will be achieved. Success is always about understanding when it is appropriate to use a particular practice, not about knowing that it exists. The problem for practitioners is that, unfortunately, a great number of those who discuss business management academically do not seem to have grasped this simple truth.

Many business writers have knowledge of what companies have done, but do not understand how to think about causality. As a result, they cannot provide practitioners with useful ways of thinking about which actions ◂ are most appropriate under given circumstances.

On Understanding

Most of the *ways of thinking* which are used in business consultancy and academic writing are poor guides to business success, because they fail to differentiate between the description of what is, or has been, and the explanation of what to do under given circumstances to achieve particular valued outcomes. This can be demonstrated if we look at a number of aids to understanding, which are commonly used in current business thinking.

One commonly used technique in personal development and the management of change is the idea that people should differentiate between the urgent and the important. By being able to differentiate between what is important and what is not, and between what is urgent and what is not, it is argued that people and companies will be more successful. This is demonstrated pictorially below:

Figure 3: **Differentiating Between the Urgent and the Important**

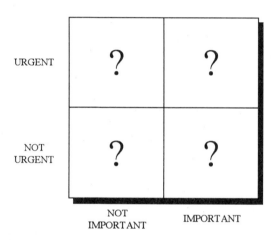

This *way of thinking* is useful at one level. That is that it has the effect of encouraging people to differentiate between a range of factors in relation to what the user may believe to be important and urgent. This is a useful heuristic device and a sensible way of ordering our thoughts.

As useful as it is however it also has major weaknesses as Figure 4 demonstrates. The most important of these is the problem that while it forces us to recognise the *need* to differentiate between things, it provides no guidance at all on *how* we should select amongst those things which might be done. For the framework to be an effective management tool it would also need to indicate *how to select* from all of the options available. The framework has no practical utility unless we

Figure 4: Deductive and Causal Explanations

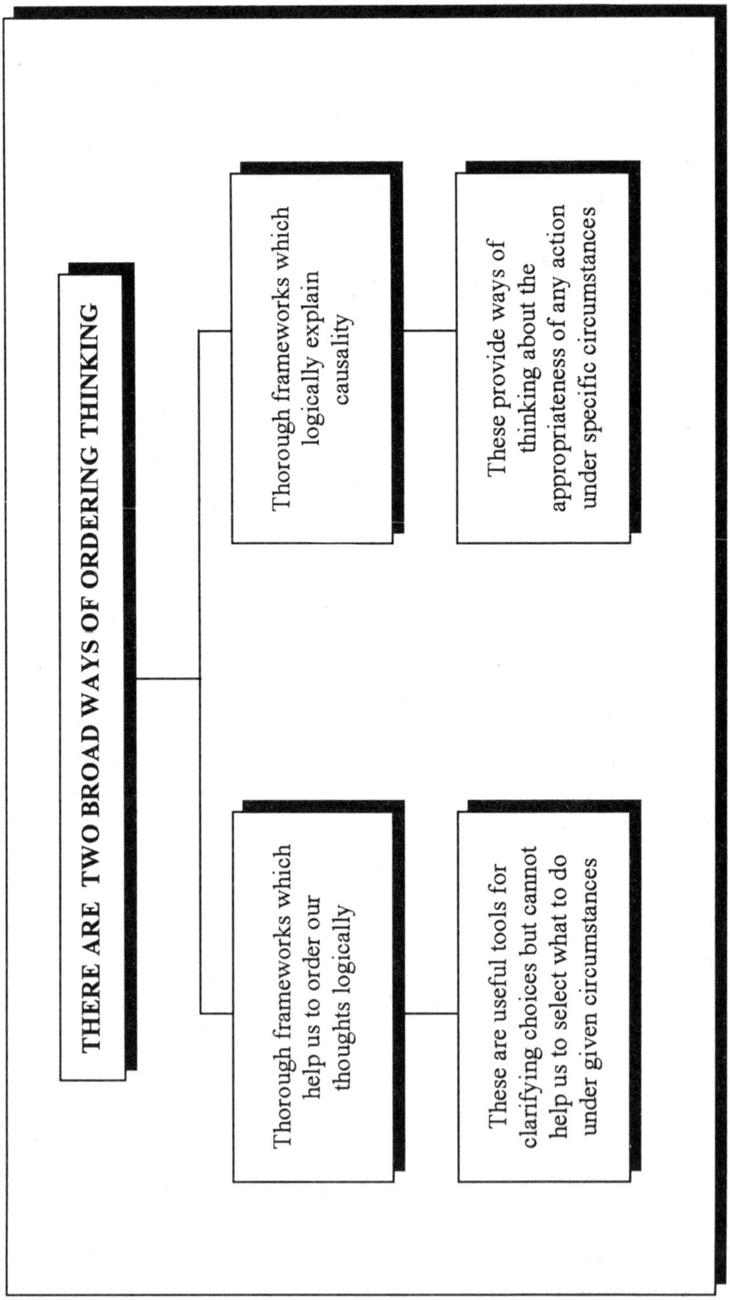

THERE ARE TWO BROAD WAYS OF ORDERING THINKING

Thorough frameworks which help us to order our thoughts logically

These are useful tools for clarifying choices but cannot help us to select what to do under given circumstances

Thorough frameworks which logically explain causality

These provide ways of thinking about the appropriateness of any action under specific circumstances

understand what *is* important and urgent under specific circumstances.

In the absence of this understanding all we have is knowledge or subjective prejudice. This can be explained simply if we think about how different representatives of functional departments in a company might fill in the 'important/urgent framework'. One might expect that an engineer would argue that introducing JIT is the most important and urgent thing that his company should do. On the other hand, someone from marketing in the same company might believe that developing a customer focused information system is the most critical thing for success. How would we know which one of these 'things to do' is urgent and important, whether both are, or whether neither are?

The engineer's experience will lead him to conclude that *best practice* is to introduce what other companies are doing at the 'leading edge' of manufacturing practice. The marketeer would surely argue that their experience tells them that a focus on the customer is absolutely critical for success.

The obvious solution to this problem of partial and subjective perspectives is to argue that it is properly the role of the CEO and the Board to know what is the most appropriate thing to do. The CEO and the Board have the role and responsibility of knowing what is strategic (important and urgent) and what is not. It is their task to recognise the subjectivity of lower tiers in the organisation, and to provide an overall focus and perspective for the company.

Obviously, in theory, this is what the CEO and the Board are supposed to do, but, just like everyone else in business, they can only do this if *they* understand causality. The CEO and the Board can only fill in the urgent and important boxes if they know what is appropriate under given circumstances. To know what is appropriate requires that the CEO and the Board, just like everyone else, must have comprehensive knowledge of all of the practices which are potentially available to them, and all of the potential circumstances which may confront them.

Only by knowing these two *necessary conditions* is it possible to begin to understand what is appropriate for an individual or a company to do. Unfortunately, these two necessary conditions, are not sufficient on their own. There is, as Figure 5 indicates, a further *sufficient condition*. The *sufficient condition* is a theory of how human beings appropriate and accumulate value from supply chains under conditions of absolute and relative scarcity.

- *Understanding in the context of business success is, therefore, defined as the capacity to know all of the potential practices which are available to a person and all of the circumstances which might confront them.*

- *But also the ability to be able to explain how human beings accumulate and appropriate value from supply chains under conditions of absolute and relative scarcity.*

Clearly, to have knowledge is a pre-requisite of having the type of understanding outlined above. The problem with knowledge is, however, that on its own it cannot provide the basis for an understanding of what is appropriate. Understanding what is appropriate involves a relationship between knowing what is potentially possible, and knowing the contingent circumstances which confront the individual and the company at any moment in time. But while knowing these two things is a necessary condition for business success, it is not sufficient on its own. The sufficient condition for understanding in business is sometimes referred to as *nous*.

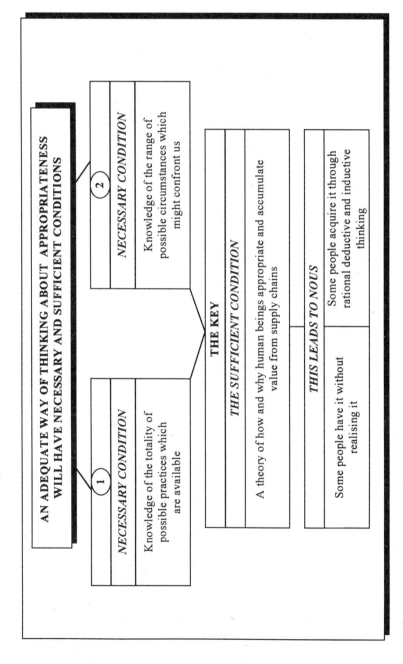

Figure 5: On Necessary and Sufficient Conditions

AN ADEQUATE WAY OF THINKING ABOUT APPROPRIATENESS WILL HAVE NECESSARY AND SUFFICIENT CONDITIONS

①

NECESSARY CONDITION

Knowledge of the totality of possible practices which are available

②

NECESSARY CONDITION

Knowledge of the range of possible circumstances which might confront us

THE KEY

THE SUFFICIENT CONDITION

A theory of how and why human beings appropriate and accumulate value from supply chains

THIS LEADS TO NOUS

Some people have it without realising it

Some people acquire it through rational deductive and inductive thinking

> *'Nous' refers to that ability which some people possess unwittingly, and which others may acquire through deductive and inductive logic, which allows them to know which factors determine the appropriation and accumulation of value in supply chains and markets.*

Some people would argue that *nous* cannot be acquired, though the position taken here is that it can. This will only be achieved, however, if people are prepared to reposition their thinking. The Figure which follows is indicative of what is necessary for the individual to do to achieve this.

Figure 6: Five Principles of Personal Development

- *Understand that the recognition of ignorance is the beginning of knowledge and understanding*

- *Accept that the more that you know, the more you will realise how much there is to know*

- *Always seek understanding rather than knowledge for its own sake*

- *Accept that there is unlikely to be a single answer, only alternatives with different consequences*

- *Seek to develop appropriate ways of thinking about what causes business success to occur*

If it is possible for individuals to adopt this open and questioning frame of mind, with its focus on understanding, then they will discover that what they first thought were certainties may not be so. If they recognise this they may come to the realisation that many of the tools and techniques which they have historically used to guide their actions may not be as appropriate as they first believed them to be.

This approach is nothing more than the development of a different *way of thinking* about the causes of business success and failure. The benefit of this open-minded *way of thinking* can be demonstrated simply by using it to question the utility of two of the most commonly used ways of thinking in modern strategic management—SWOT analysis and Business Process Re-engineering (BPR).

Figure 7: SWOT Analysis

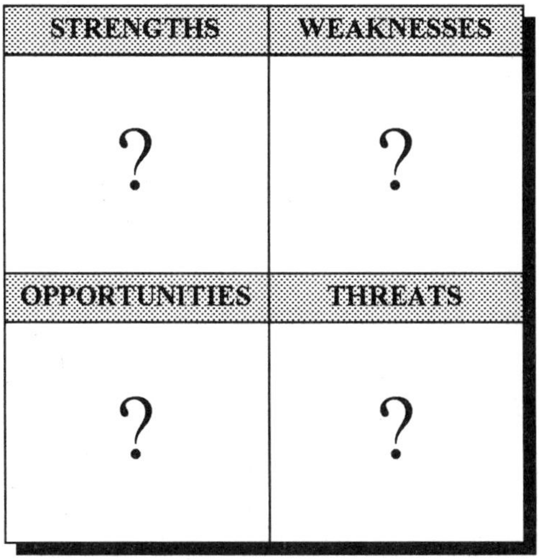

STRENGTHS	WEAKNESSES
?	?
OPPORTUNITIES	THREATS
?	?

Figure 7 reproduces the SWOT framework, which is clearly nothing more than a mechanism for ordering our thoughts logically. It is clear that it has no value in its own right unless the user has some mechanism by which he or she can bring it to life.

When most people use this framework, they fill in the boxes on the basis of their subjective perception of what is important. Yet, if the argument presented here is accepted, it is clear that this is just as likely to be wholly inappropriate as it is to be appropriate. The reason is that most people are ignorant of what causes business success under all contingent circumstances and, as a result, they are in no position to know what *is* a strength, a weakness, an opportunity or a threat. Only by having an understanding of causality can anyone fill in the SWOT framework in a practically useful way.

The same logic can be used to explain why it is highly unlikely, other than by chance, that the recent penchant for BPR programmes will achieve anything other than limited improvement in business performance.

The 'BPR fad' is based on the initial marketing of a new manifesto for business revolution by a consultancy company in the early 1990s. (Hammer & Champy, 1993) The basic recommendation of this book was that companies need to *'start over';* because of the impact of three Cs: customers are taking charge of exchange relationships, competition is intensifying, and change is becoming constant. As a result, the book recommends that all companies now need to become flexible, responsive, customer focused, and innovative, and that the way· to do this is to re-engineer all business processes. By business processes the writers mean those activities which take an input and create an output that is of value to the customer.

The central idea here is that companies have historically focused on the division of labour, economies of scale and the hierarchical control of tasks, and that they have not focused on the processes which pass value from what comes into the company and is then transferred, as a finished product or service, to the end customer. By starting from scratch and rethinking from the ground up, the writers argue, that companies can reinvent their businesses by radically redesigning the very basis on which work is organised.

The overall approach is grounded in the view that companies achieve success by having processes which allow them to be the lowest cost or best quality producers. This view has led to the simplistic and mistaken idea that companies exist to pass value to customers. Process mapping and redesign was, therefore, seen as a way to allow companies to understand where value is added internally, and to focus their activities appropriately in those areas.

The BPR revolution has certainly made some people rich but has it achieved the benefits expected? The answer is probably no. While there is no doubt that the approach has been beneficial in encouraging companies to question functional ways of thinking, most of the companies which have spent an inordinate amount of staff time and effort on process mapping and redesign will probably have failed to see significant returns from the exercise.

One has to say *probably* because, in the absence of proper empirical research, there is no evidence to make a categorical statement in either direction. It is interesting to note, however, that the original authors have recently publicly admitted that the revolution has not achieved its intended benefits, because they under-estimated the importance of people in the re-engineering process. (Hammer, 1996)

This is an interesting admission, because it can be construed either as an admission of failure, or as an attempt to justify it by blaming the people who were supposed to be implementing BPR for not understanding what was initially being proposed. There is, of course, another explanation of failure, and that is that the whole approach was *'nonsense on stilts'*. This phrase refers to a model of causal explanation which is based on truisms and half-digested and misunderstood factors, cobbled together into a wholly spurious but glitzy package, which bears so little relevance to reality that any evidence that its use leads to business success must be wholly ascribed to chance.

Why is BPR like this? The basic reason is that the reasoning on which the original book is predicated is faulty and spurious. A few examples will suffice to make the point. Nobody could disagree with the truisms that companies must be flexible, responsive, customer-focused, and innovative. If the world is contingent, then these characteristics are a pre-requisite of business survival, never mind business success, for everyone.

The problem is that Hammer and Champy argue that this is a new phenomenon when clearly it is not. They argue that the reason why companies now have to focus on these issues is a consequence of increased competition, new technology, and increasing customer demands. The difficulty one has with this view is that Hammer and Champy are not describing something that is new, they are merely describing the state of nature within which business has operated throughout the ages.

If companies and individuals have always had to operate within an environment in which change is part of the state of existence, why is it that companies should focus on process re-engineering today, rather than on other factors to achieve business success? Unfortunately, Hammer and Champy demonstrate no awareness of the totality of ways in which a company might sustain its business, or any understanding of the proximate circumstances under which any of these alternative practices might be appropriate for business success. They appear to assume that the impact of the changes they describe will be experienced in exactly the same way by all companies in all sectors and in all supply chains. This is clearly a logical nonsense.

The test of good business advice is the ability of the advisor to demonstrate a knowledge of both the generic and the specific factors which uniquely impinge upon the ability of the company to achieve value appropriation and accumulation, not a desire to impose one specific practice as a general solution across industry as a whole. Since Hammer and Champy provide no coherent explanation of why what they propose is more important than any other technique which might be available to a company for sustaining profitability, one must conclude that there can be no a priori justification for the use of a BPR approach.

Interestingly enough, while technological change regularly impacts dynamically on supply chains, Hammer and Champy appear to have completely failed to notice one of the most important factors which has threatened existing corporate profitability. This is the removal of those governmentally imposed artificial barriers to trade, which historically restricted competition within specific territorial areas of the globe. The wave of liberalisation and de-regulation has been one of the most significant factors which has challenged corporate success in recent years. One may ask, therefore, how does process re-engineering help us to understand this important phenomenon and how will its application help us to develop appropriate contingency measures to deal with its consequences?

The answer to this question is that it cannot help us to achieve either of these objectives because the thinking is faulty. The whole book is replete with half-truths and spurious generalisations. For example, it is argued that business success is about inventing new ways of doing business. The *way of thinking* developed in this volume would lead one to contend that this is a naive argument, because there are only certain, well defined ways in which human beings can appropriate and accumulate value from supply chains. The only thing that will be new, therefore, is the technological and regulatory circumstances under which these traditional value appropriation and accumulation techniques are used.

Re-engineering business processes simply cannot help us to understand what is to be done, because the thinking provides no basis for anyone to understand what are the appropriate things to do, now or in the future. The experience that most people have had of BPR is that it is simply another way of describing what *is* within the company. As a result, the existing activities of the company become a battleground for all of those functional specialists who see the process review as an opportunity to win control over even more areas of the business. It is not surprising, therefore, that BPR has had many converts. Equally, it should come as no surprise that it has provided little in the way of dramatic improvements in competitive performance.

Conclusions

The problem is clear. BPR may be a novel process-based *way of thinking* about existing functions in a business, but it is asking the wrong questions and starts from an inappropriate starting place if an understanding of the keys to sustainable business success is what is sought. It is not, however, the BPR gurus who are solely guilty of this error. As will be argued later, most of the current thinking in business management appears to be equally culpable in the way in which it approaches the analysis of business success and failure. The fundamental problem appears to be a lack of theoretical rigour, which leads to a misunderstanding by business writers of how it is possible to know what is a causal factor, and what is not, in any business circumstance.

The central argument in this book is that many writers simply do not understand what causes business success and business failure, and that they are attempting to generalise for business as a whole from a few idiosyncratic examples of what specific companies have done under unique, contingent circumstances. This is clearly neither logical nor is it likely to lead to appropriate prescriptions for business. The answer must be to recognise that explanations of causality can only be derived from a prior theorisation of the causes of business success, which can then be tested against empirical events.

To make this categorical statement, and to be able to predict in advance of implementation, why many of the things which are proposed by business writers will fail, is only possible, however, if one has already developed a prior theorisation of the causes of business success and failure. This development of a prior theory of causality provides the basis on which the present author holds views about what causes success different from the ones which others appear to hold. The remainder of this volume is devoted to introducing the reader to this *way of thinking*.

In the first major section that follows the *way of thinking* which informs the argument in this book is explained theoretically. It is argued that current business thinking is neither theoretically, nor is it epistemologically, robust and that, as a result, it fails to understand the causal factors in business success. A more theoretically robust method of analysis is presented based on the idea of *abstractive reasoning*.

In the second major section this *abstractive way of thinking* is used to develop a theory of causality in business success. This theory focuses on **asset criticality** in supply chains, and contends that entrepreneurial action is the basis of sustainable business success. Ideally, this entrepreneurial action needs, it is argued, to be focused on the use of leverage and market closure, in order that a monopoly control and ownership of **critical supply chain assets** can be achieved. In the final section a brief overview is provided to explain how this strategic *way of thinking* can be operationalised by individuals and companies. This process is called **business praxis.**

SECTION B

THE POVERTY OF THEORY IN BUSINESS THINKING

3

Ways Of Thinking About Causality And Success

It should be clear that the preface and introduction have been a way of signposting the fundamental problem which this book addresses. This problem is the belief by the author that business writing suffers from a lack of epistemological and theoretical rigour. If most ways of thinking in business are based on a lack of understanding of how to think properly about causality, it is hardly surprising that most writers do not understand which things are appropriate and which are not under given circumstances. The dilemma is simply expressed:

If business writers do not know how to think about causality their prescriptions for practitioners are unlikely to work, other than by chance.

The fundamental problem here is the way in which writers think about what causes any particular outcome to occur. To put it another way, how is that any writer knows which factors, from the multitude of potential variables that might be determinant, are more important than others. Only if the business writer has a *way of thinking* about the world that allows him or her to understand correctly, and with a high degree of certainty, which *are* the most important factors will operationally relevant advice be made available. This is because such a *way of thinking* will lead to a high probability that any behaviour adopted will be appropriate under the contingent circumstances that any individual or company faces.

There is however a major problem. There is a *dominant way of thinking* in the current business management literature. This approach starts from a research technique which is premised on the subjective observation of empirical events, and the pursuit of *best practice* through copying and adaptation. This *way of thinking* it is argued here, is flawed in one major respect. This flaw resides in a tendency *to let events speak for themselves,* and is one of the major weaknesses within business management thinking today. This *way of thinking* is sometimes referred to as **barefoot or systematic empiricism**.

It will be argued in this chapter that this *way of thinking* (which is primarily based on inductive reasoning) could, if human beings had all the time in the world, lead eventually to understanding and knowledge about what is appropriate for the achievement of business success. Since human beings do not have all of the time they require, it is argued that there is a more appropriate way of developing scientific knowledge and understanding about business success and failure. This approach is based on the fusion of deductive reasoning (in one's head though logical deduction) and inductive reasoning (in one's head from detailed observation), and requires the development and testing of a prior theorised view of business success. This *way of thinking* is called **abstractive reasoning**.

The chapter is devoted to outlining the differences between abstractive and empiricist approaches to an understanding of the causes of business success and failure. The chapter is divided into three sections. In the first section the difficulty which individuals and companies face when they adopt a benchmarking and 'fads' approach to business success is outlined. In the second section the relative utility of deductive, inductive and abstractive ways of thinking about causality are outlined. In the final section a *way of thinking* about how to operationalise the strategic ideal in an optimal manner is presented.

'Best Practice' and The Myopia of Benchmarking and 'Fads'

One of the fundamental questions which this chapter seeks to address is how do we know whether any particular operational intervention is appropriate to deliver business success? This is just another way of asking how do we know which operational behaviour constitutes *best practice*? In answering this question five basic points are developed in this book about the alignment of business strategy and operational practice and, although they have been touched on earlier, they need to be clearly stated because they inform everything which follows. They are presented in Figure 8.

It will be clear to the reader that the arguments presented in Figure 8 clearly fly in the face of much of the current dominant logic within business management thinking. Many academics and consultants argue that there are definite 'world class practices' which, if companies copy them, will inevitably lead to higher levels of sustainable business success. Indeed most of the dominant thinking in the management literature, with its recent penchants for MRP2 systems, total quality management, Outsourcing and core competence analysis, business process re-engineering and, more recently, partnership and collaborative approaches, is in this mould.

The problem with many of these 'world class' solutions is that they are proffered without any robust theoretical or empirical verification. All too often these 'fads' (newly fashionable management practices) are nothing more than simplistic generalisations which have been developed from a

Figure 8: *Five Keys to Strategic and Operational Alignment*

- *There can be no single answer to the question of what is operational 'best practice' because of the contingent nature of the world within which companies operate.*

- *If successful operational practices are necessarily contingent, successful business strategy is not. Successful companies pursue the same 'generic' business strategy.*

- *This 'generic' business strategy requires an understanding of which supply chain resources to own, control and leverage. It also requires the development of the appropriate operational practices to allow for the successful appropriation and accumulation of value from customers, employees, competitors and suppliers.*

- *If the appropriate operational practices may change, as may the resources which are necessary for ownership, control and leverage, the strategic approach, which ultimately leads to business success, does not.*

- *Strategy and operational practice are not to be regarded as separate activities. Corporate 'best practice' is the alignment of operational practices with the value appropriation and accumulation strategies of the company around critical assets in specific supply chains.*

limited number of empirically observed cases. These have often been developed without proper thought about the specific utility of the practices for particular companies, or for the unique supply chain and competitive market conditions under which they are operating.

At the same time the tendency within 'fad' thinking to focus on *operational best practices* often stands in place of a proper focus on strategy. The copying of operational practices becomes a substitute both for strategic thinking and an awareness of the appropriate strategic issues. It is hardly surprising, therefore, that companies which pursue operational 'fads' normally lose sight of strategy and fail to improve their ability to appropriate and accumulate value from their involvement in supply chains. Why is this? There are potentially three explanations.

The first reason, and the most cynical, is that most 'fads' are nothing more than marketing and sales pitches offered to hard pressed practitioners by publishers and consultants. There is clearly some truth in this assertion, but there are other potential explanations as well. There are two other possible major reasons why 'fads' fail.

As Figure 9 demonstrates the two major reasons why 'fads' fail is either because of inappropriate application or inappropriate *ways of thinking*. It may very well be that the operational practice—JIT, TQM, Lean Production, BPR or Outsourcing—is wholly appropriate. However, it is the manager who has to implement it when he does not fully understand what needs to be done that is the problem. On the other hand, it may well be that the whole approach is based on a false *way of thinking* about what companies can do to achieve success. It may be that copying and benchmarking itself is the problem because the unique conditions which proved successful in the past cannot ever be properly replicated in the future. This is because benchmarking and 'fad' approaches to management are really a form of myopia.

Figure 9: *Two Reasons for Fads to Fail*

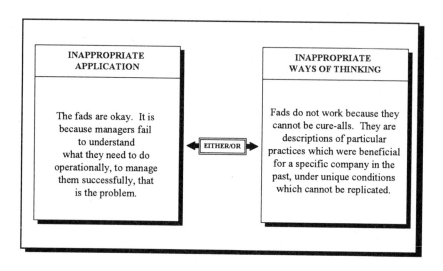

This line of reasoning can be developed further if we begin to analyse in more detail what causes 'fads', based on a benchmarking mentality, to fail in operational practice. Figure 10 provides a clear indication of some of the more proximate causes of failure which arise from an attachment to the inappropriate application of a 'fad' approach:

As the Figure demonstrates there are a whole host of reasons why managers fail to operationalise 'fads' successfully. These can range from the fact that the idea was never appropriate in the first place, through problems which arise from honest misperception and misunderstanding, to change management overload, to examples of clear obstruction on the part of managers who do not wish to see any change at all. Clearly, all of these possible causes of failure must be present whenever a new approach to business success is introduced within a company. They are not, however, likely to be the major reason for failure.

Figure 10: *Failure from Inappropriate Application*

SOME INAPPROPRIATE APPLICATIONS

- The ideas came from snake-oil salesmen

- Managers do not fully understand or misperceive what is being said

- Managers fail to understand what is required to implement any new 'fad'

- Managers do not want to implement a 'fad' and resist it operationally

- Managers "Highjack" a 'fad' and use it to achieve their own prior pre-conceived plans and goals

- Managers have to implement more than one 'fad' at the same time

- Short-term financial drivers hinder successful long-term implementation

The most important reason why 'fads' fail is because this is simply an inappropriate *way of thinking* about business success. As a result, this must be one of the major contributing factors to relative corporate and individual failure. Figure 11 below provides a summary of why this criticism is made:

Figure 11: *Failure from Inappropriate Ways of Thinking*

INAPPROPRIATE WAYS OF THINKING

- The 'fad' cannot work outside of the circumstances in which it was originally implemented in

- The 'fad' is based on a benchmarking mentality of observation of past practices and is no guide to future action

- Successful adaptation can only ever lead to a war of competitive imitation

- The approach is <u>epistemologically unsound</u> as a guide to appropriate behaviour for particular companies under specific contingent circumstances

---

As the Figure demonstrates, 'fads' often fail because they cannot be implemented outside of the circumstances in which they were first introduced. They also fail because the operational practices which were successful in the past are no certain guide to the operational practices which will lead to success in the future. Furthermore, even if it is possible to successfully copy and adapt what others have done, because these practices are imitable, they can never be the basis of sustainable success in the future.(Peteraf, 1993)

All that copying and adaptation can achieve is the development of competitive imitation and attrition. This is a process in which the ultimate beneficiary is always the customer.

If products or services are capable of imitation it is the customer who receives more and more of the value in the supply chain, rather than the individual or the company that is undertaking all of the financial risks of supply. Finally, given that sustainable success must be based on being different from other people, it would appear that the whole intellectual approach behind 'fads' and benchmarking must be myopic—it is an inappropriate *way of thinking* about sustainable business success and is based on shaky epistemological foundations.

If this is true what is the fundamental cause of this malaise in business management thinking and practice? It can be argued that the fundamental cause arises as a result of the failure of business management writers to understand the nature of scientific enquiry in the social sciences. The majority of business writing—both academic and consultant—is based on an empiricist methodology. This *way of thinking* can be divided into **bare-foot** or **systematic empiricist** schools. These two approaches are summarised in Figure 12.

It is argued here, however, that both of these approaches are flawed because they are based on a false perception of what is a proper scientific epistemology in the social sciences. The correct approach to understanding operational *best practice* for any company must be based, not on the empirical observation of what others do, now or in the past, but on a prior theorisation of the fundamental causes of business success for all companies under any, and all, contingent circumstances.

Only when such a theory of the firm has been developed (which explains why it exists and for what purposes) will it be possible to determine what are the proximate causes of success. These ideas about strategic causality cannot be generalised from observation alone. They must be part of a rational logic, pursued within the mind of the individual theorist, which seeks to explain why certain activities are more causally important than others.

Figure 12: Two Schools of Management Thinking

1. The Bare-Foot Empiricist School

This school contends that generalisations about business success can be made by observing discrete operational cases of success. Theoretical rigour is based on the idea that verification is based on the search for supporting evidence from replicable cases. If sufficient cases can be found, then generalisations are made about the operational practices which appear to lead to business success and which, it is argued, other companies should copy.

2. The Systematic Empiricist School

This school contends that guides to business success and 'best practice' can be gleaned from a deductive categorisation of the totality of potential factors which have in the past impacted on businesses and their success. This thinking normally takes place in the thinkers head and leads to the development of logical typologies of alternative practices. The thinking is still based, however, on the systematic observation (through induction) of existing empirical cases of individual or corporate behaviour.

The aim of empirical research is not, therefore, primarily to observe the regularity of occurrence of certain phenomena, but to test particular theoretical explanations of why firms are successful, and which operational practices have assisted their success under particular circumstances. This view of social science and business enquiry, which has been called **abstractive reasoning**, informs the theoretical and epistemological approach outlined in this volume.

The basic research methodology holds that, whatever causal proposition about business success is proffered as a guide to operational *best practice*, it must also be linked to an 'over-arching' and 'generic' theory of business success. Such a theory must also be capable of empirical verification or falsification (if it is to have any explanatory utility). Propositions about business success which are based simply on generalisations from one or two discrete case studies, or are based on the search for verifying rather than falsifying evidence *(a lawyers brief)*, cannot be regarded as a satisfactory, or properly scientific, explanations. Furthermore, if they are not based on rigorous theoretical and scientific foundations it is also not clear how they can provide suitable guides for operational *best practice*.

In order to understand what a company should do—in marketing, in finance, in production, in research and development and in procurement and supply management—a scientific and theoretically rigorous approach requires a different starting point. It requires that we know, deductively, what all of the determinants of business success are under all circumstances. Having achieved this, it is then possible to specify the full-range of operational tools and techniques which are potentially available to assist the company in developing its own unique migration path from where it is now to where it needs to be in the future. Only after this has been achieved is it possible to ascertain which specific operational practices are most likely to assist a particular company, under specified conditions, in the achievement of sustainable business success.

These practices would be those which are demonstrably *best practice* for that company, but for that company alone

It can also be argued that any specification of functional *best practice* must be based on a theoretical research methodology which is contingent. What this means is that any attempt to understand what constitutes *best practice* in any aspect of business management must recognise that there can never be one single operational answer for each and every company.

Since companies are idiosyncratic cultural entities, with their own unique historical antecedents, operating in very different industrial sectors and supply chains, and under widely different regulatory and competitive forces, it must be highly unlikely that any one approach to operational practice can be 'best' for everyone. Consequently we need to understand (if we are to be able to specify what is *best practice* for any individual company) what are the contingent factors, both external and internal, which companies in general (and in particular) must address if they are to be successful.

The case for the approach which is outlined here is built up in two stages. In the next section the nature of scientific enquiry in the social sciences is discussed in relation to the grounds on which knowledge is discovered, understood and developed. The grounds on which a test of theoretical and epistemological adequacy in the social sciences can be made is also outlined, and the case for a predictive and abstractive approach to business management thinking is then made. In the final section a *way of thinking* about *contingent best practice* is outlined.

Epistemology, Causality and Alternative Ways of Thinking About Success

It has been argued that there are three basic approaches to enquiry and knowledge development in the social sciences.

These three epistemological approaches, which have been defined as the **rational**, the **empiricist** and the **abstractive**, are briefly outlined below. (Willer and Willer, 1973)   Before focusing on the way in which these alternative ways of thinking have been developed it is worth stressing what epistemology means, and why it is important. This is because many readers will not necessarily be familiar with this concept. Figure 13 graphically demonstrates what epistemology means and why it is important.

Epistemology is just a word which means the theories through which human beings develop methodologies to think about knowledge and understanding. By knowledge one means the codification of all of the potential practices and circumstances which individuals and companies might experience in business. Understanding means those explanations of causality that help us to know why some companies and individuals are successful and some are not, as well as what is the most appropriate thing to do to achieve success under any given contingent circumstance.

The reason why epistemologies are important is because any actions which human beings pursue will be guided by either an implicit or an explicit theory about causality.   A theory of causality is simply a view of which things are most important in bringing about a particular outcome. The problem everyone in business faces, however, is that not all theories of causality may be equally as valid. Some epistemological approaches may be more inclusive and appropriate in explaining causality than others.   This is crucially important for an understanding of business success. For, as will be argued later in this chapter, it is essential that companies and individuals understand what *the ideal* is in achieving sustainable success. If practitioners have a faulty epistemological approach, and they arrive at the wrong *ideal*, then they will have no way of developing the appropriate operational migration path to take them from where they are now to what is *optimal* within available resources.

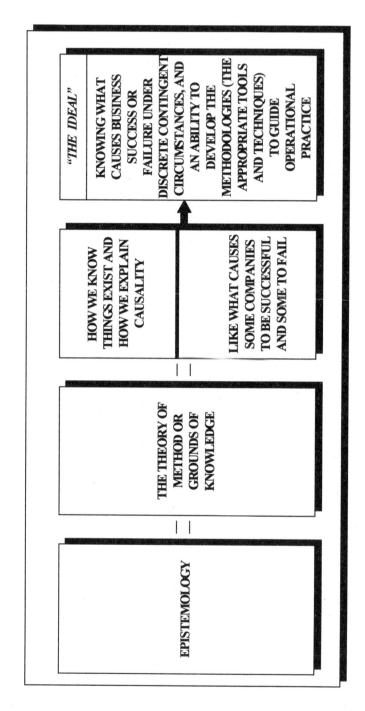

Figure 13: The Epistemology of Knowledge Development

If individuals wish to abolish ignorance and to develop knowledge and understanding, it is therefore of paramount importance that they should understand the relative strengths and weaknesses of the three major epistemological approaches to our knowledge and understanding of causality in the social sciences. Only by understanding the theoretical rigour, and explanatory utility, of these three *ways of thinking* is it possible for an informed view of business success to be developed.

The epistemology of **rational** philosophical enquiry is outlined in Figure 14. As we can see from this Figure, the methodology which philosophers utilise to explain what happens in the world is based on a deductive theorisation of causality. In this process the individual uses logical reasoning based on experience, reading, intuition and serendipity to arrive at rational ideas and concepts about causality. These rational ideas are based on the delineation of causal predictions of what will happen when pre-specified factors (the independent variables) inter-act with other intervening variables to cause particular outcomes (the dependent variables). These predictive constructs are often capable of being expressed mathematically.

Although these idealised theories of causality could be empirically tested, they are normally crafted without reference to systematic empirical observation of the real world. The utility of the philosophical theorisation is not based on its practical utility, or on an empirical test of its validity, but on the logical symmetry of the concepts built into the theory and the inclusivity of, and lack of causal ambiguity in, its predictive properties. This approach helps us to clarify the logical meaning of words and concepts without, necessarily, providing clear guidance about purposive action.

The most common methodology used in the social sciences and in business management studies is the **empiricist** approach. The epistemology of this approach is outlined in Figure 15. **Empiricism** is based on the idea that scientific explanation is about the systematic observation of discrete phenomena and the

Figure 14 : Rational Philosophical Enquiry

LOGIC OF ENQUIRY	METHODOLOGY	CHARACTERISTICS	PHILOSOPHICAL PROPONENTS
RATIONAL PHILOSOPHICAL ENQUIRY BASED ON DEDUCTION	INDEPENDENT VARIABLES / DEPENDENT VARIABLES / INTERVENING VARIABLES — IDEAS; THEORETICAL PROPOSITIONS ABOUT CAUSALITY	• "Facts" are deduced from higher-order rational principles in a systematic logical fashion • Conclusions are shown to follow from one or two general premises or postulates. • Idealised theory, or general explanatory principles, are paramount in predictive kowledge and understanding • Concepts defined without reference to empirical observation and often capable of mathematical expression • Utility of theory from rational logic and lack of casual ambiguity • No empirical test of validity	PLATO DESCARTES LEIBNITZ HEGEL

inductive theorisation of causality after the fact of observation.

Observationally defined empirical categories, which are unrelated to any prior rational, deductive theoretical construct of causality, are chosen subjectively by the analyst in this methodology. These subjectively defined categories are then observed systematically to discover if there is any regularity of pattern of specific factors (independent and intervening variables), prior to the occurrence of a particular outcome (the dependent variable). The test of validity is the fact that if, other things being equal, one observes A preceding B on a regular basis then one can make a statistically significant probability statement that A causes B.

The problems with this approach are numerous. First of all, a probability statement is not a scientific test of causality, even if it has been based on systematic empirical observations. Even if A always precedes B, the analyst can only assume that it is the causal factor in the relationship if there is already some prior theorisation (prediction) of why the two phenomena (or variables) are causally related. The reason for this is because a probability of occurrence does not tell us exactly under what conditions A will cause B.

Even if A has always preceded B in the past, there is no guarantee that this will always be the case in the future—particularly if the object of enquiry operates within a constantly changing (contingent) environment. Furthermore, observing and describing what has happened in the past—even if we can be sure we have understood the exact causal relationships—is no guide to what we should do in the future. What we need to understand is not *what happened* in the past but *why what happened* caused a particular (successful business) outcome at that specific moment in time. Arguably, this can only be achieved if one has a prior theory of causality (statement of logic about the relationship) which can be verified by empirical observation.

Figure 15: *The Empiricist Methodology*

LOGIC OF ENQUIRY	METHODOLOGY	CHARACTERISTICS	PHILOSOPHICAL PROPONENTS
EMPIRICISM BASED ON INDUCTION	INDEPENDENT VARIABLES DEPENDENT VARIABLES (EVENTS) (EVENTS) CONTINUOUS EMPIRICAL OBSERVATIONS (EVENTS) INTERVENING VARIABLES	• Subjective choice of objects of enquiry unrelated to any prior theory of causality. • Knowledge only possible through experience of the external world. • Science conceived as the accurate description, measurement and charting of external world. • Hard facts are created by systematic observation and collection of data from which theoretical observations can be induced. • Concepts driven by observation rather than theory. • Generalisations and theories about causality based on observations of past behaviour and probality statements about recurrence. • An essentially descriptive rather than predictive methodology.	ARISTOTLE LOCKE HULME J.S.MILL

The problem with the *empiricist* approach is that it starts from the wrong end of the enquiry process. The approach seeks to understand causality from the observation of what is, and has been. However, it has no rational or theoretical basis for discerning from amongst a wide array of potential factors which are truly causal (the independent variables) and which are not (the intervening and dependent variables). As a result, generalisations about what should be done in the future can only be made on the basis of recommendations about what has been done in the past, without any true test of causality having been made. It is hardly surprising, therefore, that the concepts which this atheoretical approach develops are primarily descriptive rather than prescriptive.

The business management concept of *benchmarking* falls squarely within this mould. The copying of what others are doing can, at best, lead to imitation and 'catch-up' to what others have achieved. It is doubtful, however, whether it can ever tell you what you should be doing to achieve sustainable business success ahead of your potential competitors. Only by knowing theoretically *why* certain factors cause success, rather than *what* has observably caused success in the past, can future business strategy be devised. Empirical observation may be able to tell you what has happened; but it is unlikely to tell you why it has happened or provide any guide to the longevity of current operational practices for business success. This is because:

"Empiricism when it works, works only with observations of what is and what was. It concludes that what is, is, and must be."   (Willer & Willer, 1973, p.137)

It is for this reason that a third epistemological approach has been developed known as *abstractive reasoning*. As Figure 16 demonstrates *abstractive reasoning* is based on the conscious attempt to link the inductive logic of *empiricism* with the deductive logic of rational philosophical enquiry. It is an

Figure 16: Abstractive Reasoning

LOGIC OF ENQUIRY	METHODOLOGY	CHARACTERISTICS	PHILOSOPHICAL PROPONENTS
ABSTRACTIVE THEORY BUILDING AND TESTING USING DEDUCTION AND INDUCTION	**DEDUCTIVE THEORY BUILDING** INDEPENDENT VARIABLES — DEPENDENT VARIABLES IDEAS — IDEAS — IDEAS INTERVENING VARIABLES THEORY ADAPTATATION OR REJECTION ← → SYSTEMATIC EMPIRICAL VERIFICATION **INDUCTIVE THEORY TESTING** INDEPENDENT VARIABLES — DEPENDENT VARIABLES EVENTS — EVENTS — EVENTS INTERVIEWING VARIABLES	• Theory building on the basis of higher-order rational principles, based on one or two general premises or postulates. • Creation of idealised predictive theory of causality, with internally logical and consistent concepts and principles. • Conscious and systematic attempt to test the validity of the prior idealised theory by empirical observation. • Recognition of the limits of systematic empiricism in verification. • Attachment to adaptive methodology, but acceptance of counter-factual principles for the potential rejection of the idealised theory. • Utility defined by the superiority of the internal logic and explanatory power of any theory relative to other potential theories.	POPPER KUHN STINCHCOMBE WILLER & WILLER

epistemological framework based on the view that predictive scientific knowledge can only occur if a model of explanation is created which is based on a prior rational, theorisation of causality.

This theory of causality will provide the basis for prediction about the most important variables to control and manage in the future for any given desired outcome. The methodology by which an understanding of causality is built up is through the testing of the theory of causality against observable empirical events in the real world. This test of validity must be based on an inductive research method, which uses objective observation, and which is capable of verification and refutation. In other words, the concepts and causal hypotheses underpinning the theory must be capable of counter-factual evidence. If they are, then as the model is tested empirically in the real world, the theory will generate knowledge about causality (empirical verification of the hypothesised outcomes) under particular circumstances.

It is clear, therefore, that in this epistemological approach knowledge is gathered about *the utility of the theory of explanation* through empirical observation. It is not the empirical observations themselves which are crucial but whether or not they validate or invalidate the prior theorisation of causality. Interestingly enough, even if the empirical enquiry demonstrates that the theory is sometimes invalid, the theory is not automatically invalidated unless the theory cannot be successfully adapted and modified to take account of this counter-evidence.

If the theory cannot be adapted and modified successfully, and the weight of the empirical evidence constantly refutes the theory, then the deductive search for a more inclusive rational theory must begin. Furthermore, it can be argued that, even if the rational theory of causality can be successfully adapted and modified in the light of counter-evidence, it is still possible that the theory could be disproved. This would not occur due to a single piece of counter-factual evidence, but only if an alternative rational theory was created which was better able to explain the observed facts than any existing theory or theories.

It is also worth stressing that, even if a theory is not superseded by another, more inclusive, theory it can never be argued conclusively that the new theory which the majority may currently hold to be the most appropriate is fully proven to be true. The reason for this is that the empirical methodology used is based on analysing the number of occasions, under similar or dis-similar circumstances, that particular theoretically and deductively defined variables lead to prior hypothesised outcomes. If the hypothesised outcomes do occur then the theory is proven, *but only on the basis of the current state of empirical evidence available.*

The logical consequence of this argument is that, despite the fact that we cannot know under all circumstances whether the theory is true or not (due to our inability to analyse all potential empirical cases as a result of a lack of available resources) it is axiomatic that theory must precede empirical observation rather than empirical enquiry determining theory. Obviously theory and empirical enquiry are inextricably inter-twined, but it can be argued that, while they are inter-linked, empirical enquiry should be used to test clearly defined theoretical relationships which have been hypothesised prior to observation beginning. This theoretical and abstractive approach to understanding business success can also be linked with the positivist tradition which holds that theories are broadly adequate if they fulfil the criteria outlined in Figure 17. (Cox et al., 1986)

It can be argued that an epistemology based on the combination of the insights of the positivist tradition and the abstractive approach to theory building should be the template against which each and every business writer's claims for an new approach to, or theory of, business success through *best practice* is validated. If academics and practitioners applied these tests of validity to the 'fads' of 'the gurus', who claim

Figure 17: *The Positivist Empirical Verification of Theory*

- *The theory has a clear and consistent causal explanation of success.*

- *It is capable of predicting future events.*

- *It does not require the acceptance of subjectively defined, normative and ideological principles or definitions.*

- *The empirical research on which it is based is capable of replication.*

- *It can be validated or refuted through the development of counter-factuals.*

- *It must be inclusive in its use of empirical data and not include only those cases which support the theory and omit inconvenient material.*

new generalisable insights into 'best practices for business success', then the hollowness of some of their claims would be easily understood.

Contingent Best Practice: Operationalising the Strategic Ideal

The criteria which are needed to create such an holistic and scientific approach to understanding business success and operational *best practice* are outlined in Figure 19. This Figure can be compared with the pre-scientific methodology for the analysis of *best practice* in business management which has been critiqued above and which is demonstrated in Figure 18.

In Figure 18 we can see that current business management approaches to business strategy and operational *best practice* are significantly under-developed in relation to the tests of adequacy we have outlined above. The current state of business management thinking suffers from a number of problems. These include an attachment to an atheoretical methodology, based on a **barefoot empiricist** approach. This approach leads to descriptive rather than prescriptive analysis. As a result, most of management thinking is reactive rather than proactive. It is important to note, too, that such thinking is primarily *functional* in its orientation.

By this one means that most of business management thinking divides the firm up into discrete operational functions, which academic research and teaching, as well as professional practice, reinforces. This leads to a number of significant obstacles to *best practice* in companies. Functional specialists may have tremendous expertise in their area of responsibility, but they also suffer from a tendency to functional imperialism and/or myopia, and often have a less than holistic view of business management.

Presumably, it is for this reason that academics developed MBA courses to help managers understand the concepts, methodologies and thinking of the discrete functional specialists operating within companies. It could be, however, that to adopt the MBA approach is sub-optimal, because the real problem may not be the need to understand the drivers of functional specialism, but the fact that companies are organised into functional specialisms in the first place.

Interestingly, some writers argue for cross-functionality as the way to erode the practice of functional imperialism and myopia at the operational level. They may be correct but there could be an alternative approach to this problem, which is to destroy the thinking which leads to the idea that an internal

Figure 18: The Current State of Business Thinking

FUNCTIONAL	REACTIVE	DESCRIPTIVE	SYSTEMATICALLY EMPIRICAL	ATHEORETICAL
• Business management seen as a discrete set of autonomous functions.	• No awareness of optimality in designing practical tools and techniques.	• Academic and consultants research focused on describing what practitioners do.	• Misguided reliance on evidence speaking for itself.	• Inability to provide any theoretical specification for the optimal role of any function within an organisation.
• A tendency to functional imperialism amongst academics and practitioners.	• Tendency to react to "given" organisational problems.	• Discrete case study or functional focus of analysis.	• Atheoretical research based on implicit rather than explicit, subjectively chosen criteria.	• An inability to use abstractive reasoning to test general laws.
• No holistic overview of strategy and operational practices.	• Benchmarking and fad mentality.	• Inability to link specific cases to general predictive rules or laws of business success or failure.	• Practitioner dissatisfaction with the fruits of academic and consultant knowledge.	• No theory of causality under changing contingent circumstances.

functional division of labour is the most efficient mechanism for training and developing business managers. To do this would require, however, as we indicate in Figure 19, the development of a business, market and supply and value chain specific mentality by all employees in the company.

This alternative approach to business thinking would require a clear awareness of the meaning of management. In this approach management would focus on the entrepreneurial method by which a 'sustainable position' for a company is created within specific supply and value chains, and under discrete market conditions. It would require that senior employees understood what creates and destroys value in supply chains, and how the company appropriates and accumulates value from any supply chain, by owning and controlling the key resources (**critical assets**) which determine cost, quality and innovation.

In other words, a non-functional approach to business management requires the development of a prior theory of business success, which has been properly validated and tested. In this sense, the current state of business management thinking with regard to functionalism is best characterised as pre-scientific. It contends that a functional division of labour is appropriate under all circumstances, and for all companies in all sectors, but without any clear empirical evidence to substantiate this claim.

Linked to this is a second problem related to the delineation of *best practice*. The penchant for functionalism means that the current state of thinking is essentially *reactive* rather than *proactive* to given business problems. Since there is no proper theory to guide business research or practice there is no mechanism by which companies can predict what they ought to do to deal with changing circumstances. Practitioners are forced to 'benchmark' and copy the practices of other companies because they do not understand how to differentiate

Figure 19: The Ideal Way of Thinking for Business

MARKET, SUPPLY AND VALUE CHAIN SPECIFIC	PROACTIVE	PREDICTIVE	ABSTRACTIVE	THEORETICAL
• Understanding of the importance of market perspectives and the contrast with supply and value chain perspectives.	• Ability to differentiate between "the ideal" and "the optimal".	• Focus less on what practitioners do and more on what they ought to do under contingent circumstances.	• Recognition of the importance of deductive and inductive methods.	• Clear and explicit theoretical specification of causality under contingent circumstances.
• Recognition of the unique attributes of particular markets and supply and value chains.	• Focus on market and supply and value chain opportunities, rather than reactions to existing problems.	• Robust strategic concepts, with operationally practical tools and techniques, for predictable use.	• Research seen as the testing of prior theorised causal models.	• Theory guiding the development of empirically testable hypotheses and propositions.
• Management understood as a method for achieving a sustainable position for a company.	• Innovative mind set focused on contingent circumstances not past practices.	• Prescriptive awareness of the consequences of the use of particular tools and techniques.	• Theory and adaptation through positivist counter - factual methods.	• Concepts linked to theory and not free-standing.

between what is, and what is not, appropriate for them under given circumstances.

Academics also, lacking any theory to guide their research, tend to rely instead on 'action-research'. This approach can be defined as the empirical analysis of what functionally responsible practitioners are doing, and their co-equal and direct participatory involvement in the resolution of these problems. The weakness of this *way of thinking* derives from the fact that it provides no prior theoretical basis from which to differentiate between what is currently being done within the company, and what the *ideal* solution for business success would be, given the prevailing conjuncture of supply chain and market conditions.

Unfortunately, the academic participants in 'action-research', like the practitioners they are working with, lack any theory to guide their operational interventions. As a result this approach has no greater chance of success than if practitioners were left to their own devices. The reason for this is because both the academics and the practitioners are merely choosing things to do at random, based on their own subjective hunches, or they are basing their practices on copying what others have done.

This is clearly a reactive approach to business management thinking. A proactive approach, on the other hand, would be based on the development of deductive reasoning from 'first theoretical principles' about which practices are 'best suited' to achieve business success for any specific company under particular conjunctural circumstances. Only by starting from this theoretical base is it possible to develop a *predictive* rather than *descriptive* approach to *best practice* thinking for practitioners.

What all of this implies is that *best practice* cannot be discerned by copying what others are doing through benchmarking, nor can it be gleaned from a reliance on the 'fads' which self-interested consultants and academics try to promote. On the contrary, the development of *best practice* must start from a rejection of *empiricism*.

This is because this *way of thinking* is based on a misguided reliance on *the evidence speaking for itself,* through the descriptive recording of what specific companies are doing at particular times and under discrete market and supply chain conditions. Clearly, the conjuncture of forces which impinge on any company is likely to be unique to them at that moment in time, so that copying at best can only lead to a strategy of 'catch-up' for companies operating within the same circumstances. The downside of this *empiricist* approach is that, at worst, it could lead companies operating in completely different supply chains (and under different conjunctural circumstances) to pursue wholly inappropriate strategies and operational practices. Examples of this misguided type of thinking include a melon growing company in California that invested in a MRP2 system, and a chemicals manufacturer that copied all of the operating practices of a manufacturer of consumer electronics equipment after the latter had won a national quality award.

This is not to say that understanding what others are doing is inappropriate. Clearly it is essential to use market intelligence to understand what others are doing—in particular those who are your direct competitors. There is, however, a significant difference in understanding why someone has developed a particular strategy, or operational practice, and what its contribution to profitability is for them (in their own conjuncture), and the wholesale copying of what others are doing. The key emphasis should always be on understanding *why* others are doing things rather than on understanding *what* and *how* they are doing it.

If this approach to market intelligence activities is adopted it may be possible for practitioners to improve their own performance. However, it is unlikely that this will be achieved without the development of the prior theoretical understanding of the causes of business success under specific conjunctural circumstances. A properly scientific approach to *best practice* business management can only be achieved, therefore, if there is a clear understanding of what are the contingent forces which impinge on the firm as its strives to achieve profitability in particular supply chains and markets.

One can argue on the basis of this that at the present there is no satisfactory definition of operational *best practice* for companies, nor the functions within them, because there is no effective theory of the firm in the business management literature. It is clear, therefore, that what passes for a theory of the firm in current strategic management thinking is little more than a pre-scientific under-labour. There are a number of key texts in the area. However none of these can be regarded as a proper theorisation of the proximate forces which companies must address, and the strategies they could adopt under different circumstances, to generate business success.

There are two reasons for this. The first is that they are all derived from atheoretical generalisations based upon the descriptive taxonomy of potential factors which could lead to business success. The second is that they attempt to define the causes of success on the basis of the probability of discrete empirical observations recurring. (For this approach see: Mintzberg and Quinn, 1996) It can be argued that this methodology is neither abstractive nor is it properly predictive and, as such, it can never provide the basis for a robust theoretical and practical guide to action.

The logic of this review of the epistemology of causal theory is that:

> *If one adopts an abstractive reasoning approach, it is clear that the majority of business writers completely fail to understand the shaky intellectual foundations on which many of their arguments about 'best practice' are based.*

A review of the key management texts in strategy can only lead one to conclude that most of these operate at the level of *empiricism*.

> • *Empiricism is based either on generalisations from observations of one or two cases, or upon the development of systematic a descriptive taxonomies of the range of potential operational practices which companies have used in the past.*
>
> • *These two empiricist approaches are neither abstractive, nor are they predictive. Furthermore, they are limited because they do not provide any basis by which companies might understand what could be, rather than what is.*

This final problem is, arguably, the most significant obstacle to the crafting of business success for business managers. If, as demonstrated in Figure 20, we have no methodology to understand what the *ideal* might be (what we would do if we were resource unconstrained), then we have no methodology to understand what is *optimal* (what is the best we can do within available resources and constraints). Relatedly, if we do not know what the *ideal* and the *optimal* are, we have no basis for understanding what the *migration path* should be to take us from where we are today to where we need to be in the future to achieve business success.

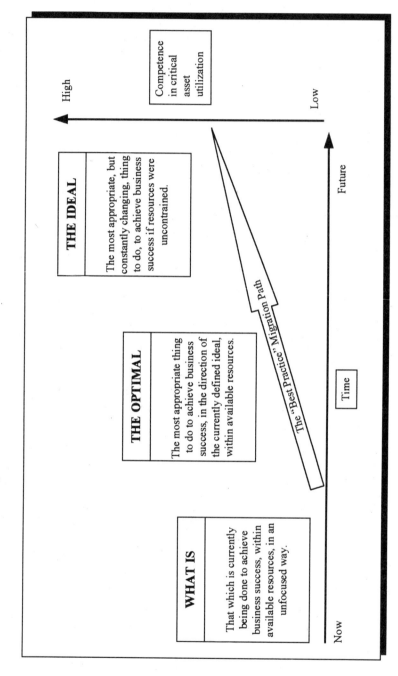

Figure 20: The Best Practice Migration Path

It would appear that the existing business strategy literature does not provide a satisfactory basis for understanding, either *what* the basis for business success *is*, nor *what could be* the basis for that success. It is theoretically and empirically immature, and does not stand the test of satisfactory descriptive and predictive utility, which is the basis of ***abstractive reasoning***. This becomes clear when we begin to appraise some of the leading business strategy texts and their theoretical and empirical underpinnings in the next two chapters.

4

The Current State of the Art in Business Thinking

In this chapter the concern is still the lack of theoretical rigour in business management writing. The focus of the discussion is on why some of the most widely accepted business thinking may not be as appropriate for all companies as it is sometimes claimed. The focus here is, once again, on the *appropriateness* of the thinking for particular companies under specific contingent circumstances.

The discussion here is necessarily selective. The writer is engaged in an extensive critical analysis of the current business management literature but only some of the key texts, which have had a seminal influence on strategy and operational practice, are discussed. Despite this it was felt that the reader might better understand the utility of the *way of thinking* which is being introduced here if they were shown how it can be used to appraise the worth of current business thinking.

It is a measure of the achievement of many of the writers whose work will be discussed here that their thinking has shaped and informed the activities and goals of many tens of thousands of business practitioners and academics around the world. This would not have been possible unless their own *ways of thinking* had not uncovered, either directly or indirectly, some of the primary causal phenomena which shape and determine business success and failure.

The writings of these authors have also had a profound impact upon the present author's own thinking, and the intellectual debt which is properly owed to them is gratefully acknowledged. Ironically, those ideas which have had the most impact on the author's own thinking are the ones which receive the most vigorous criticism. The author can only hope that these writers appreciate why extensive critical appraisal of their work has been necessary in the context of the development of the thinking presented here.

By reading their work, and that of the many extremely able thinkers whose contributions will be discussed in a subsequent volume, the author has been able to clarify his own thoughts. It is only by the honest expression of the way an individual thinks about the world, and through the individual's recognition of his or her own potential subjective partiality, that anyone can hope to learn and grow intellectually.

In having the temerity to suggest how others should think about the world, however, one must also accept that one's own thinking may be partial and, in some cases, inappropriate. If someone else is capable of demonstrating this is so, then the intelligent person must be grateful because they will have learnt something they did not know before. Furthermore if they have an open mind they will, as a result, be able to improve their own *way of thinking*. The present author accepts this potential fate with equanimity. He can only hope that those with whom he has an honest and genuine intellectual disagreement about emphasis and focus share this viewpoint.

Revolutions in Ways of Thinking and the Paradigm Shift

The inappropriateness of an idea is discovered in two ways. The first, and most obvious, is when empirical events do not conform with that which our *way of thinking* would lead us to predict. This does not necessarily mean our theory is wrong. It simply means that it does not have the ability to explain all cases. Given our current available theoretical choices this non-inclusive theory may, however, still be the most appropriate *way of thinking* about causality (i.e. business success and failure). The only way that the currently most appropriate theory of explanation can be superceded, however, is through deductive rather than inductive reasoning.

No amount of constant replication of empirical observations of conforming or non-conforming cases in relation to the current dominant theory can lead to this *way of thinking* being replaced. For the dominant theory or theories to be replaced a second event must take place. The first event is the recognition that the theory of explanation cannot account for all cases of business success and failure adequately. The second event is the creation of an *alternative way of thinking*. This *new way of thinking* will only be accepted, however, if it results in the creation of a theory which has a superior capacity to explain causality in *all cases* of business success and failure, or in *more cases* than alternative theories of explanation.

Thomas Kuhn has referred to this process in the natural sciences as a *paradigm shift*. (Kuhn, 1962) When the paradigm shift occurs, as depicted in Figure 21, a *new way of thinking* occurs which has a superior explanatory utility relative to other ways of thinking. This does not mean, of course, that the *new way of thinking* is right and all other theories (or ways of thinking) are wrong. This cannot be true logically. No theory is right: it can only be the most appropriate given our current level of deductively theorised understanding of causality, and based on the breadth of our current empirical evidence.

What this means is that, compared with other *ways of thinking*, the new approach can explain more cases than its competitors. Alternatively, it can explain in a more satisfactory way when the causal explanations offered by other theories are appropriate (or not) in particular circumstances. To put it simply, the *new way of thinking* supercedes all others because it

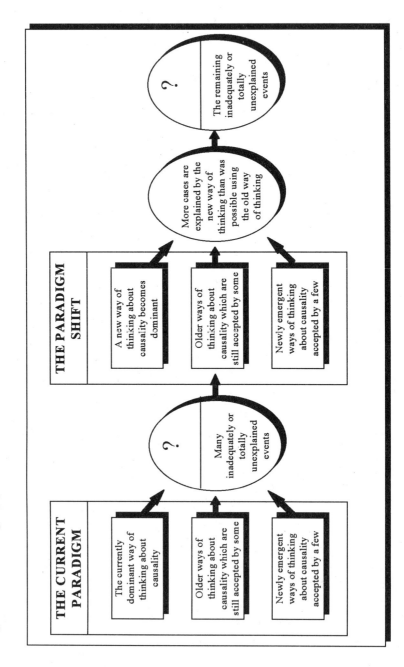

Figure 21: The Paradigm Shift

is inclusive (it can accommodate and extend the insights of all other theories) and has a more powerful predictive capacity. (See Steven Lukes, *Power: A Radical View* (1974), for an operationalisation of this *way of thinking* in relation to one of the most important concepts in human existence).

If this *way of thinking* is adopted, then it can be argued that there are no properly adequate theories of causality in relation to business success in the current economics and business management literature. The reason this view is held is because of the epistemological critique outlined earlier, and the lack of an appreciation of the need for an abstractive approach to causal explanation within current business management writing. There are, however, other reasons of which the most important are: the failure of business writers to make their theories of causality explicit; their tendency to construct a lawyer's brief (to look only for supporting rather than contradictory evidence); and, their logically irrational attempt to generalise for business as a whole from one or two specific cases.

Not all writers fall into all of these traps, and those which are discussed here have, by and large, made fewer of these errors than most. This is probably why they have succeeded in attracting so much attention in the past and have exerted so much influence on business thinking. Like successful businesses through the ages they must have been doing something right, even if they were not always aware of what it was when they were doing it. But in the same way that the actions which people take and which lead to business success cannot be based on chance, there must also be causal reasons why the leading business writers have been influential. The reasons must reside in the fact that their *ways of thinking* do uncover and explain some of the key factors which cause business success and failure. The question is however: do they explain these two phenomena in the most satisfactory way possible?

The author does not believe so and thinks that a more satisfactory explanation of causality can be constructed. The basis of this more inclusive and predictive theory has not been plucked from thin air however. The author's theory could not have been developed in this way. It has been developed, as summarised in Figure 22, from thinking about the logical and empirical strengths and weaknesses of the current explanations of business success in the social science literature in general, and in the business management, politics and economics disciplines in particular.

Figure 22: *Five Keys to the Current Lack of Rigour in Business Thinking*

FIVE KEYS TO THE CURRENT LACK OF THEORETICAL RIGOUR IN BUSINESS THINKING
(1) *A lack of awareness of the need for abstractive theorising*
(2) *A failure to make currently held theories explicit*
(3) *A lack of counter-factual empirical verification*
(4) *Inappropriate generalisations for business from a limited number of empirical cases*
(5) *Descriptive rather than predictive theories or models*

While only the outlines of this theory are presented in this short volume, and much work of theoretical clarification and empirical verification remains, the author would like to express his intellectual debt to those writers whose work has contributed to his own *way of thinking about asset criticality in supply chains and markets.* While it is impossible to acknowledge the direct and indirect contributions from the hundreds of authors whose ideas have influenced this volume, it is a pleasure to recognise the contribution of those authors whose writing has significantly influenced this *way of thinking*.

While the author will take issue with many of the writers to whom he owes the greatest intellectual debt, his own view is that the groundwork and foundations for a properly adequate theory of causality have been laid already by Aristotle (1962), Smith (1774), Machiavelli (1952), Marx (1960), Coase (1937), Penrose (1959), Porter (1980 & 1985), Williamson (1975 & 1985), Hamel and Prahalad (1993 & 1994), Peteraf (1993) and Kay (1994). As important as these writers are, however, the author's greatest intellectual debt is to the Austrian economics school associated with Schumpeter (1934), Von Mises (1949), Kirzner (1973) and Von Hayek (1976). Without their appreciation of the simple fact that business success is ultimately about *entrepreneurship*, under dynamic and contingent circumstances, rather than something called 'management', the foundations for the embryonic theory introduced here could not have been laid.

In what follows only a few selected texts are discussed, and these are mainly drawn from the business management literature. This is because the current volume is very much a work in progress. The discussion is presented, therefore, as a sample of the critique which the use of an *abstractive way of thinking* about *critical supply chain assets* provides of some of the currently dominant ideas in business thinking.

This critique is divided into a number of sections which deal with the views of some of the most highly regarded recent business thinkers. The *abstractive approach* takes issue with each of these current day thinkers on the grounds that their ideas lack theoretical rigour and cannot account for all empirical cases of business success and failure. Before discussing the ideas of each of these writers in turn it is, first, necessary to explain the grounds on which any writer's ideas should be tested. Once this has been achieved it is then possible to raise one of the major theoretical difficulties with current approaches to business thinking. This is the *false dichotomy* which current writers appear to make when they discuss causality in relation to the scope for free-will or determinism in human action.

The Adequacy of a Theory and the False Dichotomy in Business Thinking

Although there are many different perspectives about what causes success in the business management literature existing writing can be divided broadly, if not wholly satisfactorily, into two schools of thought.

The first, the **intra-firm perspective**, can be defined as that body of writing which tends to focus on those internal characteristics of the firm which allow it to be successful. In the contemporary period the *resource-based theory* of the firm can be placed primarily within this school of thought, (Montgomery, 1995), but it is not the only approach which falls historically into this camp.

The second, **the inter-firm perspective**, can be defined as that body of writing which tends to emphasise the structural properties in business success which arise from the horizontal (competitive) and vertical (supply) relationships which exist between legally separate firms. The collective work of Coase (1937), Porter (1979) and Williamson (1975 & 1985) falls into this broad school of thought, with its emphasis on external market and supply power.

Each of these two broad schools of thought tends to emphasise either the internal or the external aspects of the business environment as the most important in explaining success. Theoretically it can be argued that this *way of thinking* is unlikely to lead to a satisfactory understanding of business success, or of the appropriateness of particular actions under specific circumstances. The reason for this is because it creates

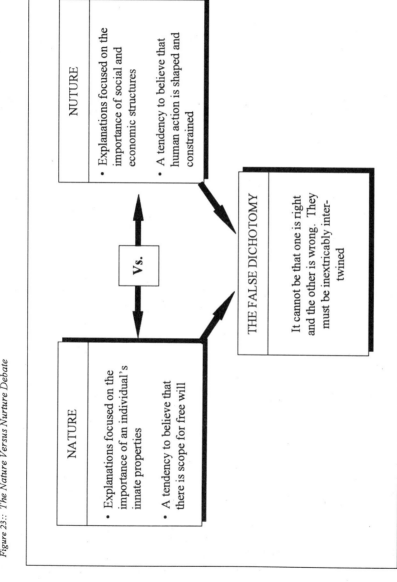

Figure 23:: The Nature Versus Nurture Debate

a *false dichotomy* between factors which must, in practice, be inextricably inter-twined. This is a common problem in social science thinking and has its roots in the debate between nature and nurture.

As Figure 23 reveals, in the social sciences there has always been a debate about the relative importance of **nature** (what an individual possess innately) and **nurture** (what an individual learns to do within the constraints of society). There has, therefore, always been a significant differentiation between theories which tend to emphasise the scope for *free will* by autonomous individuals, and those which deny the scope for free will, due to the *constraints* imposed on individuals by social and economic structures.

It is clear that **intra-firm perspectives** on business success can be broadly located within the nature school; while the **inter-firm perspective** tends to fall within the nurture philosophical approach.

While it is relatively easy to classify the ideas of business thinkers in this way, it is not so easy to overcome the pernicious impact of this type of thinking on the development of a properly holistic view of business success. Logically, the nature and nurture arguments can be nothing more than the opposite sides of the same coin. This implies that one of the tests of adequacy (or superiority) for any theory of business success must be whether it can adequately accommodate insights from both the intra and the inter-firm perspectives.

As we shall see, few theories adequately meet this test, nor do they satisfactorily meet the tests of adequacy which abstractive reasoning and positivist methodology would demand. This *way of thinking* suggests that there are ten major tests of adequacy, as presented in Figure 24. The ten key tests of a theory are that:

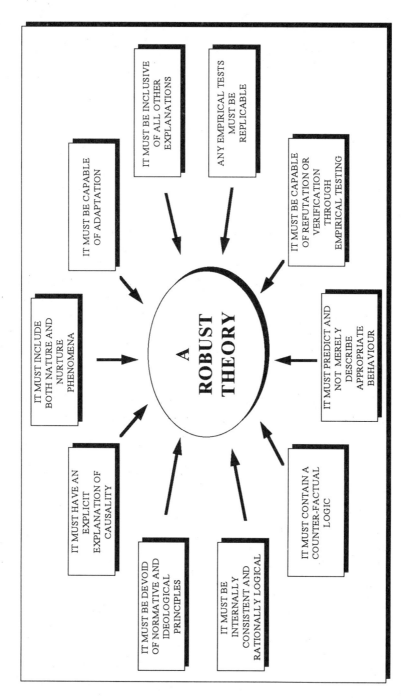

Figure 24: Ten Tests of Theoretical Adequacy

- *it has an explicit explanation of causality*
- *it must contain both explanatory phenomena relating to nature and nurture*
- *it is internally consistent and rationally logical in its use of concepts and ideas*
- *it extends but also can accommodate the explanations of causality derived from competing perspectives*
- *it is devoid of normative and ideological principles*
- *it is capable of verification and refutation any empirical testing is based on a search for confirming and non-confirming evidence*
- *the empirical test must be replicable*
- *it must be adaptive if there is non-conforming evidence*
- *it must have a predictive as well as a descriptive utility*

When we apply these tests of adequacy to the majority of the most widely read texts in business management they begin to look rather less than perfect. Most of the major texts fail to match fully the tests of adequacy outlined above and many fall down in a significant number of ways. The reason for this is arguably because the vast majority of business writing is atheoretical.

The current literature can be divided into two camps. As Figure 25 demonstrates the first of these—*the bare-foot empiricist*—attempts to make generalisations for business as a whole from the observation of a limited number of specific empirical cases. The second—*the systematic empiricist*—can be best described as an attempt to create systematic, descriptive typologies of the range of possible strategies and practices which companies could use. The methodology is based on

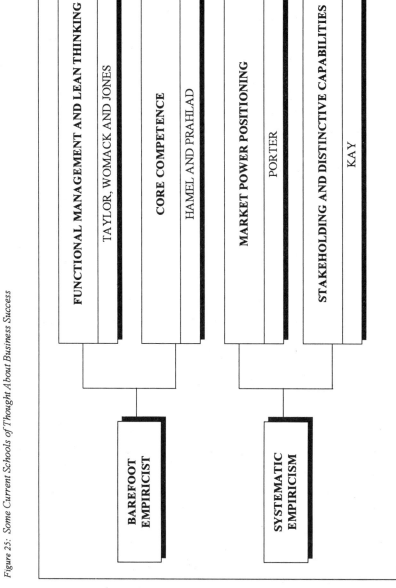

Figure 25: Some Current Schools of Thought About Business Success

inductive reasoning through a systematic observation of the observable strategies or practices which companies are using, or have used, within market competitive situations. Neither of these two approaches can be regarded as robust, because they do not meet the tests of scientific or theoretical adequacy outlined above.

Bare-foot Empiricism: The Problem of Inappropriate Generalisation and Benchmarking

In this section we discuss briefly the recurring historical problem of the tendency by which, because business writers pursue a *barefoot empiricist* approach of generalisation from specific cases, they tend to arrive at inappropriate conclusions about causality. The first example of this practice is the benchmarking and copying approach built into Taylor's scientific principles of management, and the replication of this *way of thinking* in a more contemporary setting by Womack and Jones. The second example is the *core competence* approach of Hamel and Prahalad, which is criticised for creating an atheoretical and tautological, descriptive account of business practice.

Functionalism, Scientific Management and Lean Thinking

One of the earliest exponents of management thinking about business strategy and operational practice was arguably F.W. Taylor. Taylor developed views about the scientific principles of management, which spawned the present day fixation with functional or silo management. It is interesting to note that Taylor's theory of *best practice* was in fact based primarily on analysing companies which were vertically integrated and operating in continuous process industries. It is worth remarking at this point that, for the companies which he analysed, this may very well have been a highly appropriate way of managing. This is because a functional division of labour may have been highly appropriate at the time he analysed their industrial structure and practices. (Taylor, 1911)

Whether or not vertical integration and a division of labour is the most appropriate way to organise production in the present historical conjuncture for such continuous process industries is, of course, open to question. Even if it were true that a functional division of labour is the most appropriate way to manage all process types of industry, it would be highly questionable to conclude today, or even when Taylor wrote, that this is the most appropriate way to organise business in those industries which do not have continuous processes. Presumably what is *fit for purpose* and *best practice* in these industries will be contingent on the *conjuncture of forces* (supply chain structure, market competition, regulatory forces, levels of effective demand etc.) within which particular companies are operating?

We see, therefore, straight away in Taylor's work, as demonstrated in Figure 26, the pernicious influence on business thinking of generalisations which are based on only one or two types of empirical case. There must have been any number of eminently sensible reasons why companies in the United States, like Ford's, in the early industrialisation period of the nineteenth century, chose to create a functional division of labour. Presumably this will have had something to do with the conjuncture of contingent circumstances which Ford faced at that time.

Of these contingent factors, one of the most important may have been the fact that there was an absolute shortage of skilled, craft workers available at the time. This was because most of the new immigrants to the USA were semi-literate and unskilled peasants and agricultural workers, who had been forced to emigrate or starve because of the Great European Depression in

Figure 26: The Myopia of Scientific Management and Functionalism

THE MYOPIA OF SCIENTIFIC MANAGEMENT AND FUNCTIONALISM

BASIC THESIS

- Taylor argued the case for a scientific and functional system of management based on hierarchy and a division of labour

- Taylorism based on analysing Fordist principles of vertical integration and the division of labour

FIVE THEORETICAL AND METHODOLOGICAL PROBLEMS

- A theoretical approach with no explicit theory of causality

- It is based on a bare-foot empiricism and a descriptive methodology

- Generalisations from a small number of cases

- Involves normative assumptions

- No effective empirical test of alternative ways of doing business under different contingent circumstances

agriculture in the 1880s and 1890s. In these circumstances, and because Henry Ford may have had a personal penchant for control and vertical integration, a particular system of production and management was introduced which was clearly highly appropriate for what Ford required at that particular historical moment.

Why anybody should believe it would be the best for all time, and the one that should always be copied, is beyond this author's power of comprehension. If circumstances change then *common-sense* should surely tell us that we would need to consider all of the alternative choices which might be possible, and try to work out what the likely consequences of their implementation will be for us. In thinking in this way a contingent view of the world would be adopted, which tried to find the most appropriate practices given the circumstances.

This, of course, is not the way in which the majority of human beings seem to act. Human beings appear to have an ingrained attachment to copying and imitation. This is probably because this is the way human beings begin to learn. From infancy human beings copy and imitate the actions of those whom they admire, or those whom they would like to emulate. Unfortunately, this attachment to copying never seems to leave the majority of people. It is this attachment to imitation and emulation that provides the space within which individuals who are prepared to take a chance on uncertainty, can prosper.

> *Taking a chance on uncertainty—doing things differently and in ways others have not thought of—is clearly the way in which change comes about.*

There is a lesson for those who would seek to achieve sustainable business success in this insight.

Unfortunately for the history of business thinking, because Henry Ford achieved phenomenal success with his division of labour approach to vertical integration, everyone at that time, and for a generation, appeared to fall into the trap of the 'fad' and benchmarking mentality. Ford's system of mass production and 'scientific management', based on the concept of a division of labour, appears to have been copied not only by industrialists throughout the world for more than a century, but it has also dominated the way in which business management is taught and business thinking is sub-divided academically. This is a staggering realisation. It is as if the concept of *appropriateness* had never been invented in business thinking.

This practice of generalising from the unsatisfactory epistemological base of a few idiosyncratic cases is not confined to Taylor's work however. The practice would appear to be rife within business writing at all levels. Other notable exponents of this misguided methodology include such eminent and well respected writers as Peters and Waterman (1982). More recently, the writings of Womack, Jones and Roos (1990) have left the author, as demonstrated in Figure 27, with the impression that the business community has no capacity to learn anything from the errors of its past *ways of thinking*.

Womack et al. have studied the recent phenomenal success of Toyota and other Japanese car assemblers, and their quasi-vertically integrated, just-in-time production and assembly systems. These systems have clearly assisted Japanese car assemblers in their recently successful competition against the more Fordist, vertically integrated mass production systems in the West. The lesson which Womack et al. appear to have learnt from their empirical observation of this phenomenon is the obvious fact that this is a more efficient and *lean* way of doing things, which everyone should now copy. (Womack and Jones, 1986)

Figure 27: *The Myopia of Lean Thinking*

THE MYOPIA OF LEAN THINKING

BASIC THESIS

- Womack and Jones, after observing Japanese car assemblers, argue that business success comes from lean thinking

- Lean thinking is the creation of a supply chain which delights customers by transmitting value to them effectively by eliminating waste

FIVE THEORETICAL AND METHODOLOGICAL PROBLEMS

- It is atheoretical and based on a bare-foot empiricist methodology

- It is an over-generalisation from an inappropriate number of cases

- It is based on a benchmarking mentality

- It misunderstands the logic of supply chain dominance through structured hierarchy

- It fails to differentiate between value delivery and value appropriation

No one could argue with the idea that being efficient (because this is surely all that *lean* means in practice) is desirable in business, but is it not possible that Womack and Jones are falling into exactly the same intellectual trap that Taylor did all those years ago? There must have been contingent circumstances that encouraged Toyota to do what it did. The question to ask is why does it follow that what they did then must always be appropriate for everyone else in business to do under all circumstances in the future? Despite the problems which a misguided attachment to Taylor's functionalism may still be causing to corporate effectiveness, it would appear that the sin of generalising inappropriately from one or two specific cases is still with us.

This tendency to focus on the description of current operational practices by academics and consultants can be categorised as little more than an exercise in *bare-foot empiricism*. This is the practice, described earlier, whereby researchers believe thcy will be able to provide useful recommendations for industry in general from a close, and sometimes participatory, observation of the current or developing working practices of one or more companies. It is clear however that this thinking is fundamentally flawed, as Figure 28 indicates. No amount of academic rigour expended in pursuit of such a research methodology can lead to the development of generalisable rules about the most appropriate actions for companies to take to become more competitive. The basic reasons for this are self-evident in Figure 28.

As a result of these two factors it is almost impossible to draw generalisable rules about what the proper conduct for companies should be from the analysis of any one company, or from a group of dis-similar companies. The reason for this is because, even if researchers are to discover for any one company that a particular approach to manufacturing, marketing or relationship management is highly conducive to business success, this would only be true for that particular company, with its distinct culture and standard operating practices, at that particular moment in time. Furthermore, this moment in time (or *conjuncture* of events and circumstances) is unique to the particular supply chain within which that individual company is operating and is, arguably, not fully replicable with the same business benefits by any other company at a later date.

Figure 28: The Inappropriateness of Generalisations from Benchmarking

1. Each of the cases which is the subject of any research enquiry is unique, because all companies are distinct in their culture and existing standard operating procedures, even if they are operating within the same industry and business environment.

2. Most comparative studies do not study similar companies operating within the same industrial context, but normally take cases from very different industrial contexts, where there are very different competitive forces in operation, and where the business and technological drivers in the respective supply chains are also dis-similar.

It follows from this that no amount of effort directed towards describing what individual companies are doing, or have done in the past, can provide a basis for understanding what any other company ought to do now, or in the future. The simple fact of the matter is that, even if companies are in the same industries, they start from where they are now and not from where their competitors are.

It is also highly unlikely that they will start from exactly where their currently superior competitors originally started from, to get to where they are now. Additionally, what is the logic of companies operating within the same industries trying to copy the practices of their direct competitors? Surely the logic of competition is the ability to improve upon, or to *leap-frog*, the competition rather than to constantly play *catch-up* to the current operating standards of other companies.

More problematic perhaps, is the tendency built into **bare-foot empiricicm** of business strategy conceived as *benchmarking* what others are doing. While there may be a case for a company understanding the superior practices of its direct competitors (if it can obtain this information), there is far less to be said for the current vogue for *benchmarking* the activities of other companies, whatever industry they are operating in, and whatever the current state of competition they are facing. There can surely be little logic in a company's time or effort being expended in copying, or adapting, the operating practices and priorities of companies competing in completely different market places and supply chains. The reason for this is that the logic of sustainable success is surely to come up with completely new ways of doing things, which cannot be copied, rather than imitating what others are doing.

It is clear, therefore, that all too often academic research reinforces this myopic tendency by its attempt to take the learning from one or two operational cases in a particular supply chain and to generalise from these limited empirical cases for industry as a whole. The work by Womack, Jones & Roos (1990) on the novel operating practices of the Japanese auto-assemblers is, arguably, a particular case of this tendency to *over-generalise* from one case. This has spawned a whole genre of thinking around lean production, lean enterprise and lean supply, which is currently being sold as the most effective way to manage business.

One consequence of this *way of thinking* has been a worrying tendency, over the last five years, for purchasing and supply chain academics and professionals to argue for more collaborative approaches as the way to achieve *best practice*. This argument is centrally based on the undoubted fact, which Womack, Jones and Roos have observed and recorded, that Japanese auto-assemblers have historically used more collaborative approaches to supply management than the more arms-length approaches used in the West. Since the Japanese auto-assemblers have been quite successful competitively, then it has been argued that the best way to achieve business success must, necessarily, be for all companies to use *partnership sourcing* or other variants of collaboration, like *the virtual company*. (Carlisle & Parker, 1989: Lamming, 1993; Macbeth & Ferguson, 1994; Hines, 1994; Lewis, 1990 & 1995; Moore, 1996; and, Brandenburger & Nalebuff, 1996)

The problem with this approach is that one can argue that even if Womack, Jones & Roos have properly described the causes of business success in the Japanese auto-assemblers case, there may be some doubt as to whether or not they have properly understood the basis of their success. However, even if they have it does not follow at all that this approach is appropriate for all other car producers. For example, it could be argued that there might be an even better way of managing the auto assembly supply chain given the current situation created by Japan's relative competitive dominance.

The fact that the Japanese have adopted a more hierarchical, structured and quasi-vertically integrated supply chain, when compared with the more vertically integrated, arms-length and opportunistic approach traditionally adopted in the West, does not mean that copying the Japanese approach will necessarily be the way to obtain competitive advantage in the future. The South Korean car manufacturer, Daewoo, is for instance not currently replicating the Japanese model but is innovating with unique distribution techniques to set new standards of quality and customer satisfaction, as well as reducing cost.

The significant question here is always, however, not whether we should choose either the Japanese or the South Korean approach but rather: *"under what circumstances should any approach be used by any company to achieve sustainable competitive advantage?"* If it is questionable to conclude that there is only one way to operate successfully in the car industry, it is clearly illogical to argue, as some proponents now do, that the *lean enterprise* approach adopted by the car assemblers in Japan is the way in which *all,* or even a substantial majority of, companies should base their operational practice. (Womack & Jones, 1996)

Indeed, one could go further and argue that Womack and Jones have failed to understand one of the truly causal factors in Japanese business success—*the creation of a hierarchy of structured supply chain dominance.* It is the creation of this system of domination, which limits the possibility of *'free riders'* operating opportunistically, which so clearly differentiates Asian economic practices from their Western competitors. (see Olson, 1971) This insight leads one to conclude that Womack and Jones' may not have properly *understood* what it is they are observing.

While no one could argue that what the Japanese auto-assemblers have achieved is a highly appropriate set of practices, this does not tell us under which circumstances it can be replicated, and for whom. This weakness is compounded by the fact that, in their recent writing, the authors appear to demonstrate a total lack of understanding of the basic dynamics of business at all. In their latest work, Womack and Jones (1996) argue, mistakenly in this author's view, that the essence of business success (lean thinking) is about passing value to the customer as effectively as possible.

This is clearly not the case, and demonstrates a misunderstanding of why companies exist in the first place.

Companies do not exist to delight customers or to pass value to them efficiently; companies exist to appropriate and accumulate value from customers. They will, therefore, only maximise the value which they pass to the customer if they are forced to do so by their need to operate in properly competitive markets. Adam Smith, of course, told us this two hundred years ago! Fortunately, he also told us that companies often exist as conspiracies against the consumer and that, if they are able, they will always seek mechanisms to rig markets in their favour against the consumer's interest.

> *Companies do not exist to pass value to customers or to delight them. Companies exist to appropriate and to accumulate value for themselves.*

This argument, that companies exist to appropriate and accumulate value from customers, can be seen to be deductively and logically correct if one starts from first principles. So where does this leave Womack and Jones' argument that companies actually exist to delight customers? The answer to this conundrum is clear enough. Logically it can be argued that individuals and companies will seek monopoly, or degrees of monopoly, whenever they can in order to sustain their ability to appropriate value. However, in the absence of the ability to own or to control inimitable assets in a supply chain, or to create effective barriers to supply chain entry, an individual or company will experience copying and a contested market will form.

If the market which forms is highly contested (competitive)—as the car industry has been—then the only effective alternative for an individual, or for a company, is to seek a *relatively superior competence* when compared with their competitors. If the competitors are pursuing a policy of aggressive, zero-sum competition, and the goods or services which are produced in the supply chain are easily imitable, then the only alternative facing the players is to pass increasing amounts of the value in the supply chain to their customers. Logically, this will, be increasingly necessary the more the supply chain provides the customer with a high degree of effective choice. As demonstrated here:

- *Individuals and companies will seek monopoly control of inimitable supply chain resources to achieve sustainable success.*

- *If they are unable to stop copying, and a contested market forms, then the only basis for success is the creation of a temporary monopoly. A temporary monopoly can only be created by having a relatively superior competence than existing or potential competitors.*

- *If everyone can copy new ideas quickly then the supplier is forced to compete by passing more and more of the value in the supply chain to the customer.*

Unfortunately for Womack and Jones, the idea that this strategy is the most efficacious and appropriate for all companies to pursue will simply not hold, as Michael Porter has already demonstrated. (Porter, 1996) It would seem logical, therefore, to argue that the policy of delighting the customer will only hold until such time as the players in the supply chain decide to rig the contested market back in their favour. This *predictive* idea that, under certain conditions, markets concentrate (monopoly and oligopoly) when left to their own devices, is not a new insight. Marx demonstrated it in the middle of the last century.

The lesson to be learnt from this example is plain. If thinkers start from empirical observation alone they will have no basis for knowing whether the factors which they are observing are truly causal or not. Nor, if they use this approach, will they be in a position to know if the practices that one company pursues are appropriate for other companies in completely dis-similar supply chains. It is important to keep in mind that Womack and Jones are not wrong to claim that the Toyota approach is a way of achieving business success. It clearly has been, and is at present, a highly appropriate way of achieving success in their specific supply chain. One could also go further and concede that it may also be appropriate for their direct competitors in the same supply chain to copy and adapt these practices, *if they are able to do so.* This accepted, Womack and Jones still have no robust theoretical or empirical basis for claiming, as they do, that the whole approach and *way of thinking* is highly appropriate for many, if not all, other companies.

If they are to be commended for their description of a particular approach to business success in the car industry, Womack and Jones must be criticised for their attempt to over-generalise from this **bare-foot empiricist** foundation. The primary reason why is not because what Toyota has done cannot be replicated, but because Womack and Jones have not understood what are both the necessary and the sufficient conditions for this approach to be actualised.

Space does not allow here for a proper discussion of their failure to grasp these subtle distinctions. All that one can say with certainty about *lean thinking* is that it has helped the Japanese auto-assemblers, but it is still necessary to analyse **the contingent circumstances under which this approach is appropriate.** This would help companies to understand the causes of success and failure. An attempt to try to encourage every type of company to introduce, what will clearly be an inappropriate strategy in very different contingent circumstances, will not do so.

A simple example will demonstrate the force of this argument. For B/Sky/B the need to develop a *lean* approach, which delights the customer by passing value as efficiently to them as possible, is clearly not an important consideration at all. One of the competitive strategies which Rupert Murdoch has operated, in the fight for dominance with terrestrial broadcasting in the UK, has been not to reduce costs, but in fact to raise them in the supply chain by bidding for sports activities at such a high level that other competitors (like the BBC) can no longer compete for control of the assets. This strategy appears to be working for Murdoch at the moment. However, it would be equally as fallacious, from a study of this one empirical case, to argue that *raising the stakes* is the most appropriate strategy for competitive success, as it is to argue that quasi-vertical integration and close working relationships, as practised by Japanese auto-assemblers, is the only way to operate a business successfully.

This line of reasoning leads us to the view that **barefoot empiricism** must be flawed as a basis for theorising about what the most appropriate strategies are for business success. One reason is that it has a tendency to lead to *'fad'* thinking. *'Fad'* thinking is that process by which a particular approach becomes fashionable amongst the practitioner, the consulting or the academic community and is touted (until it demonstrably fails to live up to expectations) as the *cure-all* for every business ill.

A second reason is that no amount of analysis of operational practice, in the absence of an understanding of the contingent strategic business and supply chain contexts within which these practices must operate, can provide a guide for improved business performance. It follows from this that useful guides and tools for business can only be created if analysis first starts from a prior theorisation of the key factors which drive business success in any, and all, contexts. It cannot start from an analysis of the specific and idiosyncratic factors which currently are, or have been, important in any particular company.

Competing On Core Competence

The work of Hamel and Prahalad on *core competence* has also been influential but it also suffers from an over-reliance on a limited view of epistemology. This is due to the fact that Hamel and Prahalad's central argument, as demonstrated in Figure 29, is derived from only a few empirical cases, which are presented in the form of a *lawyers brief* to substantiate the causal arguments presented. Their thinking lacks rigour because it is not based on a sound scientific research method which seeks to test out a prior deduced theory of business success through the use of counter-factuals. As a result, although there is insufficient space to go into great deal about this approach here, it is clear that the definition which Hamel and Prahalad have given of *core competence* is not soundly based theoretically. As a result, it can provide little clear guidance for future operational practice. (Hamel and Prahalad, 1990, 1993 & 1994)

Hamel and Prahalad argue that, as a result of the global competitive pressures facing organisations, an approach is needed to sustain competitive advantage which allows companies to search for new markets and to delight new customers. It follows that the primary focus of strategy should, therefore, become the mastery of competencies which allow companies to develop new, rather than to defend historic, products or services. There is much to be said for this viewpoint, because one of the primary drivers of change in recent years has been technological innovation, which poses severe threats to for strategies which focus only on the defence of traditional products and services. Having said this there may

Figure 29: The Myopia of Core Competence Thinking

THE MYOPIA OF CORE COMPETENCE THINKING

BASIC THESIS

- Hamel and Prahalad use a bare-foot empiricist method to observe a number of specific cases, and use inductive reasoning to create an explanation of business success

- Success seen to come from having internal skills and processes which allow firms to control capabilities which are competitively unique, providing fundamental customer benefits

FIVE THEORETICAL AND METHODOLOGICAL PROBLEMS

- An explicit theory of success which cannot explain cases of success when companies do not have core competencies

- If all successful companies have core competencies by definition the theory is tautological

- The theory is primarily descriptive

- It provides no predictive guide to future action

- The methodology is based on a lawyer's brief approach

be serious practical problems for corporate decision-makers who attempt to adopt this approach.

Hamel and Prahalad conceive of a *core competencies* approach to business strategy as being essentially about basing competition on the possession of a bundle of distinct and defensible skills and technologies. They refer to this as *"the sum of learning across individual skill sets and individual organisational units"* (Hamel and Prahalad, 1994, p.203) Hamel and Prahalad argue that it is this which allow a company to create the business opportunities of the future by finding new ways of leveraging markets and delighting customers. The major thrust of this thinking is that companies should focus only on those activities in which they have a *core competence*: Core competencies are defined by reference to three tests:

- *They must deliver a fundamental customer benefit.*

- *They must be based on a capability which is competitively unique.*

- *They must be extendible into an array of new products or services.*

While no one can disagree that it is a good thing to have a capability that is competitively unique, or that companies should think about the future product and service needs of consumers, this insight is hardly astounding theoretically. Furthermore, it provides little in the way of advice for the millions of companies that are attempting to compete in markets where it is not possible to develop a capability which is unique. What is the appropriate strategy for these types of companies?   Is it impossible for such companies to be successful?

An additional problem with this approach is that it does not tell us prescriptively which skills or capabilities will be needed in future to allow companies to be successful, under particular supply chain and market circumstances.   As a result the approach is merely descriptive and provides no operational guidance as to how a *core competence* can be created in the future.

> *The problem with the Hamel and Prahalad approach is that while it allows the analyst to define what the 'core competencies' in any supply chain were after the fact (by reference to who was successful), it does not provide any clear mechanism to enable companies to analyse what will be important in the future.*

The methodology provides, therefore, no real guide to allow for a prediction of which resources should be controlled in a supply chain or a market, and which skills and capabilities will allow companies to do so.   It can be argued, therefore, that it is a descriptive rather than an analytic approach to business strategy, which fails both the test of appropriateness and of prediction.

This approach also fails to address one of the key operational questions that confronts all companies.   This is the question of the effective management of external resources.   The focus throughout is primarily on developing internal skills and capabilities, rather than on understanding that effective management also involves the development of an external focus on suppliers, as well as customers, once a firm has decided what its *core competencies* are. This approach, therefore, does not address satisfactorily the key issue of how external resources can be differentiated, and how relatively complementary or residual resources outside the boundary of the firm should be handled to allow the company or individual to appropriate and accumulate value from participation in a supply chain.

There is also a further problem with this approach. Since it is difficult to define the innovative skills and capabilities *(core competencies)* which are necessary to allow us to control and dominate new markets in advance, it would appear that the operational tendency has been to equate *core* with *smaller* and *leaner*. The reason for this clearly resides in the practical difficulties of operationalising the Hamel and Prahalad approach predictively.

> *If the supply chains that companies are involved in are new, and not as yet known then, presumably, companies will need to know which of the resources within that chain are* <u>*critical*</u>*, which are* <u>*complementary*</u> *and which are of* <u>*residual*</u> *importance to value accumulation and appropriation.*

As a result, it would appear that companies adopting this approach in the 1990s have equated business success with a concentration on their *core business*. This normally means those things that they currently know most about and do reasonably well. Unfortunately, as Penrose argued many years ago, concentrating only on what you can do well today does not help the company to grow. (Penrose, 1959) For Penrose companies can only grow successfully by applying their surplus resources within new markets and supply chains. If this view is correct then it must be seen as a plea for successful diversification rather than a recommendation to concentrate on the *core business*. There seems little doubt that, in practice, the argument by Hamel and Prahalad about the need to concentrate on *core competencies* has been diluted by an operational penchant for cost reduction through headcount outsourcing.

This conclusion is interesting, because it highlights an additional problem. Even though academics and consultants may generalise from limited evidence there is a further problem. Practitioners are busy, and they often fail to fully understand the relative sophistication and nuance of some of the ideas to which they are exposed. As a result, they compound the initial problems of epistemological inadequacy and theoretical immaturity within the discipline, by implementing particular ideas and practices inappropriately and with inadequate understanding.

Sometimes, of course, they may also simply steal a particular concept or idea and use it to justify a particular practice which they had always wished to implement, and which has no direct relationship whatsoever with the original concept or idea to which they were exposed. It would be interesting to know, for instance, how many CEOs and finance directors have picked up on the *core competence* idea as a vehicle for short-term cost reduction through outsourcing.

Systematic Empiricism: Constructing Rational Descriptive Typologies

The second methodology that dominates contemporary business thinking is that associated with the systematic construction of rational, deductive typologies. This approach assumes that, by codifying all of the factors which can impact on business into descriptive categories or typologies, it will be possible to use this knowledge to assist companies to become more effective.

This approach is adopted by leading strategy writers like Ansoff and Porter. Ansoff's famous taxonomy of generic strategies is widely accepted as the basis for strategic differentiation by companies, with its focus on market penetration, product development, market development and diversification. (Ansoff, 1965 & 1988) The problem with this type of approach is, however, that although it provides a descriptive taxonomy, which catalogues potential practices, it does not provide a methodology that will allow companies to predict the strategies which will be the most appropriate to adopt under given circumstances.

Clearly, however, the development of descriptive taxonomies of the total universe of strategic and operational practices, which might be possible under all contingent circumstances, is a useful under-labour conceptually. If undertaken properly it can provide the basis around which a more predictive theory of business success can be built. It is not surprising, therefore, that the most fertile and robust lines of enquiry in business thinking that have been undertaken in recent years have been those associated with the development of descriptive, organising typologies.

The work of Porter, on the codification of the external, market-specific, factors which shape the internal business strategies of the firm, is of major importance in this respect. The work of Kay, that has codified the internal universe of capabilities which successful companies can use, also stands out as one of the most seminal contributions in business thinking in recent times. The strengths and weaknesses of each of these two ground breaking works are discussed below.

*The Five External Forces and the Tyranny of Market Fit and
Focus*

Porter's Five Forces model of the key external market forces
impacting on all companies has been widely influential as a
business text, and so has his view of the choice between
strategies based on differentiation, cost leadership and focus.
(Porter, 1980 & 1985)   The reasons for this are obvious.
Porter's Five forces model, see Figure 30, deals with five of the
invariant factors which always impact on companies in
competitive markets and in all contingent circumstances.

Figure 30: Porter's Five Forces

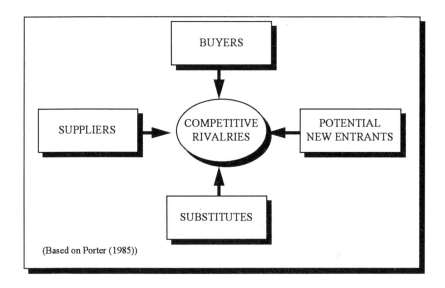

(Based on Porter (1985))

All companies in markets experience potential competitive
rivalry and the threat of substitute products and services. They
also operate in market places of buyer and supplier relative

power. The reason for Porter's standing in the profession is obvious. His work has codified some of the key factors outside the firm that are embedded within all markets and which have a contingent influence on its strategic focus. By also codifying some of the broad strategic choices, which are available to any company in relation to the scope of that strategy (see Figure 31) he has also performed a great service for practitioners and academics alike. His work has demonstrated some of the constant choices that individuals in companies can make when they attempt to decide what to do with the resources that are available to them.

Figure 31: Porter's Strategic Options

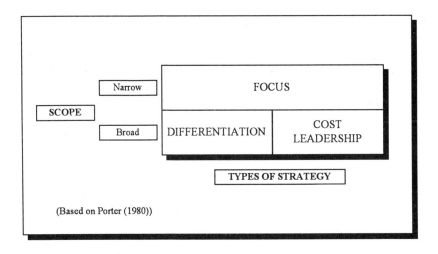

(Based on Porter (1980))

Despite this there is still one major theoretical and epistemological problem with Porter's approach as Figure 32 demonstrates. It can be argued that, despite his comprehensive treatment of many of the contingent forces in market power structures, his concern is still very much with the need for the company to *fit* itself to the existing market structure. Porter's view is that this can be achieved by the company by positioning, within this existing market structure, and defending this position through the erection of market barriers to entry. Even in his most recent writing he still conceives of the firm as a tightly defined entity that, in order to achieve its own competitive advantage, must seek out opportunities to make the most of the complementary resources available to it. (Porter 1996) This *way of thinking* is implicit in his organisationally specific conceptualisation of the value stream. (See Figure 32)

Figure 32: Porter's Value Chain

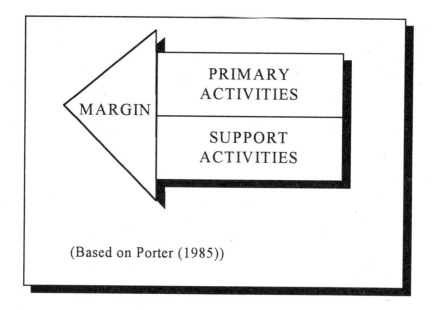

(Based on Porter (1985))

While there is nothing intrinsically wrong with this it would appear that Porter does not visualise the problem of corporate success or failure in any other terms than as a *black-box*, in which the firm uses available resources (notice his constant emphasis on the need for focus) to find distinctive and non-replicable things to do. The problem with this view of the firm is that it does not recognise the essence of entrepreneurial activity:

> ***Entrepreneurial activity is the ability to understand how the stream of value within a supply chain (not a market) can be radically changed by contingent forces, other than those which Porter defines as of central importance for markets.***

In other words, Porter's argument is correct under all circumstances, but only if it is correct to conceive of business strategy as pre-eminently about competitive market positioning. The view that focusing on competitive market *'fit'* is always the most appropriate thing for companies to do may well be incorrect. Again this is not to say that Porter's view is therefore wrong. Rather, it is to say that his view is not necessarily correct, under all circumstances.

Herein, as Figure 33 indicates, lies the major epistemological problem with Porter's seminal work. While his work has codified many of the contingent factors in market situations, it can be argued that, while this provides, a comprehensive description of a variety of potentially important external market factors, there is still something missing from his account. Although the taxonomy is comprehensive, it does not provide any real basis for us to know what a company will experience in

Figure 33: The Myopia of Market Power Positioning

THE MYOPIA OF MARKET POWER POSITIONING

BASIC THESIS

- By thinking deductively Porter has arrived at a typology of 5 key market-specific forces which impinge on all companies in all circumstances

- On the basis of these forces Porter focuses on the creation of market barriers to entry as a key to business success

FIVE THEORETICAL AND METHODOLOGICAL PROBLEMS

- A solid taxonomy of 5 forces but atheoretical with no explicit deductive theory of causality

- An essentially descriptive methodology

- An essentially reactive rather than predictive way of thinking

- The focus is primarily on external rather than internal forces

- There is no way of knowing, dynamically, which forces will be more important than others in future circumstances

the future, or for understanding what a company ought to do to mange its situation pro-actively in any particular circumstance in the future.

On these grounds alone the Porter approach, while of great significance as a work of systematic descriptive taxonomy, fails the test of predictive theorisation. It tells us what some of the important factors will always be, but it provides no guide to purposive action. The author believes that the major reason for this is because Porter has focused first on markets rather than on supply chains and, as a result, is operating with an inadequate understanding of what a value chain is. This is the tyranny which comes from a strategic focus on market *fit*. This focus has clearly caused the profession to under-estimate the full range of contingent circumstances which individuals and companies actually face externally.

Competing on Distinctive Capabilities and Resources

Nonetheless, despite these criticisms, Porter's work is one of the necessary precursors to the development of a properly abstractive and scientific approach to an understanding of business success. Until Porter's work appeared the predominant emphasis in the literature was on the analysis of business success through anecdotes, descriptive case study work and some attempts at broadly based generalisations (although often based on a limited number of cases). The reasons for this are rooted in the relatively short history of the development of business management as a discipline of academic enquiry. According to John Kay, business management has only really been a major area of academic enquiry for the last thirty years or so. (Kay, 1994)

Kay, like Porter before him, has made his name in business management by introducing the analytical rigour of traditional economic thinking into the discipline. Kay's work is of equal importance to that of Porter for the development of business thinking, because he has begun the process of systematically codifying many of the *internal* (skills and capabilities) which underpin any and all cases of business success. This work complements, even though it challenges, the earlier work on *external* market forces by Porter. Kay's contribution is broadly within the *resource based theory of the firm*, that was initially developed by Edith Penrose (1959), and which has recently dominated a great deal of American business thinking. (Montgomery, 1995).

The seminal importance of Kay's work should not be underestimated because, by systematically codifying many of the internal skills and capabilities within the firm (see Figure 34), he has created the second precursor to the development of a properly contingent and abstractive theory of business success and failure.

Figure 34: Kay's Taxonomy of Distinctive Capabilities

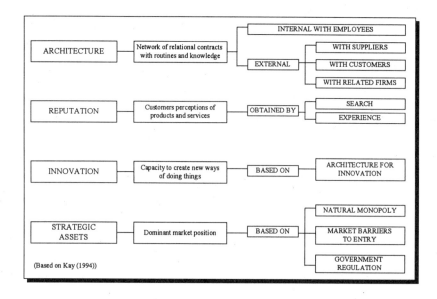

If such a theory is to be properly developed in the future, it will be necessary to codify all of the resources that an individual, or a firm, may use under different circumstances. This theory will also require an understanding of the universe of potential external constraints that individuals and companies may experience under different contingent circumstances. Kay and Porter have taken the first steps on that theoretical journey.

Kay is also to be applauded for his recognition of the immaturity and under-development of current business management thinking. His own analysis of the existing work on the causes of business success confirms that, while most of the early writers did base their arguments about success on clear empirical, operational cases, they singularly failed to distinguish between taxonomy, deductive logic and empirical observation. This, Kay has correctly argued, has led most strategy writers to fail to develop an organised framework for the study of business behaviour and success, and demonstrates that the majority of this work is based on *bare-foot empiricist ways of thinking*.

Unfortunately, despite the sophistication of his descriptive taxonomy of potential internal capabilities, and his clear insight into the epistemological problems of business management thinking, Kay's own view of the causes of business success does not really resolve the problem he highlights. The major reason for this is, as Figure 35 reveals, that Kay's own analysis is also grounded in an *empiricist*, rather than an *abstractive* and properly *theoretical*, approach to strategy and operational practice.

Kay does use a rigorous, rational and deductive, logic to construct his taxonomy of potential internal capabilities. However, he has not recognised the need to apply the same approach to the delineation and verification of his own preferred explanation of the causal factors in business success. While he (unlike Porter and Hamel and Prahalad) has a theory, he has still not accepted that causality can only be understood through the development of an explicit theory based on a priori rational,

Figure 35: The Myopia of Stakeholding and Distinctive Capabilities

THE MYOPIA OF STAKEHOLDING AND DISTINCTIVE CAPABILITIES

BASIC THESIS

- Rational deductive logic and empirical observation can create a descriptive taxonomy of the universe of resources and capabilities which can bring business success

- There is no generic business strategy but stakeholding and long-term relational contracting is seen to be the most appropriate

FIVE THEORETICAL AND METHODOLOGICAL PROBLEMS

- A solid descriptive taxonomy of capabilities, but the predictive theory is based more on inductive rather than deductive reasoning

- A tendency to use a lawyer's brief approach rather than abstractive reasoning

- A confusion of cause and effect through incommensurable logic

- A failure to understand the contingent nature of strategic means, but the determinant nature of strategic ends

- An inability to predict which distinctive capabilities should be owned and controlled in the future

deductive logic which is tested through a positivist, inductive methodology.

This leads Kay to confuse cause and effect in his own explanation of business success. He argues that, while there can be no single recipe or generic strategies for business, successful companies will be those that are able to develop stability and continuity in relationships. Furthermore, those relationships will, necessarily be devoted to the application of *distinctive capabilities* (innovation, architecture and reputation) within particular markets. This *stakeholder* (or *relational contracting*) approach, he argues, is what the Japanese in general, and BMW, Glaxo, Honda, IBM, Benetton and Marks and Spencers in particular, have used with great success to achieve sustainable competitive advantage in recent years.

The problem with this *way of thinking* is that while it has real empirical strengths, it also a number of epistemological weaknesses. On the one hand, Kay provides an inclusive, descriptive list of all of those contingent factors which may or may not be the basis for business success. He also, correctly, emphasises that companies must pay attention to all of those internal resources—*architecture, reputation, innovation* and *strategic assets*—which may help them to develop *distinctive capabilities* in relation to their competitors.

He then concludes, however, that one approach—*stakeholding and long-term relational contracting*—is the most appropriate way of arranging capabilities, managing competition and achieving sustainable business success. Unfortunately, by doing so, Kay appears to be holding two mutually incompatible views. He argues that there can be no one generic strategy that leads to success for all companies; while also maintaining that stakeholding and relational contracting is the approach which is the most appropriate for achieving success. These two views do not appear to be commensurable.

The problem of non-commensurable logic (which Kay's argument demonstrates) arises because he has slipped into the same empiricist trap within which the business management profession has historically found itself. He appears to have started from the premise that business success and operational practice is contingent and that, as a result, an understanding of all of those potential factors which support business success must first be codified properly before research can begin. This is Kay's view of taxonomy and it leads him into a cul-de-sac. The cul-de-sac is created, not by his recognition that scientific research requires a taxonomy (a classification and codification of types of action with a specification of the likely consequences from their implementation), but from his failure to acknowledge that a taxonomy is not descriptively defined.

It can be argued that a proper taxonomy of the causes of business success must be predictive. This means that a valid taxonomy can only be derived from deductive theoretical reasoning about causality in business success in advance of observation. Once a theory of the causes of business success has been derived in this way it is then possible to sub-divide the range of potential variables which the theory logically specifies are the causal factors in success. These can then be used to provide potentially predictive hypothetical propositions about how success is achieved, in relation to the relative importance of particular resources (skills and capabilities), under specified circumstances. Only when this prior theorisation has been achieved will be possible to begin the process of empirical verification.

This verification process has to be one in which the theory and the predictive causal hypotheses are transparently tested for validity. These propositions must be capable of proof and disproof (falsification) if they are to be the basis of proper scientific enquiry. Furthermore, the empirical testing of these propositions must lead, eventually, to the systematic development of a verified taxonomy of causality under particular circumstances. If none, or a substantial number, of the propositions (causal hypotheses) are invalidated by the evidence then, of course, the initial theory must be modified to take account of these facts. On the other hand, if the theory cannot be modified successfully, then it must be rejected and the search for a new explanatory theory of causality must begin.

Unfortunately, despite his desire to create a truly scientific approach to the analysis of business strategy, Kay's approach fails to meet this test of scientific validity. While it is a systematic approach it is, therefore, still firmly located within the empiricist view of theory building and taxonomy. While Kay has correctly described many of the major resources (skills and capabilities) which could be the determinants of business success, he has failed to develop a theory of causality prior to research.

As a consequence, like many business management writers before him, he appears to have created a *lawyer's brief*. By this one means that he appears to have provided only empirical cases to support his own prior view of what does lead to success. His view is that this is the creation of a set of *distinctive capabilities* linked to a strategy of stakeholding and long-term relational contracting. He has not however, scientifically tested to see if there are also significant numbers of cases in which business success is determined by other factors.

For this reason the most that one can possibly say in relation to Kay's view is that his interpretation of business success may or may not be correct. On the basis of the evidence provided by Kay we simply do not know whether or not his approach is appropriate under all circumstances, or only under some. If it is only appropriate only under some circumstances then it is still necessary to know which of these circumstances are the most conducive to stakeholding and relational contracting strategies.

To provide a few cases of successful companies and argue that, because they have had stakeholding and long-term contractual relationships with their suppliers and customers, this is the reason for their success, does not constitute scientific proof at all. On the contrary it merely indicates that these companies do, descriptively, have long-term relationships. Furthermore, the existence of these relationships does not on its own rule out other causal phenomena as the potential reasons for success. Nor does it rule out the possibility that the long-term relationships which these companies have may be a consequence, rather than a cause, of their success.

The problem with Kay's view, as with all of the other views which he criticises, is that none of them have been sufficiently tested empirically to validate whether or not they are the causes or consequences of business success. The reason for this is not, as Kay argues, because business management writers have failed to understand the need for taxonomy, deductive logic and empirical verification. The primary reason would appear to be because business writers (both academics and consultants) cannot begin to understand what causes success until the discipline develops a theory (or theories) about the role and function of the firm in society.

A proper theorisation of the role of the firm cannot start from the development of a descriptive taxonomy of all of the resources (skills and capabilities) that are potentially available to firms. Rather, a proper theorisation must start from a clear specification of the 'raison d'être' of the firm. This means that the legal status of the firm must be understood in relation to two key factors.

- *The private ownership of property under conditions of absolute and relative material scarcity; and*

- *The constraints on the ownership of material wealth which result from the relative degrees of freedom of exchange that exist in the world.*

Only if the firm is first understood theoretically in this way will it be possible to define and measure success properly. It also follows that, only by theoretically understanding why the firm exists at all, will it be possible to develop testable hypotheses, or propositions, about the causal factors behind success under specific circumstances. Furthermore, to be properly scientific, these propositions (or hypotheses) must be defined prior to any empirical test of their validity; they cannot be constructed after an empirical analysis of a particular case or cases.

This problem is highlighted most starkly if we focus on Kay's view that companies must develop *distinctive capabilities* to be successful. By this he means that companies must focus on their own unique internal character and attributes, and then try to find markets in which this *distinctiveness* can be applied successfully in ways which their competitors cannot imitate. On the face of it this seems reasonable enough as a guide to business success. However, on further reflection, it can be argued that this view provides no predictive guide whatsoever to what a company could or should do.

The problem is that Kay's approach provides a description of what companies do—by definition—to be successful: they develop things which others cannot imitate. These, Kay tells us, are *distinctive capabilities*. The problem is that Kay's approach allow us to know what these were descriptively in the past, but it provides no basis, whatsoever, to allow us to predict which *distinctive capabilities* will be needed to allow us to be successful in the future. Unless the stakeholding view can be substantiated, Kay's approach clearly lacks any predictive utility. It is, therefore, like Hamel and Prahalad's *core competence* perspective, a post-hoc, descriptive and atheoretical methodology for analysing business success.

The major reason for this conclusion is that Kay's approach merely describes what companies are doing, without providing any guide to what the *ideal* configuration of corporate resources and assets could, or should, be in the future. In specifying what these might be, it is necessary to recognise that what is *ideal* in achieving sustainable advantage, for the wide diversity of companies that exist, will be a function of the distinct supply chains which they operate in under contingent market circumstances. Kay is not, however, the most culpable in this respect. Kay has at least recognised the need to develop a taxonomy of resources (skills and capabilities), and a theory of explanation. In this way his work has made a significant contribution to the clearing of the ground intellectually to allow for what may then follow.

The majority of business writers still seem, however, to be some way from the insights of Kay. Furthermore, they appear to believe that the empirical observation of any particular operational practice, in companies that are more or less successful than others, is the appropriate empirical basis for the development of a *new theory* (sic) of business success. It would appear that the real problem in much of business management writing is that thinkers do not really understand what a properly scientific theory of business success would look like.

Hopefully, the analysis presented here will have gone some of the way in explaining how an abstractive and contingent theory of success and failure could be developed. The next stage is to lay out the reasoning behind the ***theory of asset criticality*** which is informed by the abstractive *way of thinking* in this volume. This is the task of the three chapters in the next section.

AN ENTREPRENEURIAL WAY OF THINKING ABOUT SUSTAINABLE BUSINESS SUCCESS

5

On Scarcity, Value Appropriation And Effective Leverage

In the last chapter it was argued that there are some seminal texts in business thinking, but that none of them satisfy the tests of theoretical and epistemological rigour. While the works of Kay and Porter are close to the ideal, it was argued that they failed to provide an adequate predictive theory of business success. In this chapter and the next two, starting from *first principles*, a theory of the firm is developed. This theory is based on a series of propositions about what firms have to do to be successful.

These propositions were not constructed after the systematic direct observation of the activities of firms, but are derived from a process of deductive thinking, based on the inductive acquisition of knowledge through the author's own personal experiences. This deductive and inductive process has, however, been informed by his observation of human behaviour in public and private sector organisations over many years. It has also been developed from extensive reading about the *ways of thinking* of commentators on the human condition in a wide array of historically specific social, economic and political circumstances. It is by this process of deductive and inductive thinking that the author has arrived at the conclusion that current business thinkers have failed to grasp fully what is one of the primary causal phenomena of business success. This is can be summarised quite easily:

- *The ability of individuals or companies to understand which existing, and which future, supply chain resources they should own, control and leverage to allow them to appropriate value.*

- *A recognition by individuals or companies that they must act entrepreneurially, and seek conditions of permanent or temporary monopoly, in supply chains.*

- *An understanding by individuals or companies of how supply chain resources can become critical assets.*

In this chapter the basic ideas which inform this abstractive and theoretical *way of thinking* are outlined. In the first part the problem of the **dominant paradigm** is introduced. This is shown to be an attachment to market-based thinking. It is argued, theoretically, and from first principles, that this *way of thinking* is largely due to the seminal influence of the work of Adam Smith on economic and business thinking. In parts two and three the important, but partial contributions of Adam Smith and Karl Marx are outlined. From this critique a more inclusive theory of the conditions for business success is developed. This theory is based on an understanding of the importance for business success of material scarcity, monopoly and the leverage of intellectual property in supply chains by entreprenurial individuals or companies.

The Problem of the Dominant Paradigm

The *way of thinking* which the author has developed is based on the idea that the fundamental problem with all business management and economic thinking is that it starts from the wrong place. As excellent as the work of Kay and Porter is it is located within a particular paradigm—*way of thinking*—about the relative importance of things. This thinking provides a filter through which certain phenomena, rather than others, are selected and chosen for analysis. In selecting in this way academic thinkers are providing a filtering process which becomes the guide through which practitioners understand what it is that they should do. Practitioners are, however, unlikely to appreciate that their actions are rarely based on their own conscious choices. Rather, as Keynes said long ago, they are often made as a direct consequence of the previous filtering and selection process of some philosopher or academic writer.

The fact that practitioners are not aware that they are basing their actions on the *way of thinking* of others is not necessarily important. The reason for this is because *different ways of thinking* are always in competition with one another. What practitioners normally do, without fully understanding it, is to operate within the dominant paradigm. This is the *way of thinking* which has the best fit with reality of all of the currently competing ways of thinking. This *best fit* is based on the observable fact that, if the practitioner operates within this *way of thinking*, things normally work out successfully more times than they do not. This, by definition, is why this *way of thinking* is currently the dominant paradigm for human action. It is the best guide to success and failure.

It does not normally matter, therefore, that practitioners do not fully understand the epistemological and intellectual foundations of the theories which directly and indirectly shape their thoughts and actions. Practitioners can be successful without understanding theoretically why some of their actions are more appropriate than others. There is no problem, as long as their experience (the empirical observation that if they do a certain thing it will normally lead to a valued outcome) continues to reaffirm their currently held assumptions about causality. The reason is that the dominant paradigm (*way of thinking*) is the guide by which everyone else is operating.

A problem only occurs for the dominant paradigm when a better (more inclusive and predictive) *way of thinking* emerges. If there is a *better way of thinking* about causality which clarifies more of the inadequately explained causes of business success and failure, then it is crucial that practitioners do begin to understand the intellectual and epistemological foundations of their *ways of thinking*. The reason is that *ways of thinking* are, potentially, extremely valuable commodities. Without any doubt the possession of the *currently most appropriate way of thinking* about causality could, if it was possible to create an absolute, or even partial, monopoly over this *way of thinking*, be a **critical asset** (from which its owner could appropriate and accumulate material wealth).

The control of the intellectual property of thinking in this way is of course problematic because, as soon as someone explains the *new way of thinking*, everyone else has the potential to copy it for themselves. Nevertheless, since a *new way of thinking* may provide the basis for a more efficient focus on the truly causal factors in success and failure, the possession of it will potentially provide a competitive and, in some cases, a sustainable advantage over others. For this reason, all practitioners need to understand the *new way of thinking* because the possession of it provides them with a potential opportunity for value appropriation and accumulation from others. Those who master the *new way of thinking* first, will also have the opportunity to use it to focus their activities more *appropriately*.

The problem is, of course, that those who adopt the *new way of thinking* have to be risk takers. The reason is obvious. When the *new way of thinking* is first developed it is untested. This must be so because the ideas must first have been developed in someone's mind. This will have been on the basis of abstractive reasoning through a process of rational, deductive logic and inductive validation. When the *new way of thinking* is formalised, however, it is nothing more than a theory that the original thinker has developed. Only when it is tested in the real world will evidence about its practical utility be discovered. If the *new way of thinking* is more appropriate than the existing ways of thinking then, gradually, there will be a **paradigm shift,** as more and more people come to accept that it is superior to previous ways of thinking.

The difficulty for practitioners is, however, that they have to make decisions about what they should do in an environment in which there is no certainty that what the *new way of thinking* proposes will in fact be successful. This is because, when it appears, it is only a theory in the mind of an individual, and there can be no guarantee that its implementation will lead to beneficial outcomes. There is just as much chance that the theory will be incorrect as correct. Consequently, the practitioner, seeking certainty, will wait until somebody else takes the initiative and risks failure. Once the theory has been tested and validated by others, the risk averse practitioner will then rush to implement it and to copy those related operational practices which have been proven to be beneficial in the past. This is what most practitioners regard as good business practice and effective business management.

It will be obvious to the reader by now where this line of reasoning takes us. Many business thinkers, and the bulk of the practitioner community, have a belief that business success has something to do with effective management. In this author's view, while this is an important aspect of business success, it can never be the key to it. The reasons are obvious:

- *Effective management is, at heart, about the copying of the operational practices of previous risk-takers who, apparently, have been successful.*

- *It is about creating standardised and routinised processes through which regular patterns of behaviour can be organised to deliver pre-specified, and already known, outcomes.*

- *This may help individuals and companies to manage existing ways of thinking but, arguably, it has very little to do with long-term, sustainable business success.*

In this writer's view the key to business success is firmly rooted in the capacity of individuals (and therefore companies) to take chances with uncertainty. At its very heart, business success is therefore about *entrepreneurial action*. By this is meant two things.

- *The capacity of individuals to understand, in advance of others, which things should be acquired in order to control the appropriation, accumulation and allocation of value.*

- *Since it is difficult to know for certain what should be acquired and controlled in the future, business success requires that the individual is willing to take educated risks with uncertainty.*

Figure 36: Business Success and Entrepreneurial Action

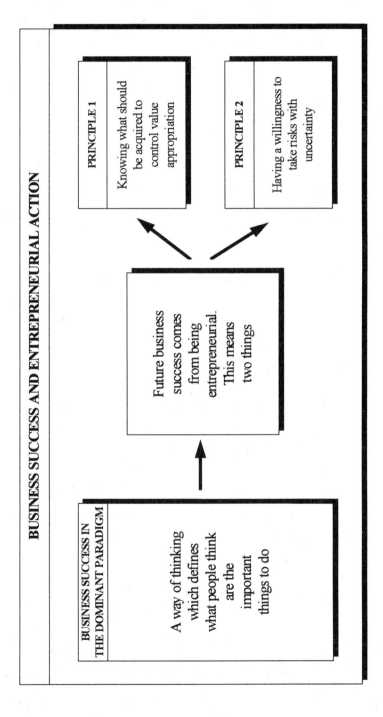

BUSINESS SUCCESS AND ENTREPRENEURIAL ACTION

BUSINESS SUCCESS IN THE DOMINANT PARADIGM

A way of thinking which defines what people think are the important things to do

Future business success comes from being entrepreneurial. This means two things

PRINCIPLE 1

Knowing what should be acquired to control value appropriation

PRINCIPLE 2

Having a willingness to take risks with uncertainty

The focus here, as Figure 36 demonstrates, is on the acquisition of those things which allow individuals and, therefore, companies to *steal a march* on their rivals. It should be plain, therefore, that the approach to business success which is outlined here is not based primarily on the making of recommendations about the copying, or benchmarking, of what other people are doing. By definition, such an approach can rarely be the basis for sustainable competitive advantage. The problem for practitioners is that, since the majority of them are risk averse, they will only consider a *new way of thinking* when it has demonstrably been successful in practice for others. Unfortunately, when practitioners benchmark what others are doing, and then copy or adapt the *new way of thinking* to their own purposes, they have often already lost the game to their competitors. This is the ***practitioner's dilemma*** (see Figures 37 and 38).

The practitioner's dilemma is in three parts.

Figure 37: *The Practitioner's Dilemma*

- *Practitioners want to know, with certainty, that a new way of thinking will lead to business success before they are willing to accept it.*

- *Practitioners want clearly defined operational guides to action, with clearly calibrated probability statements about potential outcomes, before they will adopt a new way of thinking.*

- *If validated practical guides to operational action exist for new ways of thinking, and they are freely available and tested, then it is unlikely that they will provide any sustainable competitive advantage for the practitioner.*

Figure 38: The Safe-Bet and the Long-Shot

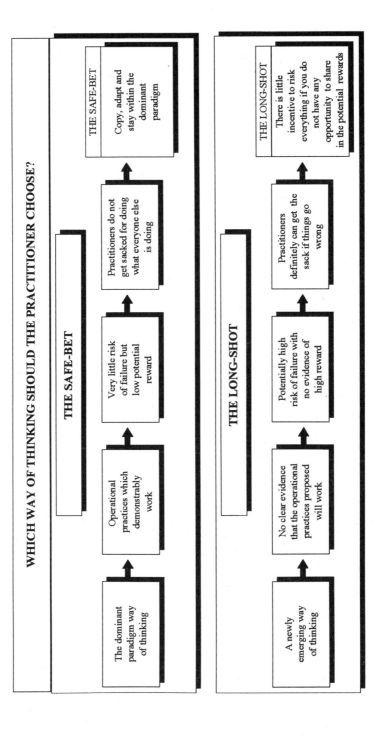

WHICH WAY OF THINKING SHOULD THE PRACTITIONER CHOOSE?

THE SAFE-BET

The dominant paradigm way of thinking → Operational practices which demonstrably work → Very little risk of failure but low potential reward → Practitioners do not get sacked for doing what everyone else is doing → THE SAFE-BET: Copy, adapt and stay within the dominant paradigm

THE LONG-SHOT

A newly emerging way of thinking → No clear evidence that the operational practices proposed will work → Potentially high risk of failure with no evidence of high reward → Practitioners definitely can get the sack if things go wrong → THE LONG-SHOT: There is little incentive to risk everything if you do not have any opportunity to share in the potential rewards

It is through trying to understand these types of operational problems from first principles that the author has arrived at his own view of what causes business success. It has led him to the view that it is not just practitioners who do not know what are the primary conditions for achieving business success. The majority of business writers and thinkers are similarly afflicted. This is not to say that everyone is wrong. On the contrary, there are many business and economics writers who have isolated most, and perhaps all, of the factors which can account for business success in competitive market situations. It is, however, the strength which comes from the current *way of thinking* about operating within competitive markets that also accounts for this dominant paradigm's greatest explanatory weakness.

This weakness is the fact that, throughout the history of modern business thinking, the dominant paradigm used by academics, consultants and practitioners alike, has been conditioned by a short-term *market-focused way of thinking*. The current writer believes that it is a result of this fact that most people cannot see what is before them. What is before them is a simple truth. It is a truth of which the business community and many a politician and academic dare not speak. This truth is the fact that:

> *The ideal way to achieve sustainable business success, in a society of absolute and relative material scarcity, is through the creation of absolute, or relative degrees of, monopoly.*

This is the essential truth which Peteraf wrote about in a recent seminal article. (Peteraf, 1993) It is also a truth which, although they wrote from very different perspectives, Adam Smith, David Ricardo and Karl Marx understood in the eighteenth and nineteenth centuries.

If this simple truth holds, then it is plain, as Figure 39 indicates, that *the goal of business is not to operate successfully within competitive markets, but to stop competitive markets operating.* Given absolute and relative scarcity, and the possibility of learning and imitative behaviour by individuals and companies, the ultimate *strategic goal* of all companies under all circumstances should be the same. It should be to find ways of controlling the key resources within a supply chain in such a way that a contested and competitive market cannot be created. It therefore, follows, that:

> *Strategic thinking is the ability to understand the conditions under which it is possible to create either permanent monopoly or temporary monopoly on a serial basis in supply chains..*

This, theoretically and logically, must be the ideal strategic condition which all individuals and companies seek, because it is the only certain way of achieving sustainable business success. If this is so, why is it, that most of the current literature on business and economics focuses so single-mindedly on competitive market thinking? The answer to this apparent conundrum is discussed in the next section in relation to the seminal influence of Adam Smith on business and economics thinking.

This discussion is followed by an analysis from *first principles* of the human condition under scarcity, looking at the contribution which Karl Marx has made to our understanding of

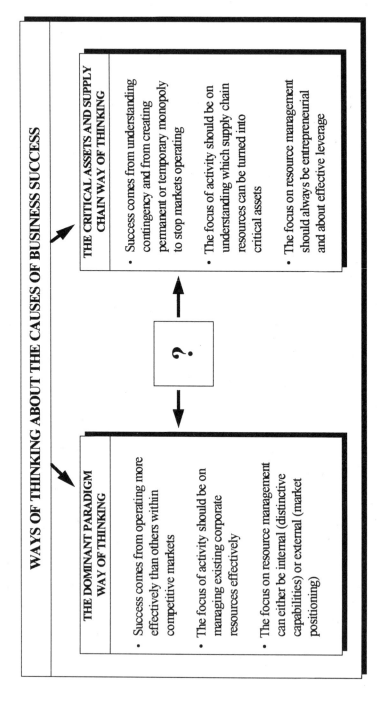

Figure 39: Alternative Ways of Thinking About the Causes of Business Success

the conditions under which business success and failure occur. This general discussion of political economy then leads into an introduction to a *way of thinking* about **critical supply chain assets**, which the author believes is a *missing link* in current business thinking.

On Adam Smith and 'The Wealth of Nations'

In an article to be published shortly Leslie Hannah has asked the question why is it that so very few companies, which were formerly successful, survive and prosper? Unfortunately, while Hannah demonstrates that very few of the top 100 companies in 1912 have survived to the present day, he is unable to provide a satisfactory explanation of why this is so. His article provides a rigorous and systematic description of the phenomena of corporate failure, but it does not provide any clear explanation of what are the causes of success or failure. (Hannah, 1997 forthcoming)

Hannah's article is an exceptionally good example of the atheoretical problematic within which current *ways of thinking* operate. The epistemological methodology which Hannah uses is one based squarely within the **barefoot empiricist** school. His article collates the descriptive data on the performance of the top 100 companies in 1912 and then analyses how many have survived to the present day. Hannah then observes the data and, presumably, hopes that *the facts will speak for themselves*. This means that he is hoping that an inductive process of observation will allow him to deduce, from the data, what causes corporate success and failure. In the end, he has to conclude that this process has not been beneficial. His conclusion, from observing the data, is that failure comes about because there are competitive markets, which are a check on the long-term growth potential of large firms.

This is an interesting finding, because it equates with the basic philosophical and rational-deductive logic in Adam Smith's book *The Wealth of Nations*. Writing towards the end of the eighteenth century, Smith argued that when markets, are left to their own devices, and not constrained by artificial barriers and protective restrictions, they will ensure the maximisation of the welfare of all citizens and the development of higher levels of national prosperity. Smith was obviously on to something, and his work has had a profound impact upon the thinking in economics and business management in the last two centuries.   Indeed, it is unquestionable that Smith's *way of thinking* has been the **dominant paradigm** in capitalist countries since that time.   The question which needs to be raised here, however, is whether or not Smith's argument was correct at the time he wrote and, even if it was, whether his thinking is still appropriate today.

It should be clear to the reader that the author takes a *contingent* view of the world.   This simply means that the author believes that what should be done *depends on the circumstances which face us*, and not those which we would like to believe exist.   The problem human beings face, however, is that they do not know objectively the circumstances which face them.   They only know what *is* through their observations, which cannot be understood except through an *abstractive process of reasoning*. There is no doubt whatsoever that Smith used an abstractive process of reasoning from first principles, and that Marx, as we shall see, did the same thing. Why is this an important thing to know?

The reason is simple enough. Human beings do not, in the author's view at least, think about anything in a void. Human beings may be condemned to live in a world of absolute and relative scarcity, but the technological and environmental circumstances within which they experience this fixed condition do change. This change in the circumstances of life takes place because human beings help to create the conditions within which they live, and their thoughts and actions can alter their experience, if not the fixed conditions, of scarcity. This is a simple point, but an important one nevertheless. Its importance is rooted in the fact that what human beings take to be important, and worthy of their consideration and thought, is not independent of the material (technological and environmental) circumstances which they experience.

This line of reasoning takes us back to the nurture versus nature debate which was discussed earlier. The link between human thought and purposive action is always contingent on the circumstances which human beings experience. If this is so then human thought and action are indivisible. As the deductive and inductive principles of abstractive reasoning demonstrate they cannot be separated. Nevertheless, even though the *ways of thinking* which human beings develop will always, in this sense, be contingent, this does not mean that everything which people think is equally acceptable or appropriate as a guide to action. What is appropriate will always, of course, depend on what it is that the individual is attempting to achieve.

In any epoch, however, it will fall to some thinkers to use rational-deductive logic to make sense of the contingent circumstances which everyone is experiencing inductively. What makes a person a *great thinker* is then easily understood. It is that person who, amongst all of the other people in the world who are also struggling to make sense of an immensely complex reality, is best able to clarify the complexity. It is also the person who is able to define what appears to be an eternal truth of human existence. Examples of the latter might be Aristotle, who demonstrated that there are only three 'ideal-typical' forms of political rule, or Einstein, who demonstrated some of the essential principles of physical existence.

The important learning point here is that there may well be different types of *great thinkers*. Presumably, if the logic above is correct, and as Figure 40 indicates, there may well be thinkers who discover invariant and eternal truths, and thinkers who discover truths which are only appropriate given the contingent circumstances which face us.

Figure 40: **Types of Great Thinking**

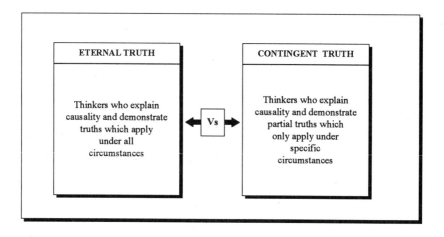

In the context of the discussion here, this insight is of crucial importance because there is a need to know whether Smith was demonstrating eternal or contingent truths about the human condition. It is this author's view that Smith has described three eternal truths about the human condition under material scarcity, see Figure 41, but that the bulk of his writing was essentially contingent.

The first eternal truth that Smith uncovered was the fact that, in the absence of artificial barriers to the ownership and control of things, people will compete against one another to own and control those things which are valuable. This is the essential truth built into the notion of the pursuit of self-interest, and it must follow logically from the recognition that the human condition is to live in a state of absolute and relative scarcity. Smith also uncovered a second eternal truth for those who live under conditions of material scarcity. This is the idea of ***the tyranny of the supplier***:

This holds that, left to their own devices, those who control material scarcity as monopolists will always use their ownership and control to appropriate value in their own interests at the expense of the those whom they supply (the consumer). The third eternal principle follows from this: namely, that an absence of monopoly control over an asset always ensures that, with perfect competition and a contested market, the buyer (consumer) rather than the supplier will determine the allocation of value. In this dependent situation the supplier will always be forced to pass more and more of the value in what is supplied to the customer in order to survive. This situation can be referred to as the ***tyranny of the buyer***.

Figure 41: Smith's Three Eternal Principles of Scarcity

- *Under conditions of scarcity human beings will compete with one another to own and control those things which they hold to be valuable.*

- *Those who own and control valuable things will use this power to appropriate and accumulate value for themselves at the expense of their customers.*

- *If it is not possible to own and control things as a monopolist, then human beings will be forced to compete and, in so doing, the power of value appropriation and accumulation will pass from the supplier to the buyer.*

It is one thing to accept that Smith pointed to certain eternal principles about how human beings living under conditions of scarcity will behave, but it is altogether another thing to argue that everything he wrote is, therefore, correct. It would appear that much of what he wrote was in fact contingent and based upon his need to understand the specific problems which confronted mankind at the time of his writing. This is in no way to denigrate what he wrote or to say he was wrong at that time. It is merely to recognise that he was only dealing with a particular set of contingent circumstances.

That Smith provided a *way of thinking* which has become the dominant intellectual paradigm over the last two hundred years is testament, in fact, to the quality of his mind and the superiority of his intellect. To recognise his intellectual stature does not mean, however, that his writing has laid bare all of the eternal truths of human existence.

If we adopt this *contingent way of thinking* about knowledge and human understanding, we can see immediately that the longevity of the appeal of Smith's writings must be based on two key factors:

- *He uncovered three invariant principles of human existence under scarcity.*

- *His way of thinking about the effective management of the contingent circumstances which faced mankind was, and has been since that time, regarded as the most appropriate by many people.*

This does not mean, however, that his *way of thinking* will necessarily be appropriate under all contingent circumstances.

In fact, it may not be appropriate at all under certain sets of circumstances.

The force of this insight can be most effectively demonstrated if one thinks for a moment about the contingent circumstances in which Smith was living, and the problems for which he was trying to find a solution. Smith's major work is entitled: *The Wealth of Nations*. This tells us immediately what it was that taxed Smith's mind and helped to shape his *way of thinking*. Smith wanted to know how social, political and economic circumstances could be re-ordered to improve the sum of human welfare within a given nation-state.

When he observed the world around him he saw that the old feudal system, with its dominant mode of production in land ownership and cultivation, was being eroded by the development of a manufacturing system based on the creation and sale of commodities. The problem, as he saw it, was that this new system, which he correctly identified as a system which could immeasurably improve the welfare of people by abolishing some of the material scarcities of the past, was being retarded by the traditional systems of appropriation, accumulation and allocation of value.

This traditional feudal system was based on an inter-locking system of deference, duty and obligation, in which the political, social and economic systems were collectively controlled by those few individuals who owned the means of production and exchange. In other words, since land was a finite and scarce commodity, from which most things of value were created (food, clothes and raw materials), those who owned the land were able to leverage their ownership in order to appropriate and accumulate material value for themselves. This system, in which a few people controlled the scarce material means of existence, was also replicated at the political level, with the landowners, by and large, dominating all of the major instruments of national, regional and local political power.

The landowners wrote the laws which allocated value within society and ensured that the whole society accepted the hierarchical structure which was created to support those laws. This hierarchical structure was reinforced, at lower levels, by the creation of guilds of skilled workers who, through exclusion, were able to create an artificial scarcity in their skills and thereby claim a monopoly rent from their possession of those skills. Being a member of a guild was a scarce commodity which allowed the favoured to appropriate and accumulate value.

This was the system against which Smith railed, but not simply because he woke up one morning and had a bright idea. The reality is that Smith was living through a period when the unforeseen consequences of a million different decisions were showing people that human beings could modify and change the material conditions which faced them. The human being is inherently inventive, and new ways of doing things were constantly challenging the old feudal systems of hierarchy and control. It seems clear that a desire to open up and manage supply chains more effectively was one of the most important reasons for this challenge to the old order of things, although this fact has, as yet, never been properly recognised by scholars and commentators.

The activities of Marco Polo and other explorers were clearly of major significance in recent human history. This is widely recognised by historians, but the fact that these activities were essentially supply chain phenomena is not appreciated. If one thinks about the activities of Marco Polo and other explorers it is clear that what motivated them was their desire to profit from scarcity, either by finding alternative sources of what was already scarce, or by finding new, items which could be sold profitably as a result of their relative scarcity. It is clear, therefore, that the existing mechanisms for the allocation of the relative scarcity of the material things of life within existing nation-states forced people to seek alternative sources of supply. In the process, this acquistive imperative stimulated those trading activities between nations which are, today, becoming global supply chain relationships.

This process of exchange between individuals, involving those things which were abundant in one part of the globe but scarce in others, was the force which ultimately challenged the traditional structure of feudal society. This trade in goods and services, which relative scarcity had spawned, created new opportunities for invention and value appropriation and accumulation. It also led to new means for the appropriation of material wealth different from those based on the immediate ownership and control of land.

While much of the material wealth which traders were able to acquire may ultimately have been derived from the product of the ownership of land, as it always has been, the development of extensive trading relationships allowed new ways of appropriation to arise. These did not arise primarily from the monopolisation of land but from the ability of the *middleman* to monopolise the physical trading relationships and information about them. In the final analysis, many of the early trading monopolies were based either on ignorance about relative scarcity on the part of the ultimate buyers and sellers in the exchange, on the unwillingness of others to take the risks, or on their unwillingness to control the appropriate trade routes physically.

Not surprisingly, in the early days of modern commercial relationships many of the trading companies were granted protection through national monopoly charters, protected by the authority of a particular nation state (as in the case of Britain and the Hudson Bay Company, the Levant Company and the East Indies Company). These companies of merchant adventurers were clearly risk-takers, who sought out opportunities for enrichment through their rights to monopolise trade (supply chains) within specifically defined parts of the globe, backed (in the British case) by the authority and the physical coercive power of the Crown.

What is interesting about all of this, however, is the fact that by supporting these monopolies the traditional feudal state was, unknowingly, sowing the seeds of its own destruction. The reason for this is obvious with hindsight, and it was what Smith was astutely reflecting on at the end of the eighteenth century. As Smith recognised, when an entrepreneur sought, he was also inadvertently providing opportunities for others to enrich themselves. This can be shown with a simple example.

When the slave traders of Liverpool went to Africa they brought black people from merchants and forcibly shipped them to the American colonies where they were sold to landowners growing cotton on plantations. The cotton crop was brought back by ship to Liverpool, where it was used by the newly emergent entrepreneurs in Lancashire to spin and weave cheap clothing, using machinery in industrial factories. The finished goods undercut the selling price of woollen goods and became a major export commodity for the British economy through their sale in other countries, like India, which were part of the British Empire. The British authorities in these countries often ensured that the indigenous cotton industry was restricted so as not to compete with and undercut imported British goods.

Smith, ruminating on these developments, concluded that it was not through monopoly or restriction that the material welfare of the people of Britain would be improved, but through the development of a *laissez-faire* economy and society. By this Smith meant that the old feudal restrictions, which created a rigid form of social, economic and political control in Britain, should be removed. The reason why was manifestly obvious to Smith. He argued that the old system of value allocation and appropriation was inimical to the process of industrialisation, and held back the innovations through which the pursuit of self-interest would raise the material welfare of all of the people in the national economy. The wealth of the nation would be immeasurably improved, he argued, by a direct attack on restrictive monopolies and through a process of liberalisation and the pursuit of individual self-interest.

It is on the basis of this analysis of the contingent circumstances which faced Britain at the end of the eighteenth century, and the fact that he had uncovered three eternal truths about the human condition, that Smith's claim to greatness is based. It is a claim to intellectual standing which cannot be denied. At the time when he wrote Smith wrote his analysis was undoubtedly the most astute then available. As a result many politicians and buraucats began to implement the policy recommendations which emanated from his strictures (like Huskisson at the Board of Trade in the 1820s).

The problem is, however, that Smith's claim to intellectual greatness is on much shakier ground when we expose his thinking to the test of eternal as opposed to contingent truth. Smith did recognise, theoretically, that buyers (consumers) will always benefit from a situation in which the supplier is forced to compete in a properly contested market place in which goods are perfectly inter-changeable. It is, however, one thing to argue that this is logically true, and altogether another to argue that it was as a result of this reasoning, and the eventual adoption of *laissez-faire* style competition, that Britain's industrial and commercial supremacy in the middle of the nineteenth century was created. This line of reasoning simply does not hold, because it does scant justice to the real causes of Britain's nineteenth century industrial supremacy.

Arguably, the most important reason for Britain's supremacy was not that Smith wrote a book canonising the principles of a *laissez-faire* economy and society, but the fact that for nearly a century Britain had a relative monopoly control of (sustainable competitive advantage in) the most important industrial and commercial supply chains in the world. The reasons for this were, of course, highly contingent. Nobody, not even Smith, could have foreseen the French Revolution and the rise to power of Napoleon.

While the French Revolution and the coming to power of Napoleon may initially have been heralded as a victory for nationalism, liberalism, and democracy, it would have been difficult to appreciate at the time that his activities also served to retard industrial innovation on the continent of Europe for almost half a century. Similarly, no one could have foreseen, at the time, that the new industrial and technological innovations which were allowed to develop in Britain—protected from war and invasion by its island location—would also, fortuitously, occur in a nation which already possessed the largest territorial empire and was the dominant maritime power and commercial centre in the world. With hindsight, we can see that Britain was already the leading commercial centre in the world well before it also became the leading industrial nation.

It is worth dwelling on these factors for a moment, and linking them to what was said earlier about the mutually reinforcing factors behind British trading and industrialisation relationships. The thing that stands out about Britain's unique position at the end of the eighteenth century, and in its period of industrial supremacy in the early nineteenth century, is that it was not a liberal or *laissez-faire* economy at all. Britain may have moved in this direction evenutally but at the time it can be argued that:

> *British financiers, merchants and manufacturers were relative monopolists in all of the major supply chains which controlled international exchange.*

British citizens, not exclusively, but certainly pre-eminently at that time, monopolised global supply and, thereby, controlled global value appropriation and accumulation. The example of the slave trade given above demonstrates this fact clearly. British merchants made money by plying their trade between Britain, Africa, the Colonies and elsewhere. These traders took *a turn* on all of the trade that passed through the Empire, and were well placed to underwrite all of the trading activities around the globe. This was how London became the maritime and financial centre of the world for almost three centuries after 1660.

This hegemonic pre-eminence was not eroded until the Second World War when American interests became *the relative monopolists* of the most significant global supply chains. Since the 1970s, the hegemonic position of the USA has been challenged, if not replaced, by what may, eventually, turn out to be a temporary pre-eminence on the part of Japanese and other East Asian interests in some of the world's leading manufacturing supply chains. What is interesting here is the fluidity and dynamism of this process of relative supremacy and decline of the interests which control supply chains. National pre-eminence can only occur, because some national interests are able, whether it be for relatively short or relatively long periods, to monopolise the process of value appropriation and accumulation in specific global supply chains.

It was, and continues to be, therefore, the capacity of British, European, American and Asian individuals and companies to monopolise (temporarily or permanently) value allocation, appropriation and accumulation in global supply chains which accounts for national success. It is not, if this *way of thinking* is correct, the creation of competitive markets which accounts for sustainable national advantage. Presumably, the key to *The Wealth of the Nation* for national governments is for them to know in which global supply chains their people and companies have a realistic chance of becoming relative monopolists.

There can be little doubt, therefore, that for Britain in the period 1780 to 1850 this pre-eminence came from *first-mover* advantages, and from the possession of a relative monopoly control over allocative scarcity in the major supply chains of the world economy. What is also apparent is that what destroyed this supremacy was not necessarily the inertia which comes from monopoly but from the commitment to free markets and competition which Smith was advocating. Thus, it can be argued that:

> *Britain's economic advantage as a nation was eroded by the very competitive forces which Smith argued would actually lead to the creation of the Wealth of the Nation!*

This erosion of British supremacy did not arise just as a result of superior competitive forces; it also came about because many of the nation-states which had to face competition from superior British goods (like the USA, France and Prussia) built protective barriers against them. The reasons for their doing this are obvious. The indigenous populations of these countries wanted access to the new trading supply chains which had been created domestically and internationally, and they were not about to allow the British to take control of their domestic markets with superior products.

Nation-states, and the political systems which manage them, are just another way in which individuals can control and allocate material scarcity. It is hardly surprising, therefore, that one group of people will seek ways of denying access to their domestic markets to another group of people who are seeking to appropriate and accumulate value from trading relationships, particularly if this places them in a dependent or subservient position. They will only accept this dependency if they are forced to; they will not do so if they can find alternative ways of avoiding this situation.

This line of reasoning leads us then to the conclusion that, while Smith may have correctly identified some of the eternal truths of the human condition, he was not necessarily correct in arguing that the pursuit of *laisse-faire* policies is a certain way to achieve material wealth for everyone. The history of industrial development is replete with examples of nation-states that have not adopted this *laissez-faire way of thinking*, but have nontheless managed to achieve substantial material improvement in *The Wealth of the Nation*.

The rapid rise to pre-eminence of Japan and South Korea in recent times provides ample testament to the benefits of capitalist industrialisation *without liberal cultural values*, and in the absence of effective democracy. It is likely that China will also follow this non-liberal, anti-democratic path to successful and rapid capitalist industrialisation in the twenty-first century. This should not be surprising because Britain was neither democratic, nor liberal, when it made its rapid transition to industrialisation in the eighteenth and early nineteenth century.

The facts appear to speak for themselves, but only when one has an appropriate *way of thinking* about causality. Smith may have been a *great thinker* but many of his ideas were contingent and normatively based, rather than being based on eternal truths. One may conclude, therefore, that, as Figure 42 indicates, while Smith recognised three eternal truths about demand and supply, he failed to recognise the significance of perhaps the most important of these. This eternal truth is implicit in his analysis but it is clear that he was not concerned to understand it because his focus was elsewhere. Smith implicitly recognised that sustained business success (for the individual or the corporation) can occur only through the creation of relative degrees of monopoly. He explicitly chose to ignore this,

Figure 42: The Contribution of Adam Smith

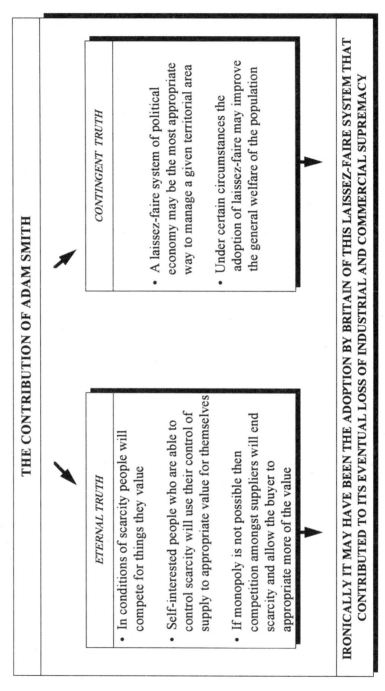

THE CONTRIBUTION OF ADAM SMITH

ETERNAL TRUTH

- In conditions of scarcity people will compete for things they value

- Self-interested people who are able to control scarcity will use their control of supply to appropriate value for themselves

- If monopoly is not possible then competition amongst suppliers will end scarcity and allow the buyer to appropriate more of the value

CONTINGENT TRUTH

- A laissez-faire system of political economy may be the most appropriate way to manage a given territorial area

- Under certain circumstances the adoption of laissez-faire may improve the general welfare of the population

IRONICALLY IT MAY HAVE BEEN THE ADOPTION BY BRITAIN OF THIS LAISSEZ-FAIRE SYSTEM THAT CONTRIBUTED TO ITS EVENTUAL LOSS OF INDUSTRIAL AND COMMERCIAL SUPREMACY

however, because he normatively believed that competition and the pursuit of self-interest would provide the basis for everyone to prosper.

Unfortunately, his thinking was based on analysing only part of the human condition. He failed to recognise from first principles that the human condition can never be about everyone prospering, but only about the ways in which relative material scarcity is allocated. People can be materially better off in absolute terms, and they can be relatively better off then they were in the past, but this is not the same as arguing that relative material scarcity has been abolished. What Smith did not seem to recognise was that, at whatever level of absolute material wealth, there would still be an allocative scramble for scarcity at any new level of material abundance.

This may not have been important for Smith's *way of thinking*—he was, after all, only really concerned with improving the general welfare of nations. However, it is critically important for those whose task it is to understand what are the causes of sustainable business success. Leslie Hannah's recent work, which was discussed earlier, demonstrates these difficulties. Hannah's analysis appears to be locked into the Smithian mind-set—namely, that success comes from operating within competitive markets—and this is why he finds it so difficult to explain why companies are rarely permanently successful. Yet the answer to his problem is very simple.

Hannah's forthcoming article reaffirms what Smith demonstrated to be an eternal truth two centuries earlier; namely, that perfect competition always puts power in the hands of the buyer, forcing the supplier to pass value to the consumer. As Hannah recognises, this objective condition can rarely be the basis for long-term individual or corporate success, because the power in the relationship is always with the buyer. The problem with buyer power is that it always squeezes supplier margins. There is, as a result, a simple explanation for business success and failure. This is to recognise, as Hannah does, that if it is competition that causes failure, then logically it is degrees of monopoly which will be the cause of sustainable business success. One can hypothesise deductively from this insight that:

> **The reason why most of the top 100 companies have not survived since 1912 is primarily due to the fact that the supply chains that they were operating in were not conducive to sustainable degrees of monopoly.**

The reason why the author can frame this hypothesis, and be reasonably confident that it may prove correct when tested empirically, is that his *way of thinking,* and the object of his own enquiry, is not the same as Smith's or Hannah's. Both of these writers are caught up in a paradigm which believes that *laissez-faire* is always the most effective way of managing business relationships. They are also both caught up in a paradigm which leads them to think that understanding how and why nation-states can be successful is one of the proper goals of intellectual endeavour.

This, the current author believes, is one of the major reasons why neither writer can properly see what is before them. By taking this approach they are failing to adopt a properly holistic view of how value appropriation and accumulation occurs. This is another way of saying that they are framing their focus of enquiry on an inadequate understanding of some of the eternal truths of human existence.

Scarcity, Value and the Human Condition

A useful way to understand the problem of a lack of holistic focus in Smith and other writers, is to start from *first principles*. By this one means that analysis must start from an understanding of the objective conditions which face human beings and, from this starting point, rationally and logically deduce the choices which are available to them under any given circumstance which they may have to face. Only in this way, is it possible to arrive at a proper understanding of the eternal truths of human existence under contingent circumstances.

The starting point for any enquiry into the causes of business success should, the author believes, be a recognition that the human condition it is to live in a state of relative and absolute scarcity. Things are scarce, because their supply is finite. Even though it is possible to drain the sea from the land, and to build barriers against the tides, the land area of the globe is relatively fixed. This means that land is, ultimately, a finite resource and that it will attract a scarcity value as a consequence. This scarcity value is likely to increase if the land area remains fixed and the population of the globe continues to increase. This is because what is in scarce supply is normally highly valued, and also because there is no easy way to increase the area of land that is available.

If land has a scarcity value because its supply is finite, there are other things which have a scarcity value as a result of variations in their supply, or because, as Figure 43 indicates, the supply is artificially reduced by individual or collective action. In the early nineteenth century, apprentice boys in Lancashire cotton mills went on strike because they were being forced to eat salmon at every meal. The reason was that there was a glut of salmon. Until the recent introduction of fish farming, salmon was in relatively short supply and attracted a scarcity value. Today salmon is still relatively expensive but it does not attract the same scarcity value as it did two decades ago.

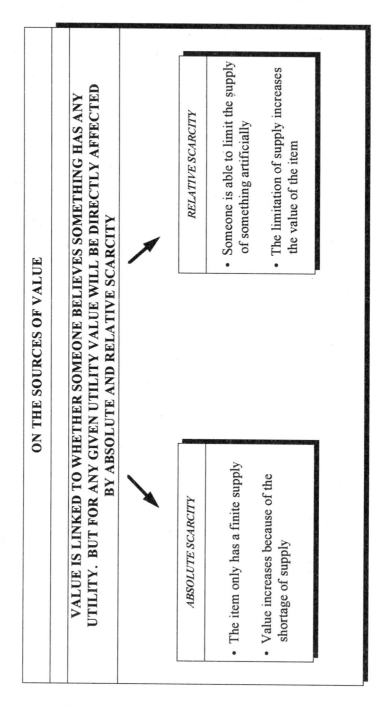

Figure 43: On the Sources of Value

The scarcity value attached to diamonds is apparently artificially induced by a diamond cartel operated by the major South African and Russian producers. This artificially created scarcity is engineered in order to keep the value of diamonds higher than it would be if they were made freely available to the market. The relatively total control of these mineral assets grants a monopoly right to the diamond cartel which owns them. These examples explain how value is appropriated by a temporary or an induced, rather than an absolute, scarcity of supply.

There are many other examples of value being ascribed to something because of an artificial action being taken to limit supply by individuals or by governments. The regulation of French wines under the Medoc system in Bordeaux is an example of this practice. The system has been in place since 1855 and has only be reviewed once since that time. There can be little doubt that the value which the wine of Bordeaux attracts is as much to do with the scarcity induced by the regulation of the industry, than it is to do with the overall quality of all of the wines that attract a particular status in the official rankings. This is not to argue that all of the ranked wines are not of high quality, because many will be of exceptional quality, rather it is to recognise that it is the scarcity value of the ranking which significantly increases the value of the wine, irrespective of its inherent quality.

There are, of course, things which people value which are not scarce. To recognise this is not, however, to invalidate the claim that, other things being equal, people value things which are scarce. Everyone values clothing, a place to shelter from the elements, and sufficient food to eat and water to drink. These are the necessities of life. They are valued because without them we could not survive. The fact that they are valued as necessities does not, however, invalidate the rule that people value what is scarce. Even if many people currently have these necessities in abundance, and may take them for granted, this does not mean that they do not value what is scarce. Clearly, if any of these necessities were to become scarce, their potential value as necessities would be far in excess of non-essential things.

The truism that people value what is scarce is reinforced if we consider the apparently irrational behaviour of modern day consumers, who pay three or four times the true production costs for designer label clothing. Prior to the 'off the peg' sale of designer label clothing, there were designers who created bespoke costumes for individual consumers. The individual was prepared to pay a scarcity price for the clothing because it was unique. There would only ever be one, or a limited number, of the item. Today, however, clothing manufacturers have discovered that, even if they are still supplying mass produced goods, it is still possible to sell them for more if they attach a fashionable label, or brand name, to the garment. Consumers are willing to pay more for the garment, because it associates them with something exclusive—their ability to pay more for clothing. This appears irrational at one level, but perfectly rational at another, when we recognise the value which human beings attach to scarcity.

Many more examples of the human penchant for valuing what is scarce could be provided, but a lack of space prevent us from doing so. Nevertheless, the examples given should be sufficient to demonstrate that it is the human condition to live within a situation of absolute and relative scarcity. Furthermore, they also show that, although there will always be exceptions to this general rule, the majority of people have always striven to obtain the things which they value. Since human beings tend to value what is scarce, and because what is scarce cannot be obtained by everyone, then the human condition is to struggle to own and control those things which are scarce. By owning those things which are scarce, as Figure 44 reveals, individuals, companies and governments are able to

Figure 44: The Importance of Monopoly and Scarcity in Business Success

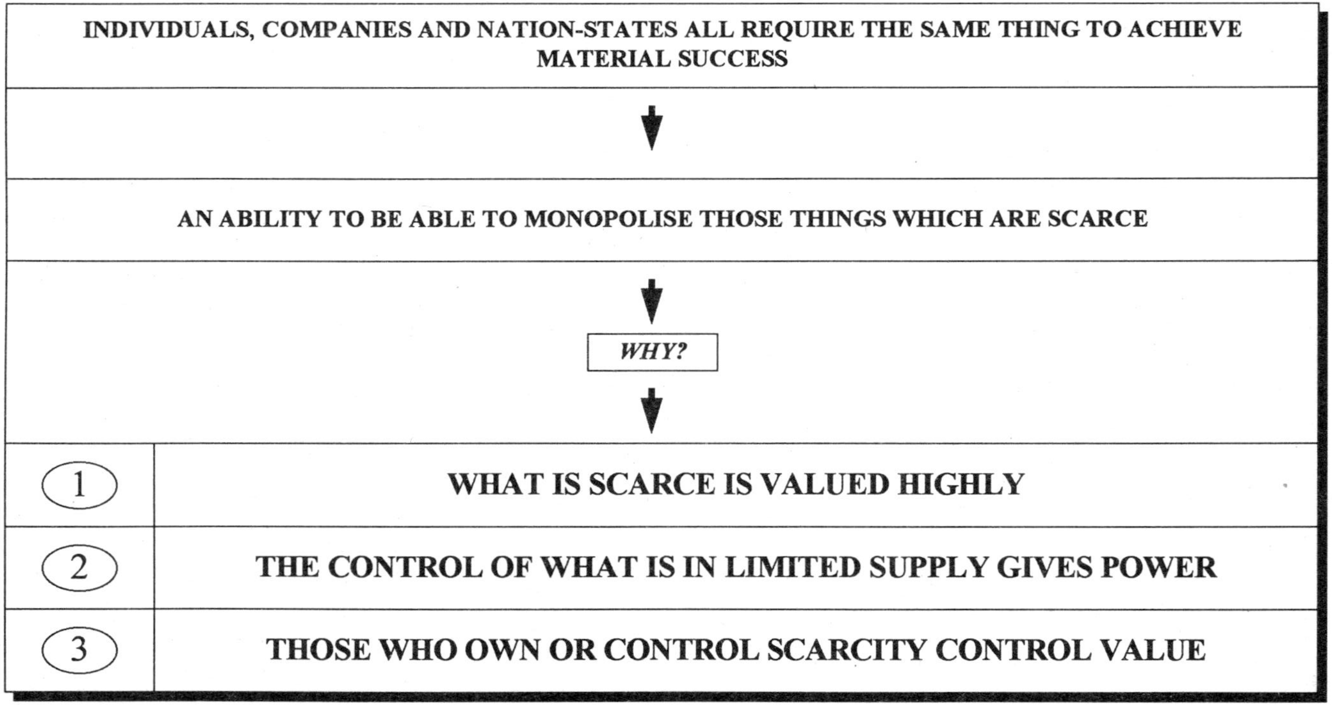

INDIVIDUALS, COMPANIES AND NATION-STATES ALL REQUIRE THE SAME THING TO ACHIEVE MATERIAL SUCCESS

AN ABILITY TO BE ABLE TO MONOPOLISE THOSE THINGS WHICH ARE SCARCE

WHY?

① WHAT IS SCARCE IS VALUED HIGHLY

② THE CONTROL OF WHAT IS IN LIMITED SUPPLY GIVES POWER

③ THOSE WHO OWN OR CONTROL SCARCITY CONTROL VALUE

control the allocation, appropriation and accumulation of value in society.

This is an interesting line of reasoning, because it allows us to understand why it is that people fight wars over land. It reveals that people are not actually fighting wars over land they are, in fact, fighting wars for the control of those scarce resources which will allow them to appropriate and accumulate value in a particular territorial area. Even though the major nation-states do not currently fight wars over land, it is only just over 50 years since they stopped doing so. In areas like the former Yugoslavia and Africa there are, however, still significant conflicts taking place over the ownership of land.

There are many reasons for these conflicts but one of the primary drivers must undoubtedly be the fact that the people living in these areas still subsist on a primarily agricultural basis. As a result, land ownership is still a significant mechanism through which value can be appropriated and accumulated. The importance of this insight is not that the people of these lands are backward, but that if land ownership became the major source of value appropriation in the future in the West, then the people of the currently advanced industrial nations would begin to fight over land ownership.

To say that people value what is scarce and will struggle and compete to obtain those things which are in limited supply, does not, however, mean that all people are the same. To argue this would be a logical nonsense. Human beings are idiosyncratic and they have different propensities. Some people are more caring and kind than others; while some people are totally selfish and cruel. To recognise this does not, however, invalidate the claim that most people value and compete for things which are in scarce supply. Even though people have different needs and wants, and different threshold levels of avarice and love, the majority of people will fight to survive in a disaster situation. The recurring stories of selfishness that survivors recount after life-threatening disasters, are testament to this fact of life. What is taking place is a natural tendency by the human species to survive under all circumstances. The fact that, faced with these circumstances, some people may choose to die does not invalidate the general rule that most people will struggle to survive if they have to.

This is an important point because it helps us to understand why it is that human beings are naturally competitive, and also to understand why there must be regular patterns to their behaviour under the same contingent circumstances. If, in general terms, people struggle to obtain the things which are scarce, not everyone has the same desire to maximise their control and ownership of scarcity. This line of reasoning is based on the psychological principles associated with the idea of the **hierarchy of needs**. This holds that everyone will have a hierarchy of needs but that, at certain levels, as some needs are satisfied, people will not pursue these as maximisers but will satisfice themselves. When they have achieved the satisfaction of one need they will choose to replace this with another need, and then maximise their pursuit of this new need until they have satisfied this second order need, and so on.

This is, surely, one of the keys to understanding why individuals and companies succeed and fail. It is rooted in the propensities of human need. People will compete for the ownership and control of material needs, but not everyone will have the same desire to maximise their control and ownership over these material resources. At a certain point, some people will stop maximising their need for material security and will instead pursue non-material goals like art or social work. In this situation, they are immediately vulnerable to those who are pursuing maximising behaviour in order to control resources which are materially scarce.

It is logical to argue, therefore, that, as demonstrated in Figure 45, other things being equal, it will be those who are *maximisers* rather than *satisficers* who will ultimately control and own the material resources within society. Only if those

Figure 45: Maximisers, Satisficers and the Hierarchy of Needs

MAXIMISERS	SOME POTENTIAL HUMAN NEEDS	THE HIERARCHY OF NEEDS	THE IMPERATIVE OF COMPETITION	THE ENTREPRENEUR
Always seek to achieve maximum control over the available resources of the things they need	• Sustenance • Survival • Shelter • Love • Comradeship • Status • Material Wealth • Recognition • Control of others • Leisure • Innovation	• Each individual has a unique personal hierarchy of needs • For somethings they may be maximisers, for others they may be satisficers • As one need is satisfied people tend to move to the satisfaction of other needs	Other things being equal, without controls on human behaviour, and with absolute and relative scarcity, for any potential available resource, maximisers rather than satisficers will tend to control the resources they value	Maximisers pursuring material wealth will tend to be people who become entrepreneurs
Vs				
SATISFICERS Only seek to achieve a satisfactory level of control over any potentially available resources of the things they need				

who are satisficers, and who wish to pursue non-material goals, are able to continue indefinitely to monopolise control over material resources, will they be able to withstand the permanent search by those pursuing maximising behaviour for ownership and control of the resources which determine material wealth.

On the Contribution of Marx to Business Thinking

This type of rational-deductive analysis of human behaviour explains why it is that Marx arrived at a conclusion different from that of Adam Smith. Writing shortly after Smith, and strongly influenced by his *way of thinking*, Marx disagreed with Smith's optimistic view of the future of the human condition under capitalist exchange relationships. He also disagreed with his analysis of the driving forces behind the cumulative social, economic and political changes which both writers were trying to understand between 1760 and the end of the nineteenth century. While there is insufficient space here to discuss this disagreement in detail, it is important to touch on it briefly because it highlights the author's general point that, while both Smith and Marx were exceptional thinkers, both tended to focus on only certain aspects of the human condition.

Marx took the view that in a state of nature, the human condition would be one in which people would be loving, kind and collaborative. It was the artificially induced scarcity of material wealth, which allowed certain individuals to appropriate and accumulate value for themselves, that, according to Marx, caused the problems of human existence. Marx felt that the industrial system was capable of providing material abundance for all, but that this was not possible because, in all ages, those who had been able to own and control the material means of production and exchange had used that ability to retain the surplus value from production for themselves. Marx looked at the past and concluded that, under

Feudalism landowners had appropriated value from their possession and control of land, which was the dominant means of value creation. He predicted, therefore, that value appropriation in the newly emerging society would be dominated by those who owned the *industrial* means of value creation.

For Marx, therefore, the villains of the piece under industrialisation would be the owners of the new, industrial means of production. In Marx's view, they would replace landowners as the dominant force in society, and appropriate and accumulate value from their ability to exploit their own workers. This was so because, Marx argued (mistakenly in this author's view), that all value was created by the exploitation of the labour of dependent human beings. For Marx, exploitation was defined in relation to the *surplus value* which was left over from the sale price of a commodity, after all of the inputs into the production process had been taken into account. Since the *surplus value* was retained by the capitalist owner, and not shared with the employees of the company, Marx concluded that capitalist owners were exploiters, and that profits were made exclusively as a result of the employer failing to redistribute surplus value to his workers.

History has shown that, in reality, the capitalist system has developed in a far more complex way than Marx could have predicted. What is interesting, however, is the fact that, although Marx may have been wrong in many respects, his ideas have been of tremendous influence in the history of the world. The reason for this is that, in the author's view at least, he touched either upon some eternal truths, or upon some contingent truths, in his complex analysis of the circumstances surrounding the transition from feudalism to capitalist industrialisation.

Like Smith before him, it is possible to argue that the true intellectual standing of Marx is related to the fact that he touched on a number of eternal rather than contingent truths.

The paucity of contingent truths in Marxist thinking can be seen in the fact that much of what he predicted contingently has not come true, and that the capitalist system has adapted and changed in ways that his original theory could not have predicted.

So, what are the eternal truths that Marx touched upon? It seems clear that Marx uncovered a central fact of the human condition when he argued that Smith was wrong to conclude that markets, when left to their own devices, would necessarily lead to the maximisation of everyone's welfare. Marx argued, on the contrary, that when left to their own devices markets have a tendency to concentration rather than competition. It was for this reason that he rejected the idea that market forces could ever solve the problem of redistribution and welfare. Marx took the view that maximising behaviour by individuals, in a situation of absolute and relative scarcity, must lead to concentration, and that, as Smith also accepted, monopoly would always lead to a situation of *the tyranny of the supplier over the buyer*.

There are clearly strong parallels between Smith and Marx here, although Smith was optimistic about the possibilities of market competition being sustained against monopoly, while Marx was not. Marx may well have been on to something, as Figure 46 indicates, because there seems little doubt that sustained business success can only arise as a result of the maintenance of some form of monopoly, or through the restriction of effective competition. The problem with his insight, however, is that it may not be as absolute a condition as he supposed. This reinforces one of the greatest weaknesses in Marx's writings, namely his tendency to be dogmatic about causality. He tended to believe that there were determinant forces which always applied, and there is little doubt that this *way of thinking* undermined the subtlety of his reasoning.

As will be argued later, Marx may have been correct to argue that concentration provides one of the bases for business

Figure 46: The Contribution of Karl Marx

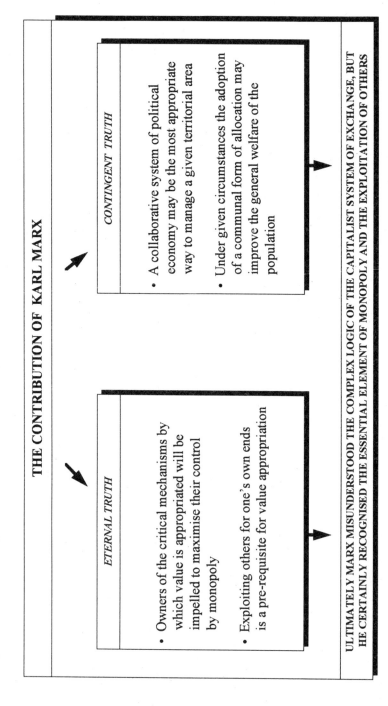

THE CONTRIBUTION OF KARL MARX

ETERNAL TRUTH

- Owners of the critical mechanisms by which value is appropriated will be impelled to maximise their control by monopoly

- Exploiting others for one's own ends is a pre-requisite for value appropriation

CONTINGENT TRUTH

- A collaborative system of political economy may be the most appropriate way to manage a given territorial area

- Under given circumstances the adoption of a communal form of allocation may improve the general welfare of the population

ULTIMATELY MARX MISUNDERSTOOD THE COMPLEX LOGIC OF THE CAPITALIST SYSTEM OF EXCHANGE, BUT HE CERTAINLY RECOGNISED THE ESSENTIAL ELEMENT OF MONOPOLY AND THE EXPLOITATION OF OTHERS

success, but the capacity for individuals and companies to engineer these arrangements in a sustainable way is much more operationally circumscribed and constrained than Marx recognised. The reason for this is that, if the focus of our enquiry shifts, as it must, from the analysis of markets to the analysis of supply chains, it readily becomes apparent that some supply chains can be much more easily monopolised than others. Theoretically, we can argue, therefore, that:

- *Those supply chains in which the sunk costs and switching costs of operation are high will be those in which the barriers to entry are also highest.*

- *These supply chains, when compared to those without these costs, and in which products and services are easily imitable and replicable, will be the ones in which the highest propensity to concentration is likely to be found.*

What is being argued here is that the emphasis on markets, which was the concern of both Smith and Marx, should not necessarily be the starting point of enquiry if we are trying to understand how individuals and companies successfully appropriate and accumulate value over time. The implication here is that the proper focus of any enquiry into the sustainability of value appropriation will be the properties of the supply chain, rather than those of the market. It is in this light that we can understand the seminal influence of Marx in helping us to think about the causes of business success. The contribution of Marx comes despite himself, because he clearly did not like the fact that employers did not redistribute wealth to their employees. Whether we share his personal view or not, in recognising this fact, he has aided our understanding.

Marx clearly understood, from a supply chain perspective, one of the eternal truths of human existence. This truth can be encapsulated in the proposition that value appropriation and accumulation comes from the exploitation of the skills and capabilities of others:

> ***One key to business success is the ability to exploit the skills and capabilities of others for one's own benefit.***

If we suspend the normatively emotive word— *exploitation*—for a moment, and concentrate objectively on what Marx is saying, he is clearly focusing on the relationship which exists between those who own and control the key resource (***critical assets***) within a supply chain and those who work for them as employees. Business success must come, ultimately, for owners and risk-takers from their ability to buy the goods, services and human input they require at a price lower than that at which they can be sold for. If this is so, then logically, one of the most significant ways in which individuals and companies can appropriate value for themselves must be by leveraging the skills and capabilities of their own employees.

If an employee did not provide this opportunity for the owners of a company, then the company would, by definition, be incapable of generating a profit and would quickly go out of business. This situation of *objective exploitation* of the employees must, therefore, be logically true, even if the employees of a company are more than satisfied with their personal salaries and terms and conditions, and do not feel exploited.

Indeed, in the modern world there must be situations in which the general level of business acumen of many of the personnel working for the monopoly, or oligopoly companies operating within global supply chains is so low (relative to the remuneration of these employees) that they are the objective beneficiaries of a *cattle show*. In such a *cattle show*, it is not the activities of the employee which determine their remuneration, but the simple fact that they are the unwitting beneficiaries of a *fashion parade*. This *fashion parade* allows the employee to believe that they are the cause of their own material success. Objectively, however, their material success has everything to do with the relatively monopolistic position of the company for which they are working, and has virtually nothing to do with their own personal business skills and capabilities.

In this way, although he failed to recognise that some workers may be extremely contented in their condition of exploitation, Marx provided a valuable insight into the ways in which value appropriation and accumulation occurs. Nevertheless, his overall analysis can still be criticised for being overly deterministic and for its failure to properly understand the range of contingent forces shaping capitalist supply chains and markets.

In particular, Marx failed, as Smith had done before him, to recognise the problem that individuals and companies have in ensuring that they can always control the behaviour of their suppliers. This is a serious, and continuing, gap in our theoretical understanding of business success, and one which this volume attempts to rectify theoretically. This is necessaary because the effective control of supplier power has always been central to effective value appropriation and accumulation. It is interesting to note that the leading contemporary business writers, Porter and Kay, have both recognised this phenomenon without adequately explaining the contingent circumstances under which value appropriation and accumulation can be achieved by the use of different forms of supply relationships, in discrete types of supply chains. (Porter 1979 & Kay 1994)

On Types of Monopoly and Effective Supply Chain Leverage

What is clearly apparent from this short discussion of Smith and Marx, is that there do appear to be some eternal truths which can be gleaned from an analysis of some of the most important writings in political economy, even though the focus of enquiry of these writings is historically on the nation-state or the employee, rather than on the individual or the company. These eternal truths relate to the fact that sustained business success for individuals and companies, and ultimately for nation-states, can only occur if there is a possibility for continuous value appropriation and accumulation. How is this achieved?

- *Since there is absolute and relative material scarcity in the world, sustained business success must be linked to the ability of the individual (or the company) to find ways to monopolise supply chains and restrict the operation of a contested market.*

- *It is clear that this process of market closure can either occur in a permanent (or absolute) way or it can be induced temporarily.*

As Figure 47 demonstrates, it is possible for companies or individuals to achieve market closure on a relatively permanent

Figure 47: Types of Monopoly

DEGREES OF SUSTAINABILITY	
PERMANENT MONOPOLY	*TEMPORARY MONOPOLY*
KNOWABLE BUT NOT REPLICABLE	REPLICABLE BUT NOT CURRENTLY KNOWN
• Based on the possession and control of inimitable, non-replicable resources which others cannot obtain	• Based on the temporary possession of a relatively superior competence in value leverage, through the discovery of new ways of doing things which can eventually be copied
• Government regulated rights • Patent protections • Natural monopolies • Technical standards • Unique brand image	• JIT *(leveraging suppliers)* • Employee Associations not Trades • Unions *(leveraging employees)* • Marketing hype *(leveraging customers)* • Horizontal merger and acquisition *(leveraging competitors)*

basis if they can create and own inimitable, or non-replicable, resources. These are supply chain resources for which there is a high level of effective demand, which may be knowable, but which cannot be copied, or which can be copied, but only with very great difficulty over a relatively long period of time. Examples of these types of supply chain resource include: site specific rights which are granted by governments (oil drilling rights); international and national patent protections (e.g. Tagamet and Zantac); natural monopolies (e.g. a water and sewage system); system monopolies (technical standards for operating systems); and unique brand images (e.g. Levis and Coca Cola)

The problem for most people is that these types of permanent monopolies are not readily available to everyone. Furthermore, since they are only available to the few, first mover advantages may be of critical importance in securing ownership or control of them. Since these unique *structural* types of supply chain resources, which can be defined as ***critical supply chain assets,*** are in limited supply, most of business activity takes place over *contested* supply chain resources which are, potentially replicable. Competition in business, therefore, occurs primarily over the ability to own and control those highly imitable resources in such a way that they could become ***critical assets*** in a supply chain. ***Critical assets*** in the supply chain are, by definition of two types:

- ***Structural resources that attract a large effective demand but which are not copyable, even when known; or,***

- ***Contested resources that attract a large effective demand and which, although potentially imitable if known, are not currently being copied by others.***

Eventually, if they can be, all of these contested types of ***critical assets*** will be copied, because the intellectual property in them cannot be controlled effectively.   When they can be easily copied in this way by many people the supply chain resources in question cease to be ***critical assets*** because no monopoly control exists in the supply chain. The reason for this is because the way of doing things, which is implicit in the ***critical asset***, has become a commodity, which many people are now competing to produce.

When this happens the monopoly rent which the ***critical asset*** attracts will disappear, and the margins for this supply chain resource will collapse. The reason for this is because, in a contested market, the balance of power between the buyer and the supplier shifts from the supplier (as temporary monopolist) to the buyer. This shift in ***the balance of supply chain power*** is solely due to the increase in effective, competitive supply. This is what always happens when *the tyranny of the buyer* replaces *the tyranny of the supplier*.

> ***Business success for individuals, companies and nation-states must, therefore, be about either the creation of permanent monopoly, or the development of a flexible approach to the contingent opportunities for temporary monopoly.***

While permanent monopoly is always desirable for those seeking sustainable business success it is extremely difficult to achieve because it becomes transparent, and is normally regulated as a consequence. Arguably, it is therefore more realistic for individuals, companies and nation-states to seek out the opportunities for temporary monopoly. This can be achieved through the development of a **relatively superior competence** in owning, controlling and leveraging existing supply chain resources. Examples of how this can be achieved are legion: the development of JIT rather than vertical integration in the automotive industry; the development of employee associations rather than antagonistic trades unions for employees in Asian companies; the marketing hype of existing products and services by most companies; and, the merger and acquisition of horizontal competitors.

In each of the cases outlined above, however, the underlying goal of the activity is a desire to create the conditions for a temporary (and even in some cases a permanent) monopoly. This goal is desired because it is only through the temporary or permanent closure of the competitive forces within the market that significant value appropriation and accumulation is likely to be achievable. It follows, therefore, that any individual or company trying to understand how to accumulate value effectively would do well to start from *first principles*. This will involve a recognition of how value is appropriated within supply chains through effective leverage. It has very little to do, therefore, with the optimistic participation in, and copying of, others in a freely contested market.

- *Business success **must** be about understanding how relatively superior competence can be achieved vis-à-vis actual or potential competitors.*

- *This must be based on owning and controlling supply chain resources in such a way that, by making the resource scarce, its value will increase, and competitors will be excluded from the market.*

- *If monopoly is not achievable then oligopoly must be the secondary goal.*

It is important to recognise, however, that the development of this ***relatively superior competence***, which provides the temporary opportunity to operate as if a condition of absolute monopoly or oligopoly exists, is only possible if individuals and companies are able to acquire two things.

- ***An ability to understand what is important in the supply chains which currently exist, and why.***

- ***An understanding of which things will be important in the supply chains of the future, and why.***

This is called ***nous***. ***Nous*** is only useful, however, if an individual has the ability to know what ***the four principles of effective leverage*** are, and how to operationalise these under contingent circumstances to achieve value appropriation and accumulation

In Figure 47 four examples of effective temporary monopoly were provided to illuminate the discussion. These four examples were not randomly chosen; they were chosen because they are examples of ***the four principles of effective leverage***. The first example chosen was that of JIT versus vertical integration in the auto-industry. This example demonstrates why Toyota and other Japanese car assemblers have been successful in recent years. They have found an alternative way of effectively leveraging their suppliers in the car assembly supply chain than through the traditional techniques of vertical integration.

The adoption of this type of approach to assembly is not primarily a production issue, although it is often debated as such in the West. In the author's view JIT is clearly a demonstration of a *relatively superior competence* by the Japanese auto-assemblers in the way in which they leverage their suppliers. It is not better than vertical integration, because the suppliers like it; it is a system which is used because the Japanese car assemblers find it a more effective way of leveraging cost and quality improvements from their internal and external supply chains. In other words, it is a superior form of value appropriation to those alternatives which the Japanese car assemblers believe are available to them. This leaves two interesting questions for those who are inclined to benchmarking to try to answer:

- *Have the Japanese invented a completely new and superior way of manufacturing production and supply management which everyone should copy?*

- *Even if it is demonstrably true that the approach is beneficial for Japanese car assemblers, can it be replicated successfully in the West and, even if it can, is it necessarily the best way of appropriating value in industries other than car assembly?*

The second example provided in Figure 47 was of the development in Asia of company employee associations, rather than the employee trades unions which have traditionally existed in the West. This example provides an insight into two alternative ways of leveraging employee skills and capabilities. The Asian model is used to bind the workers to the goals and aspirations of the company, and to create a tight corporate loyalty. It is based on the principles of obligation, deference and hierarchy. It is a very different way of organising employees when compared with the liberal and adversarial trades unionism that has traditionally been allowed to develop in some countries in the West. This leads to two more key questions for those who are inclined to use benchmarking to try to answer:

- *Are Japanese employee associations a more effective way of leveraging employees than adversarial trades unionism?*

- *Even if we believe that Japanese style employee associations are a better way of leveraging employees, can they be replicated successfully in the West, and under which contingent circumstances?*

The third example in Figure 47 is the marketing hype of currently owned resources (products or services). This is clearly an example of the effective leverage of the customer. The acceptance that this technique—of implying that the product or service adds more value to the customer than it actually does—is an essential tool in the armoury of all companies competing on the basis of replicable products and services in contested markets. The hype is used to try to create a temporary monopoly for a particular product or service, on the basis that a non-unique product is in fact a unique one.

This technique, which is in common use in all companies, brings into stark relief the idea that companies exist to *delight customers*. Companies clearly do not exist to delight customers; they exist to satisfy them and, in so doing they hope to be able to retain as much of the value in a supply chain as is possible for themselves. The way this is achieved is by creating a brand image which excludes their competitors from the market. This also has the benefit of allowing the successful 'own brand' company to sell a non-unique product at an inflated price. Marketing hype is one of the most useful techniques in creating an effective demand for a product, irrespective of the 'real' utility of the product or service to the end consumer. This leads to two further interesting questions for those who are inclined to use benchmarking to try to answer:

> - *If marketing hype is a tool which can be used effectively to leverage customers should all companies use it?*
>
> - *Are there some products and services (and some individuals and companies) that might benefit in the long-run from not using hype, and how would you know which ones they are?*

The fourth example provided in Figure 47 is the effective leverage of horizontal competitors by the use of merger and acquisition techniques. This operational practice is often undertaken by individuals and companies when they recognise that they cannot obtain any significant increase in value appropriation through head-on competition over similar products and services. It will also normally arise when it is realised that the use of marketing hype cannot effectively differentiate replicable products or services. In this circumstance, since the customers, suppliers and employees cannot be leveraged effectively, it is competitors who have to be dealt with.

Merger and acquisition is, therefore, an attempt to control a larger share of a contested market by rationalising the duplicated supply chain resources owned by competitors. The *appropriate way of thinking* here, as in all of the four cases outlined above, is directed towards the leverage of relationships so that a relatively monopolistic and controlling situation in the supply chain can be created by the company. Two important questions for those who are inclined to use benchmarking flow from this case:

> - *If merger and acquisition can create conditions for permanent or temporary monopoly, should all companies use this technique to achieve business success?*
>
> - *Is the use of a merger and acquisition approach likely to be equally successful in all types of supply chains and markets, or is this approach more appropriate in some supply chains and markets than others?*

Conclusions

In the previous section an attempt has been made to explain what is meant by *the four principles of effective leverage*. As is demonstrated in Figure 47, the strategic goal of the individual or the company is always to maximise the appropriation and accumulation of value from participation within a supply chain. What is meant by a supply chain, and how it is different from a value chain, is discussed in the next chapter. For our purposes here, however, it should be clear that maximising behaviour is of critical importance in understanding business success. Although the owners and controllers of companies may have differences in their propensities to maximise or to satisfice themselves materially the logic of the system itself is one in which those who are maximisers will, if allowed to, be those who dominate value appropriation and accumulation.

This must, inherently, be how the drive for monopoly and concentration comes about in supply chains. Ironically, it can be argued that the process of concentration and monopoly is built into competitive market forces too. If individuals and companies can only make small margins because of competition they will be forced to seek an increase in their volume share as a way of erecting barriers to market entry. By erecting such 'scale' barriers they are effectively creating monopoly or oligopoly (a relatively superior competence) through size. This is, presumably, the only resort for companies seeking sustainable value appropriation under conditions of easy imitability.

Whatever the ultimate driver of concentration, it is clear that to be successful those who seek to maximise their ownership and control of particular resources within supply chains must always have an operational focus which is based on the effective leverage of others. *Effective leverage* is not the same thing as *management*. The following definition reveals that it is a very different thing:

> *Effective leverage means attention, at all times, to the ways in which contingent circumstances provide opportunities for the entrepreneurially inclined to own and control supply chain resources, in such a way as to allow for the appropriation and accumulation of value, through the creation of situations of permanent or temporary monopoly or oligopoly.*

Figure 48: The Four Principles of Effective Leverage

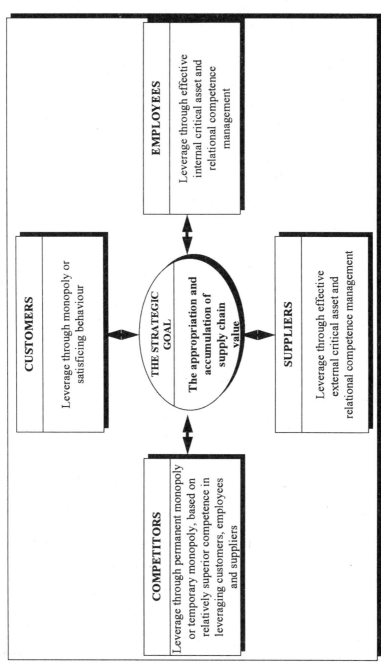

Thus, as Figure 48 illustrates, if individuals, companies and even nation-states are to be successful, it is necessary for them to pay attention to *the four principles of effective leverage*. Successful companies will be those, by definition, that understand that strategy is ultimately about value appropriation and nothing else. Such companies will also be able to recognise that operational practice is about embedding, within the ways of working and ways of thinking of employees, the routines, processes and habits which allow them to understand when they have an opportunity to leverage customers, suppliers and competitors. This means having within the company individuals who know how to answer the questions posed, but unanswered, in this chapter. It is worth stressing, however, that having such people in the company is not without its risks and problems.

Much the most difficult of the four principles to manage effectively is, however, employee leverage. The reason is that, without any doubt, the most valuable resource which a company has is the skills and capabilities of the staff. This is because this human competence can become the *critical asset* in both a supply chain and in a company. Unfortunately, employees exist in a state of permanent tension with their companies, because although the owners of a company require them to leverage others, although they also need to appropriate value from employing them. Those companies which manage this trade-off successfully, and teach their employees *the principles of effective leverage*, and still retain their services, will, arguably, be those which survive and prosper.

> *After all, business success is not about doing any particular thing; it is about understanding what it is that should be done to appropriate value under changing circumstances.*

How this can be achieved is outlined in the next chapter.

6

The Missing Link of Critical
Supply Chain Assets

In the last chapter the idea, that success can only ever be achieved if individuals know what it is that is appropriate for them to do under changing circumstances, was developed. Furthermore, it was argued, that success in business is about always knowing how to achieve effective leverage over customers, competitors, employees and suppliers. Clearly, if people do not know how this should be done, as things change, then they will fail to be successful.

It is clear, from the work of Hannah, on the fate of the leading 100 companies since 1912, that most people do not appear to achieve the necessary levels of understanding or, if they do, they do not pass it on to others. The evidence which supports this line of argument is that formerly dominant companies have consistently failed to survive as leading players in world markets. The explanation for this failure is, presumably, that they did not understand the concept of **strategic metamorphosis**:

- *Strategic metamorphosis refers to that process by which companies embed a <u>way of thinking</u> within their operational practices.*

- *This <u>way of thinking</u> allows them to know when and how they should reinvent themselves in order to maximise value appropriation and accumulation.*

There are companies that have survived and prospered, and which have developed this *way of thinking*. General Electric in the USA is a classic example. The company appears to deploy a fairly simple operational practice which ensures that **strategic metamorphosis** will take place. This metamorphosis seems to take place in such a way that the company always controls **critical supply chain assets,** with **relatively superior competence** over its competitors, and in relatively closed market situations. This is not to say that General Electric is a monopolist in all of the supply chains in which it operates. Rather, it is to argue that it has an operational practice which has a high probability of ensuring that all of its diversified units are more than likely to be successful in the supply chains and markets in which they compete.

How do individuals and companies develop the skill of **strategic metamorphosis?** The answer is, of course, that they do so with great difficulty. If it was easy then everybody would be doing it. To begin to understand how it might be achieved, however, one must start at the beginning and not at the end. The starting point for anyone who wishes to understand how to operationalise **strategic metamorphosis** is the recognition of two simple truths. These are, first, the need to recognise that effective leverage is the key to business success, and second, that this knowledge in its own right is of little value unless something else is understood. This something else is a missing link in business thinking. The author has called this particular missing link **critical supply chain assets**.

On Supply Chain Ways of Thinking

To understand what this concept means, the reader must begin by accepting that *market-based thinking* is not the proper starting place for an understanding of what causes business success. The reason for this is that, by focusing on what already exists in a supply chain—normally a contested market for similar products and services—practitioners and academics fail to understand the fundamental processes at work in business. To understand these fundamental processes one must start from a *supply chain way of thinking*.

> *A supply chain way of thinking involves an understanding, from first principles, of why it is that supply always precedes demand in business.*

For some readers, this statement will hardly constitute a novel insight, but for others it will be fiercely contested and refuted. Whenever the author talks at a conference, or workshop, of practitioners or academics he often asks the audience which comes first, demand or supply. There are normally four types of response. The majority of respondents normally declare unhesitatingly that demand always precedes supply. A smaller number declare that it is always symbiotic. Only one or two gingerly claim that supply comes first. There are, of course, always a number of people who do not respond at all. Presumably this is either because they do not know or they do not want to provide the wrong answer and, thereby, appear to be ignorant (unenlightened).

This pattern of responses has been repeated whenever the author has asked the same question. Why are these responses important in the context of the discussion being presented here? The nature of the responses demonstrates, at least as far as the author is concerned, the insidious impact of the *way of thinking* associated with the dominant, market-based paradigm of business success. Many practitioners, and many academics, believe that demand must come first because that is how they observe reality. Practitioners believe that demand comes first, because for them business practice is about the direct copying, or adapting, of the initial actions of others. This insight can be summarised as follows:

> *For most individuals and companies, the process of business is about trying to compete with companies or individuals who have already taken risks with uncertainty.*

What the generalisation above implies is that, before any product or service generates an effective demand for itself, a number of things must already have taken place. If we adopt a *supply chain way of thinking*, it is clear that what must have taken place is a process of innovation. It can be argued that the process of innovation always consists of the three stages of conception, gestation and scoping. This supply chain process is demonstrated in Figure 49. As the Figure reveals, for a new product or service to be created, or for a new way of more effectively leveraging the four sources of value appropriation to be conceived, someone must have developed a new *way of thinking* about a problem.

The first thing that must occur in this process is **the conception phase**, in which the development of this *new way of thinking* provides a new idea about effective value appropriation and accumulation. For our purposes, it is not the new product or service that is particularly significant; rather; it is the fact that an individual must have had *an original idea* which allowed them to arrive at a novel approach to value appropriation. This

Figure 49: *The Supply Chain as an Innovative Idea*

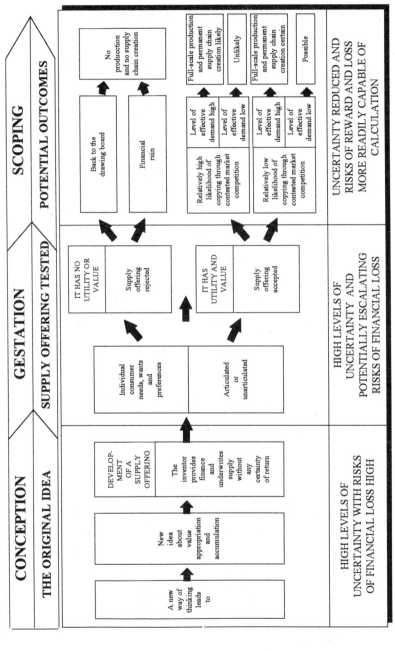

new idea will always be about supplying existing or potential demand (whether articulated or unarticulated) in a different way.

In this first stage of the creation of a new supply chain, for any given product or service, there are high levels of uncertainty and considerable risk of financial loss. Those involved in this process must be risk-takers because they have to bear all of the costs of innovation, and all of the costs of the development of a *supply offering*, without any certainty of a financial return.

> *A supply offering simply means the physical creation of the product or service which the original idea has spawned.*

This conception stage can be a very expensive business, and the costs of creation continue to rise as the supply chain is further developed into the gestation phase

The gestation phase refers to that period in the development of a supply chain when the physical product or service, which was generated from the original idea, is offered to potential consumers. It is clear that this is always a supply relationship, and that it always precedes the development of effective demand. The entrepreneur (individual or company) is making a *supply offering* to test whether there is likely to be *effective demand* for the product. For *effective demand* to be recorded for the initial supply offering, two things must occur:

> • *the supply offering must be recognised by potential consumers as providing a desired utility (i.e. it must be seen as being of value to them).*

> • *it must, also, result in a sufficient number of consumers willing to part with money for the goods or services to be worth producing on a full-scale basis.*

The final stage of the creation of a new supply chain is *the scoping phase*. In this stage of the process, after the *supply offering* has been made, a range of potential outcomes become possible.

First there could be a rejection of the offering. If this occurs then two additional outcomes are possible. The innovator (individual or company) can return to the drawing board and start again from scratch. On the other hand, if the failure of the *supply offering* was great, it might, conceivably, lead to the financial ruin of the innovator and risk-taker. In either case, there is unlikely to be the creation of a permanent supply chain or the full-scale production of the particular good or service. If, however, the *supply offering* is accepted then any decision by the innovator will be related directly to the additional risks that might arise from full-scale production.

Even if the original testing of the *supply offering* has been positive there is still a range of potential outcomes. First of all, even though there may have been a demonstration of effective demand, it may have been at a very low or at a very high level. If the response is high, this means that the new product or service has a very broad utility for a wide range of consumers. Thus, given sufficient financial resources, it is likely that consumers will buy the product or service in sufficient numbers to warrant extensive, full-scale production. In this case, the creation of a permanent supply chain for the product or service is highly likely. On the other hand, if the level of effective demand is relatively low then the decision as to whether the innovator should proceed will be much more debatable.

It should be clear from this discussion that the decision to proceed is primarily an entrepreneurial one. This is because the innovator is always operating with relatively high levels of uncertainty and risk. This risk and uncertainty increases all the way through the conception and gestation phases, and only becomes more manageable and amenable to calculation in the scoping phase. Even in the scoping phase, however, the amount of risk associated with the creation of a newly dedicated supply chain for a particular product or service is still high. Part of the reason for this is that the innovator still does not know whether the level of effective demand will be constant, or whether it will decline after a short period. There is, however, a much greater problem than risk and uncertainty, and this is *the tyranny of copying.*

> *The tyranny of copying is the possibility, which all original innovators have to recognise, that others will imitate or improve on what they have originally created.*

This problem faces all innovators when they make an initial *supply offering.* As soon as they bring their product or service to the attention of the consumer, they are also bringing its existence to the attention of their potential competitors. It is at this point that the possibility of the innovator being able to reap the rewards of invention are most directly tested. If the innovator can control knowledge (about processes, resources and techniques) in such a way that they cannot be copied by others, then, at whatever level of demand that exists, the innovator will be able to monopolise the supply chain. By doing so, the innovator will be able to control supply relative to the level of effective demand, and to appropriate value freely for as long as demand is sustained.

If, on the other hand, the innovator cannot control the process of copying, and is not able to retain control through whatever means are available to him or her, then a contested market is likely to develop. The number of competitors (copyists) in the contested market will, be high or low, as a direct result of the relative costs of supply chain entry, and the overall expected levels of sustainable effective demand, for the given supply chain product or service.

If a contested market develops in the supply chain, and the number of competitors is high, then it is more likely that the innovator will be unable to reap the full rewards for his or her risk taking. In these circumstances, it is much more likely that the final consumer will retain the power of the supply chain. In these circumstances the consumer will be able to force suppliers to compete on the basis of passing more and more of the value locked in the supply chain directly to the buyer. Some of the contingent circumstances, and the choices available to the innovator in these cases, are illustrated in Figure 50.

Which of these outcomes is most likely to occur for any new *supply offering* is not fully predictable in advance, because one can never be absolutely sure what consumers will think of a particular product or service when it is offered to them. It should be clear, however, that if the *way of thinking* recommended in this volume is used, it does become possible for practitioners to know, logically, which variables are likely to be the most important ones to be managed in any particular circumstance. If this first step—of recognising that this process is essentially supply rather than demand drive—is taken, then it becomes easier to make effective plans for implementation under any and all contingent circumstances.

Figure 50: The Logic of Demand and Supply for the Innovator under Monopoly and Contested Market Situations

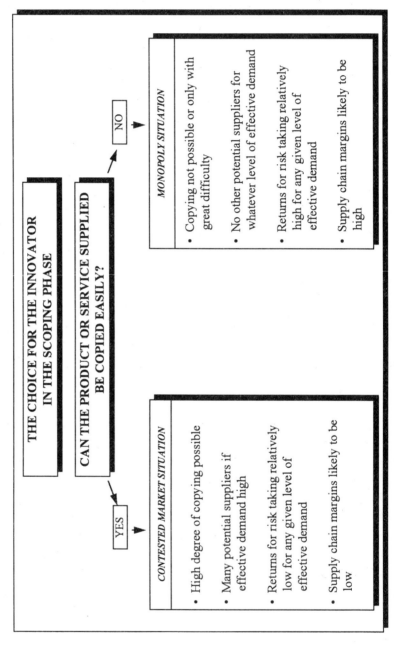

The key learning point from this discussion should also now be obvious.

> *Everything that has been discussed demonstrates the simple logical truth that; if business success is to be achieved in the future, it will necessarily involve innovation by someone. This means that supply must always precede demand in the first instance.*

The reason why most practitioners, and many academics, do not recognise this fact is a result of the fact that they are locked into a mind-set which conceives of business success as being based on the copying or adaptation of what others are doing. If this is what practitioners are doing operationally, then logically this view of the world will be correct for them. For those who copy in this way, demand always does precede supply. This is because, for the practitioners involved, their conception of strategy is always to be striving to copy what already exists, and often with exactly the same tools and techniques used by those with whom they wish to compete.

To argue that this is not the primary basis on which future business success will be achieved, does not mean, of course, that individuals and companies cannot become extremely successful by copying and adapting the things that others have already done. Clearly, *first movers* do not always reap the rewards of innovation, particularly if other people are able to adapt and improve on their initial *supply offering*. The point is, however, that this adaptive improvement can only be achieved if the individual or the company following the initiator also takes a risk with uncertainty. Logically, the follower must be supplying something which, while still a variation on an existing theme, is newly supplied at the time of the follower's initial *supply offering*.

> ***Even successful adaptation within an existing supply chain which has a contested market involves innovation, and therefore must, by definition, require that supply precedes effective demand.***

It is difficult, therefore, to see how anyone could be successful in either an existing or a newly emergent supply chain in the absence of this process of adaptive innovation. In a newly emergent supply chain innovation is a self-evident thing. Even in existing supply chains, however, where there may already be a contested market, those who follow and copy cannot oust the innovator without taking risks of their own with uncertainty and supply. At some point, there has to be a risk taken with uncertainty by someone. Logically, it can be argued that this will always involve an innovative *supply offering* of some kind whenever it occurs.

This means that the proper focus for those who are concerned to understand the causes of business success and failure, must be on the scope for entrepreneurial action embedded within supply chains. To summarise the argument so far it can be argued that there are five keys to understanding business success:

Figure 51: *Five Keys to Understanding Business Success*

- *Business success is linked to the scope for entrepreneurial action that exists within the structure of supply chains, not in the markets which develop to contest ownership and control of supply chain value*

- *Markets cannot, logically, be the basis for an understanding of the possibilities for entrepreneurial action, because the market is, by definition, the demonstration of competition rather than the cause of entrepreneurial innovation.*

- *Entrepreneurial action is always generated as a direct result of the development of new ways of thinking about supply by individuals, either on their own or in companies.*

- *Business success is always about the ability of the individual (or the company) to link a new supply offering with effective demand, in such a way that control over supply chain value is retained.*

- *The most successful will always tend to be those entrepreneurs (or entrepreneurial companies) who understand the need for innovation, but who also know how to leverage it effectively against customers, competitors, employees and suppliers within a specific supply chain.*

On the Meaning of the Supply Chain and the Value Chain

There is, however, a final important point which this *first principle* discussion of supply and demand forces us to recognise. There is a pressing need to clarify exactly what is meant by the concepts of the *supply chain* and the *value chain*. This is an important discussion, because many practitioners and academics appear to confuse these two concepts, or to use them as if they were interchangeable.

The problem here is linked to the lack of theoretical and epistemological rigour in business thinking, which was discussed earlier. Concepts cannot stand on their own as ideas plucked from thin air by the analyst. Concepts are words or phrases which have a meaning, but only within the context of a specific *way of thinking* about causality and reality.

> *Concepts are not, therefore, separate from theory; they are the means by which theory is articulated and understood.*

Many academics in the social sciences fail to grasp this simple point, and pursue their research as if concepts are independent things which can be used in whatever way that the analyst may desire. The problem with this *way of thinking* is evident whenever an argument begins in a bar. Although people may be using the same words and phrases (concepts) they cannot agree because these concepts (art, religion, Christianity, Socialism etc.) mean different things to each of the protagonists. Since the protagonists mean different things by the concepts which they are using, they can never agree about anything, because they are in fact talking about different things, even though they are using the same concept to describe these things.

The reason why this happens is because, while people generally do understand that concepts must have a logical meaning, they completely fail to recognise that this logical meaning is only explicable within the context of the theory of causality (*way of thinking about reality*) which the individual is using. The reason why there is so much discussion between academics and practitioners about the meaning of concepts is, therefore, transparent. It is not because there are lots of different theories about causality, but because most academics and practitioners do not recognise that they think in a *bare-foot empiricist* way.

Most academics and practitioners do have implicit theories of causality in their heads, even if they do not recognise this fact consciously. When the academic or practitioner uses a particular concept, its meaning will, in fact, be informed by their implicit, unconscious, *way of thinking* about causality. As a result, what a concept means to them will based upon their own subjective view of the world and their own, non-explicit, theory of causality. This is why human beings spend most of their lives disagreeing about things. They fail to recognise that the concepts which they use are subjectively defined, and that they often have meanings quite distinct from those ascribed to them by others.

It is primarily for this reason that it is of critical importance that the reader understands why it is necessary to define precisely what the two concepts—*the supply chain* and *the value chain*—actually mean. There are, however, other reasons why it is important to clarify the meaning of these concepts. First, the reader needs to be clear what the words actually mean when this author uses them. Second, if words and concepts are to have separate meanings, a *supply chain* must be distinct from a *value chain*, and the reader needs to know how the author explains this difference. Third, most academics and practitioners either use the concepts to mean very different things from that meant by the present author, or they use the concepts as if they were interchangeable. Finally, and crucially, the two concepts have a meaning which, the reader needs to understand, is defined explicitly by the theory of human action under conditions of relative and absolute scarcity, which informs the *way of thinking* developed in this volume.

Figure 52 demonstrates graphically what these two concepts refer to in relation to the *way of thinking* adopted in this text. The problem with the supply chain and value chain concepts as they are used elsewhere, is either that people do not define them from *first theoretical principles,* or that they appropriate the concepts for their own purposes. Michael Porter, for example, has used the idea of a *value chain,* but he uses it in a very different way to that which is used in this book. (Porter, 1985) Porter's use of the concept of the *value chain* (see Figure 33) is linked to his desire to describe the successive internal stages of the production process within the company. The aim is to provide a tool to aid an understanding of what are the key drivers of cost within the process. The focus throughout is, therefore, on the idea that business success is about finding those key points within the process which could be managed more efficiently and could, thereby, add value to the company's output.

This *way of thinking* is not necessarily wrong. Clearly, if companies can find the key points in their processes where costs are incurred, and then finds ways in which these costs can be reduced significantly, they will have a major opportunity to increase their value appropriation. The interesting thing, of course, is that knowing where the significant costs are, does not necessarily tell us how to go about reducing them. Knowing how to achieve this requires someone to innovate. This innovative process always requires that someone use rational deductive and inductive logic *(abstractive reasoning)* to come

Figure 52: The Supply Chain and the Value Chain

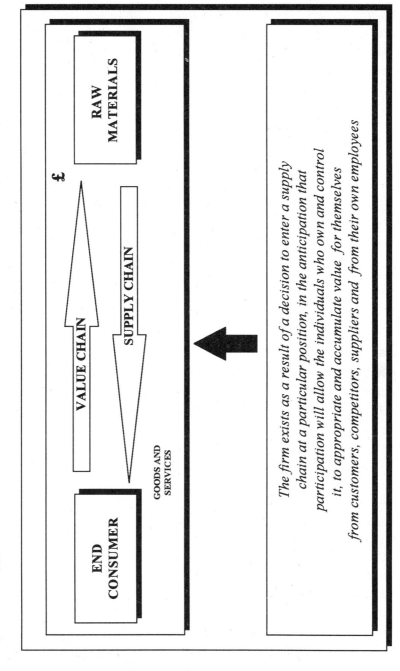

RAW MATERIALS

£

VALUE CHAIN

SUPPLY CHAIN

END CONSUMER

GOODS AND SERVICES

The firm exists as a result of a decision to enter a supply chain at a particular position, in the anticipation that participation will allow the individuals who own and control it, to appropriate and accumulate value for themselves from customers, competitors, suppliers and from their own employees

up with *a new way of thinking* about how to do the things that are currently being produced and supplied, but in a different way. It requires, in other words, entrepreneurial action focused on the supply of something new. This process will always involve a more effective way of leveraging someone in the supply chain. Furthermore, and this is a very important point:

> **While a description of the cost incurring process within the existing boundaries of the company (Porter's value chain concept) tells us what is, it can never tell us <u>what to do</u> to change this reality to our advantage.**

It is for this reason that the concept of the *value chain,* as described in Figure 52, is used differently in this volume. The *value chain,* refers to the process by which money is exchanged through a *supply chain,* after an initial *supply offering* has been made. The thinking here is straight forward enough. If we start from a recognition of the fact that supply always precedes demand then it follows logically that someone has to take a risk on the supply of physical goods and services to a customer. This is the *supply chain.* The *supply chain* is that complex and interconnected network of relationships which exist between individuals and companies, in order to transmit physical products and services *in exchange* for value (money). These networks of relationships, based on the transmission of physical products or services to the ultimate consumer (after they have first passed through an initial raw material stage and then through a series of successive semi-finished stages) only exist because of this *exchange of value*.

The *supply chain* is, then, a metaphor which describes the physical production process for both goods and services. This, process must, logically, precede the operation of the *value chain*. The reason for this, theoretically and practically, is because buyers rarely pay for supply before they have received physical goods or services. This is not to say that people never pay in advance of supply, but that they will normally only do so if they have a reasonable certainty of legal redress to recover their money if there is a subsequent failure of supply. The general rule in business, although there are some significant exceptions, is that people supply goods and services before they are paid for them. This is why there are normally standard operating procedures in exchange relationships dealing with the length of time the buyer has before he or she has to pay the supplier.

Some readers may disagree with this view, and may argue that they, as customers, often pay in advance of supply. For example, people often pay in advance for an airline or theatre ticket. If the reader dwells on these two examples for a moment, however, it will quickly be realised that what appear to be cases of demand preceding supply are, in fact, not really so. In each of these two cases, the customer only pays for a ticket in advance, because there is the possibility of a lack of supply through excess demand. Furthermore, although the ticket is bought before the service being offered, the airline and the theatre company have already had to supply the necessary physical infrastructure and personnel in advance. Only by doing this, can they provide the degree of certainty demanded by the customer that what is being offered can reasonably be expected to be supplied. Even if it is not supplied, the customer knows that, barring a corporate collapse, there is a very high certainty that all money paid in advance will be refunded.

The two examples given above, refer to the process by which direct supply is replaced by a high degree of certainty that someone has *the capacity to supply* what is being offered. The possession of a capacity to supply involves someone having the resources to provide a product or service, even though the actual product or service does not exist at the time it is offered. The airline and theatre tickets are good examples of this, as is the practice that some entrepreneurial companies use of offering a product to the public when it does not, and never has, existed. This practice is commonly used as a marketing technique by mail-order companies, when they offer a picture of something that has not yet been mass-produced, and only produce it if, and when, the level of effective demand is known. This practice can be extended to the creation of a mock-up of a product which has never existed, but which will be if there is sufficient effective demand.

In each of these two examples, it is clear that consumers are being asked to part with their money before the supply of a product or service. Despite this objective fact, these examples do not invalidate the general claim that supply precedes payment. The reason for this is that, even if the money is provided in advance of supply, there is an implicit contract in the exchange that the money will be repaid if the product or service is not eventually supplied. The money does not, therefore, belong to the supplier legally until the act of supply has been consummated with the buyer. Obviously, if the company holding the money fails or goes bankrupt before the supply event takes place, then the buyer will have to forfeit his or her money. That this is so does not, however, invalidate the general rule that successful companies normally have to supply things before they are paid. If, in the absence of supply, the supplier can only keep the money by going into liquidation, this can hardly be seen as an effective business strategy for long-term corporate sustainability.

If the *supply chain* refers to the physical process of supply, the *value chain* logically refers to that complex network of payment relationships which exist in parallel with, and normally after the fact of, this physical supply. Despite the caveats made above, generally speaking the *value chain* will only come into operation when the ultimate and final consumer puts money into the chain by paying the proximate supplier of the final product or service. Therefore, even though it logically follows supply, the *value chain* is the key focus of business activity in this *way of thinking*, because it is the energising force which provides the fuel by which the *supply chain* can exist. In the absence of an expectation, on the part of entrepreneurs, that this energising force will be forthcoming, innovation will stop and there will be no supply offerings

The two concepts of the supply and value can, therefore, be summarised in this *way of thinking:*

THE SUPPLY CHAIN

The supply chain precedes the creation of the value chain, and refers to the complex network of relationships that are required in order to turn raw materials into physical products and services for ultimate consumption.

THE VALUE CHAIN

The value chain operates in parallel with, but normally after the fact of, the supply chain, and refers to that complex network of payment relationships which, through anticipated reward, energises the supply chain.

This point about the *energising role* of value exchange is critical to our understanding of what makes things happen in a world of absolute and relative scarcity, where people have to take risks with uncertainty. Many writers seem to believe that anything is possible in this world, and that if people want something then it can be provided for them. In a recent book, Womack and Jones have called on companies to fulfil people's *dreams* about the things they would ideally like to have supplied to them. Their message is clear. If you give the people what they want, then corporate success will be secured, because delighting customers and passing value to them effectively and efficiently is the basis for all corporate success. (Womack & Jones, 1996)

This is an immensely appealing *way of thinking* for companies and for the people who work in them. The reason is that it provides them with a view that what they are doing is essentially moral and ethical, and leads them to believe that the ultimate purpose of business is *to delight the customer*. Appealing as this vision may be, it is, if the arguments presented here have any validity, only a partial view of the fundamental causes of business success.

Day-Dreaming or Purposive Actualisation?

It was argued earlier that the ultimate goal of business is to appropriate and accumulate value through the effective leverage of customers, suppliers, competitors and employees in supply chains. This was reinforced, in Figure 52, by the claim that individuals and companies only enter supply chains, and take the risks of participation, because they anticipate that it will lead to reward. Reward can be achieved in many ways but in business it is normal to conceive of the reward that is being sought in material terms. Individuals are seeking to participate in supply chains in the anticipation of being able to appropriate and accumulate value for themselves through a process of exchange. The ultimate reason, of course, is that they hope to use the value that they accumulate to appropriate those material things which they most value.

It is interesting in this context to dwell on why it was, if success is based on individuals pursuing their own accumulation strategies, that people decided to work together to create limited liability, joint stock companies as a mechanism for value appropriation in the nineteenth. The limited liability company has had a relatively short life since its creation by government regulations in the middle of the nineteenth century. There also appears to be a great deal of interesting debate, at the present time, about the true role and purpose of these types of organisation. In the UK, this has spawned a debate about stakeholding and corporate governance. There is a view that companies exist to serve some purpose higher than that for which they were created. To set the record straight, in the author's view at least, it should be clearly understood that the limited liability, joint stock company is nothing more than a device. It is a means to an end, not an end in itself.

> *The limited liability, joint stock company is not an end in itself; it is merely a means to an end. The end is always the appropriation and accumulation of value for specified individuals.*

The limited liability company was clearly a contingent response by powerful human beings to some of the specific opportunities and problems which they were experiencing in their attempts to appropriate value from supply chains in the early part of the nineteenth century. The specific opportunity was the fact that, in the early nineteenth century, there had been an expansion in the opportunities to appropriate value from commodity exchange. This was primarily due to the fact that, due to the expansion of western control of global territories, and the opportunities for the production and logistical movement of cheaper goods and services, global supply chains were now in existence. As a result, the sources of material wealth—the supply of commodities—could now be produced in a potentially infinite manner, so long as there was effective demand for what could be supplied.

Before then value appropriation had always been limited by three factors. These three factors were:

- *The finite nature of land and what could be produced from it.*

- *The weakly developed logistical supply chains between different areas of the world.*

- *The inefficient and limited technological means of production.*

In the eighteenth and early nineteenth centuries, however, the limited opportunities for value appropriation and accumulation within defined national territorial areas were radically challenged. These challenges came from a number of sources.

The most important of these were the developments in transportation and communications, which created global supply and value chains. The creation of these global supply and value chains provided the opportunity for entrepreneurs to use new and more plentiful sources of raw materials, and new technological means of production, to supply an ever expanding portion of the globe. This widening of the scope of already existing, but previously nationally constrained, supply and value chains, increased the total level of effective demand and prompted new innovations in supply. This process, also generated completely new types of supply and value chains. The international financial system created in the City of London is a classic example of this process at work, as is the creation in the nineteenth century of Thomas Cook's, the very first travel agency company.

Under the commodity exchange system, which has been in existence since the beginning of human history, and the essentials of which are described in the definitions of the supply and the value chain presented above, the eighteenth and nineteenth centuries ushered in a new epoch. Now, for the first time, the scope and breadth of supply and value chains began an inexorable process of expansion. This process, by means of which individuals saw opportunities for their own enrichment, is still working its way through the world today.

The fact that companies today are operationally concerned with supply chain issues, and are struggling to understand what globalisation means for them, is perfectly explicable in this context. It is just another graphic example of the working out, but on a much wider stage, of those historic exchange processes, linked to value appropriation, which have always been at work within supply and value chains.

While the dynamics of the contested markets which develop within these supply and value chains are well understood, it can be argued that the critically important supply and value chain processes which underpin markets are still some of the most poorly understood phenomena in contemporary business thinking.

The reason for this is that most commentators have focused on markets as the key factor in understanding this process of supply and value chain expansion. This is because one of the most obvious manifestations of the expansion of supply and value chains is *the entrepreneurial contest* which takes place within each one *after* it has been created.

The author believes while this is an understandable reaction by commentators, it may not necessarily be the most appropriate starting point from which to understand what are the truly dynamic factors within this process. If the properly dynamic factors in the process are not being focused on, then it is unlikely that the analyst will be able to isolate the truly causal phenomena in business success. It is for this reason that the author has started from *first principles* in trying to understand business success, rather than from an analysis of the markets which are created as the secondary consequence of supply innovation. This reasoning can be summarised simply enough:

> *Entrepreneurial innovation is the dynamic cause of supply and value chain creation and expansion. Market competition is a secondary effect not the cause of this phenomenon.*

By starting from this point of departure it becomes apparent that the internationalisation, or globalisation, process is not primarily a market phenomenon at all; it is a supply and value chain phenomenon. Globalisation is at heart a process by which individuals seek opportunities to expand the scope and breadth of value appropriation under conditions of absolute and relative scarcity. The major difference today is that the possibilities for value appropriation and accumulation are now globally, as opposed to locally and regionally, defined.

In the eighteenth and nineteenth centuries, there were new opportunities to expand the breadth and scope of supply and value chains.   However, these opportunities were still circumscribed by a multiplicity of local, regional and national rules and regulations protecting certain individuals' rights to control indigenous supply and value chains.   Globalisation, which has primarily been stimulated by the political decision to deregulate the protection of certain individuals' rights to control particular supply and value chains, is simply the working through of a process which has always been inherent in the appropriation and accumulation of value.   Logically, it can be argued that the process of value appropriation and accumulation has only ever been circumscribed by environmental constraints (such as limits on the availability of raw materials and space), by political restrictions (such as governmental closure of access to participation in supply and value chains within given territorial areas), and by the ability and propensity of human beings to consume.

> *Globalisation is driven by entrepreneurial actions within supply and value chains. It is not primarily a phenomenon of markets. Markets are the consequence of entrepreneurial supply and value chain actions, not the cause of them.*

These comments may seem a long way away from our starting point in this section, which was to explain why the limited liability, joint stock company was created and why it has survived. But, by starting from this *way of thinking,* about the dynamic, entrepreneurial factors within supply and value chains, the reason why the limited liability, joint stock company was created becomes relatively easy to understand.

While the development of new avenues through which to appropriate value, in the form of expanding and newly emerging supply and value chains was an opportunity for entrepreneurs in the nineteenth century, it also created a number of contingent problems. Foremost amongst these was the fact that the risks associated with expanding existing, or establishing new, supply and value chains, and of controlling those critical points on the chain which allowed for the maximisation of value appropriation, were very high indeed. The costs of creating new factories, and of installing new machines, which was at that time was one of the most appropriate means by which to appropriate and accumulate value, were prohibitive. In the past entrepreneurs could have underwritten the costs of supply, either on their own, or through loose partnership arrangements with others. Now, with the massive increase in the costs of supply chain management the risks of loss were disproportionate to the immediate gains which could be realised.

A simple device was needed, therefore, to allow people to take risks with supply and innovation without there being a direct threat to the entrepreneur's accumulated wealth. This device was, and is, the limited liability company. Before the limited liability company was created, individuals had been liable for all of the losses that they incurred in business. Indeed, they could be imprisoned for not paying their debts, and would not be released until these debts were paid in full. Obviously, while this may have been an appropriate way of dealing with errant entrepreneurs under simple forms of supply and value chain management, under the potentially vast, global supply chain arrangements which were being created at that time, this way of regulating society was gradually seen to be inappropriate. Eventually, therefore, the idea developed that innovation and risk-taking would be immeasurably aided by the creation of the limited liability and joint stock company.

> *As always, in life, necessity was the mother of invention.*

By this device, it became possible to allow people to raise revenue for investment in new, speculative innovations, while also limiting the liability of those whose money was invested in the company. The accumulated personal wealth of the owners of these new enterprises was no longer threatened directly by the fact that their risk-taking might lead to financial collapse and debts. In the event of bankruptcy, the company's debts would be written-off by its customers (in the form of supplies foregone), and by its suppliers (in the form of payments not received). The limited liability and joint stock company was, and is, therefore, a device to allow those who own or control the stock the ability to take risks with uncertainty, in order that they can appropriate value for themselves. It is not a higher form of social or political organisation, and it has, arguably, no other purpose than that for which it was created:

> *The limited liability, joint stock company is nothing more than a device to make it easier for entrepreneurs to appropriate value from supply chains by taking risks with uncertainty, but with other people's money.*

In making this claim there is no intention to pass a moral judgement. Whether this new form of organisation, if what has been argued is true, is a good thing or bad thing cannot be stated categorically. This is because what one thinks about this device, depends entirely on what the individual values and wishes to achieve. All that one can say is that the limited liability company exists for a particular purpose, in response to specific contingent circumstances. The future of this device does not depend on what people may wish. What will determine whether it persists or not, will be whether it is still fit for its original purpose. If it is not, then presumably, human beings will invent a more appropriate way of accumulating value for themselves from supply chains.

This is an important insight, because it allows us to explain (to know and to understand) why it is that so many commentators today are discussing the growth of collaboration and strategic alliances amongst companies. It is to the credit of most commentators that they are clearly describing an important phenomenon. This phenomenon is not, however, what many of them appear to believe it is. Many commentators see what is happening, and claim that we are witnessing something completely new and innovative in the nature of business. They argue that they have discerned an essential truth in the nature of business, and then claim that, if all companies copy what others are doing, they will have the keys to business success. The problem is that while these commentators may be describing *what* is happening, they demonstrate very little understanding of *why* these things are happening.

The reason why there is a move towards ever greater collaboration and alliance formation in many supply and value chains, is that globalisation provides the same dilemma for large multinational companies today as it did for the individual entrepreneur in the eighteenth and nineteenth centuries. This dilemma is that, while there are opportunities in expansion and globalisation, there are also significant risks. The problem can be summarised easily enough:

> *Under the conditions of ever expanding scale and breadth in supply and value chains, the major companies which are seeking to participate in these chains on a global basis now have to decide whether to risk the potential costs of independence, or to share the potential rewards, by minimising these risks through alliances.*

This is not, however, a new problem. A moment's reflection will reveal that it is a recurring dilemma which has faced human beings throughout the ages. The difference today is that it is being played out on a much broader scale. Despite what self-interested commentators, may claim this is not a new phenomenon at all. Companies are being forced to consider alliances and collaboration, because they are having to take risks with uncertainty. It is clear that this is exactly the same dilemma, with the same range of choices available to human beings, which faced entrepreneurs in the eighteenth and nineteenth centuries. If the entrepreneur or the company goes it alone, and monopolises the supply and value chain, all of the material rewards to be reaped will be retained by them alone. If, on the other hand, they collaborate, any potential rewards will have to be shared with others. To recognise this is simply to understand that, under conditions of scarcity and uncertainty, the dilemmas facing those in business will always be the same.

To recognise the eternal nature of these dilemmas is important, because it should help us to understand a simple truth. This truth is that the human condition does not change:

> **The human condition is to live in a world of absolute and relative scarcity, and to compete to possess those things which are of value to individual human beings.**

What changes are not the age-old dilemmas of life (such as the need to take risks with uncertainty, or the problem that human beings tend to value most those things which are scarce), but the material and technological circumstances within which we experience these dilemmas. This realisation leads one back to an understanding that what it is appropriate for human beings to do will be contingent on the circumstances which face them:

> **The human condition never changes. The only thing which changes are the material and technological circumstances under which it is experienced.**

This means that, while the limited liability company was, and is, an appropriate response to a specific set of contingent circumstances, it was not, and is not, necessarily the only possible response for the entrepreneur. Some individuals create joint stock companies and prosper, other people create them and fail. The learning point here must be, therefore, that:

> **It is not what people do which is important, but whether or not what they are doing is appropriate under the circumstances which face them.**

Clearly, the use of strategic alliances, and other forms of collaboration, will be extremely beneficial for some companies, but for others this way of working will not be appropriate. Arguably, the key determinant of success will not be the knowledge that these collaborative ways of working exist, but whether or not the individual understands why it is appropriate to enter into them in the first place, and for what purpose. The key learning point here is self-evident:

> *There are many ways to achieve valued outcomes, and it is valuable to know what are all of the potential options. More important, however, is not a knowledge of the possibilities, but an awareness of which, of the universe of possible options, will be the most appropriate to use under given circumstances.*

The point here is that successful human beings can find the way to do what is appropriate. The problem with *appropriateness* is, however, that most people appear not to understand what it means. Appropriateness does not mean doing those things which we would like to do, despite the circumstances which confront us. This is *day-dreaming*. This means the tendency in human beings to dream about all of the things that they would like to see happen, and which they value, but without knowing how, or whether, it is possible to achieve the object of their desire.

Appropriateness is different from this, in that it means doing those things which can be achieved within the circumstances which actually confront us. There is a significant difference in these two *ways of thinking*, and the realisation of this takes the discussion back to the claim made earlier that rather than ***day-dreaming***, we should understand ***appropriateness***.

Day-dreaming means thinking about those things which one would most like to do, without really understanding whether or not it is possible to achieve the valued outcome, and then doing those things in the hope that they might work.

Appropriateness means understanding what actually confronts us, and choosing wisely, from amongst the universe of possible things that might be done. Then doing those things which have a realistic chance of successful implementation.

It should be clear from the brief discussion of the development of the limited liability joint stock company, that this was an appropriate thing to do at the time, but not necessarily for everyone. It was appropriate for many people, however, because it provided a new device by which individuals could accumulate value. It was by definition *fit for its purpose.* If it had not been, it would have been discarded and something else would have replaced it. The problem with the Womack and Jones view, and the views of those writers who recommend a more collaborative approach to business through alliances, is that their *way of thinking* fails to recognise the concept of appropriateness. These writers seem to take the view that, whatever customers most value, should, and can, be the proper focus for corporate endeavour. The problem with this *way of thinking* is that it does not recognise the importance of the concept of ***purposive actualisation***.

This sounds complex, but it is not. In general terms this concept refers to the fact that what can be done is not just a function of what people would ideally like to possess or consume. If anything is to be created in the material world an exchange relationship must take place. The exchange does not have to be about money, but it will normally involve a trading relationship of some kind. It will, therefore, involve a buyer and supplier relationship of one form or another. What can be created in the world will not, however, just be a function of what either the potential buyer or the potential supplier would like to see happen. What can be achieved will be partly a function of what buyers desire and value, and it will also be partly a function of what the supplier believes can be created. A large measure of what is done will ultimately, however, be a function of the material circumstances of risk, uncertainty, and reward which confront all of the people who must come together, within the supply chain, to make anything happen. This is part of the ***conjuncture of forces*** within which human beings act.

As Figure 53 shows a *conjuncture of forces* will always exist when human beings make decisions about what they should do. This *conjuncture of forces* contains supply and demand characteristics and, if anything is to be done of a practical kind, it will involve human beings who understand *the art of the possible* in the real world. These people are the linchpins of purposive human action. These people, who are in the middle, between the infinite possibilities of potential supply and the infinite aspirations of demand, are entrepreneurs. They are those people in the real world whose self-seeking and self-interested behaviour creates *purposive actualisation*. It is unlikely that these people will actually understand theoretically what this concept means, but they are the human embodiment of its manifestation in the world.

Figure 53: Purposive Actualisation

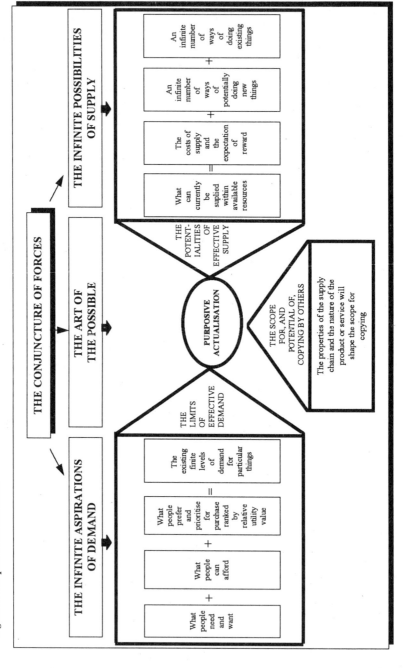

THE CONJUNCTURE OF FORCES

THE INFINITE ASPIRATIONS OF DEMAND

THE ART OF THE POSSIBLE

THE INFINITE POSSIBILITIES OF SUPPLY

What people need and want + What people can afford + What people prefer and prioritise for purchase ranked by relative utility value = The existing finite levels of demand for particular things

THE LIMITS OF EFFECTIVE DEMAND

PURPOSIVE ACTUALISATION

THE POTENT-IALITIES OF EFFECTIVE SUPPLY

What can currently be suplied within available resources = The costs of supply and the expectation of reward + An infinite number of ways of potentially doing new things + An infinite number of ways of doing existing things

THE SCOPE FOR, AND POTENTIAL OF, COPYING BY OTHERS

The properties of the supply chain and the nature of the product or service will shape the scope for copying

The role of the entrepreneur has been well documented by Schumpeter and others in the Austrian economics school. (Schumpeter, 1934, Kirzner, 1973) It is interesting to note, however, that the role of the entrepreneur is given very little attention in mainstream economics and business management texts. This is a surprising omission, because there can be little doubt that, as Schumpeter recognised long ago, the ghost in the machine of business success is always entrepreneurial activity. The role of the entrepreneur is easily understood in the context of our discussion here. The entrepreneur is the bearer of ***purposive actualisation***. He, or she, is the person who innovates and who takes risks with uncertainty.

The successful entrepreneur will not, however, be an inveterate gambler. As Figure 53 reveals, the choices facing the entrepreneur, about where to invest his or her time and money, will be based on either an intuitive, or an explicit, understanding of the processes at work in the concept of ***purposive actualisation***. By this concept we mean that the entrepreneur is the human being who is able to understand *the limits of effective demand* and *the potentialities of effective supply*.

Entrepreneurial individuals and companies would soon fail, however, if they did not understand that what people value and aspire to consume is not the same as *effective demand*. What people value may be infinite. People have literally thousands of articulated and unarticulated needs and wants. They also know that they cannot afford to purchase everything that they would ideally prefer to consume. The availability of each individual's own personal store of material resource (accumulated value) defines the limits of what is possible for the supply of anything, but this is not the end of the matter. The individual does not value the same things in the same way as everyone else. Human beings see utility in many different things, and rank order their preferences on the basis of their own view of the relative utility of things.

This means that entrepreneurs always have a chance of increasing the level of *effective demand* for their own specific products or services, if they can supply something which the potential consumer might value more highly than the other things which are currently available. However, at any moment in time, there is, relatively speaking, a finite level of effective demand for what could be supplied. This is what the entrepreneur has to recognise on the demand side of the equation. The entrepreneur has to make a judgement about the possibility of any act of supply generating a sufficiently high level of effective demand to justify the original money invested in it. This must always be a calculation made on the basis of relative degrees of uncertainty.

The entrepreneur has similarly difficult calculations and judgements to make on the supply side of the *purposive actualisation* equation. The entrepreneur knows that there are currently many different ways of doing things and that there are, potentially, many new ways in which things could be supplied. He or she may also be aware of completely new products and services, which could be supplied if there was an effective demand for them. The problem for the entrepreneur is that there is no certain way in which he or she can know whether a new way of meeting demand will lead to *effective demand* until the *supply offering* has been made. This is the perennial problem of uncertainty, which is at the heart of all business success and failure.

It is clear, as Figure 54 reveals, that, as a result of this constant dilemma, new things are normally only done if someone is prepared to take a chance on uncertainty. Someone may take a chance on uncertainty, because they do not understand the risks they are running. In most circumstances, however, people do have a reasonable knowledge of the fact that they may be running risks, and they are normally acutely aware of the potential losses that could result. For supply innovation to occur, therefore, a *purposive act* must take place.

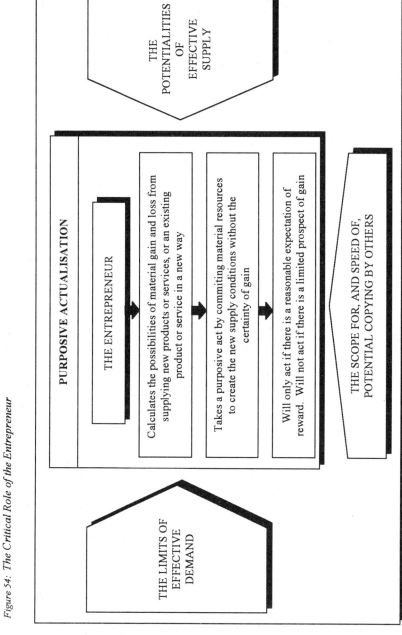

Figure 54: The Critical Role of the Entrepreneur

THE POTENTIALITIES OF EFFECTIVE SUPPLY

PURPOSIVE ACTUALISATION

THE ENTREPRENEUR

Calculates the possibilities of material gain and loss from supplying new products or services, or an existing product or service in a new way

Takes a purposive act by commiting material resources to create the new supply conditions without the certainty of gain

Will only act if there is a reasonable expectation of reward. Will not act if there is a limited prospect of gain

THE SCOPE FOR, AND SPEED OF, POTENTIAL COPYING BY OTHERS

THE LIMITS OF EFFECTIVE DEMAND

This *purposive act* will normally be driven by material self-interest rather than humanitarian altruism. The *purposive act* will also involve expectations of material gain, from running the potential risks of loss, which go with supplying new products and services in a situation of uncertainty. This does not preclude humanitarian altruism as a cause of supply innovation; but it merely states the probability that, in an environment of absolute and relative material scarcity, human beings will normally place material considerations ahead of the other considerations in their own personal *hierarchy of needs*.

If this view is correct, then it should be clear why it is that the author disagrees with Womack and Jones about *dreaming dreams* about what customers might wish to buy. There is, of course, nothing wrong with understanding what things human beings might potentially want to consume, but this is altogether a different thing from assuming that, because people want these things, it is possible to provide them. It will only be possible to provide them if a situation of ***purposive actualisation*** exists. This is a situation in which there are a sufficient number of consumers, who are willing to part with enough of their actual (or potential) store of accumulated wealth, to pay the entrepreneur (individual or company) the return which must be made in order for the supply chain to be created in the first place. The entrepreneur must also have a reasonable expectation that a sufficient return can be made for long enough, before other entrepreneurs copy what is being done. This insight can be summarised as follows:

> *Purposive actualisation exists when the fit between the expected level of effective demand, and the supply potential which currently exists, is sufficiently strong for the entrepreneur to risk the immediate loss of material resources to create a new supply offering, or a new supply chain, in the expectation of a much higher material return in the future.*

This discussion, about the role of the entrepreneur and the purposive act which must be made to create a new supply chain, or to supply an existing product or service in a new way, is at the heart of the general argument developed here. One of the key weaknesses of current economics and business management writing is its apparent lack of interest in the role of the entrepreneur. This is staggering thing to have to say because, if the arguments presented here have any validity, then business success must always start and end with entrepreneurial action by someone within the supply chains that are, and have been, created to deliver goods and services to end customers. It is only by innovating within those supply chains which exist, or by creating completely new supply chains, that the conditions for permanent or temporary monopoly, which are the bases of sustainable advantage, can be created. This *way of thinking* entrepreneurially is outlined in Figure 55.

Given that so little has been written in the key business texts about the role of the entrepreneur, it is hardly surprising, that there is evidence of managers using concepts and ideas inappropriately in their day-to-day activities. The fact that practitioners often do not really know what they ought to be doing to achieve sustainable advantage, should not, therefore, surprise us. This lack of awareness is obviously a result of the fact that practitioners are extremely busy dealing with their immediate problems. It is also related to the immaturity of the discipline, and the commensurate lack of a proper theory (or theories) of business success in the literature.

Despite this general malaise, in recent years there has been an encouraging theoretical development with the creation of what has been termed the *resource-based* school of business strategy. Based on the work of Penrose (1959), the basic thinking of this school is that companies must develop unique and distinctive capabilities from the wide number of resources which are available to them, as they compete with one another. It is argued that it is only through the development of effective

Figure 55: Five Keys to Entrepreneurial Thinking

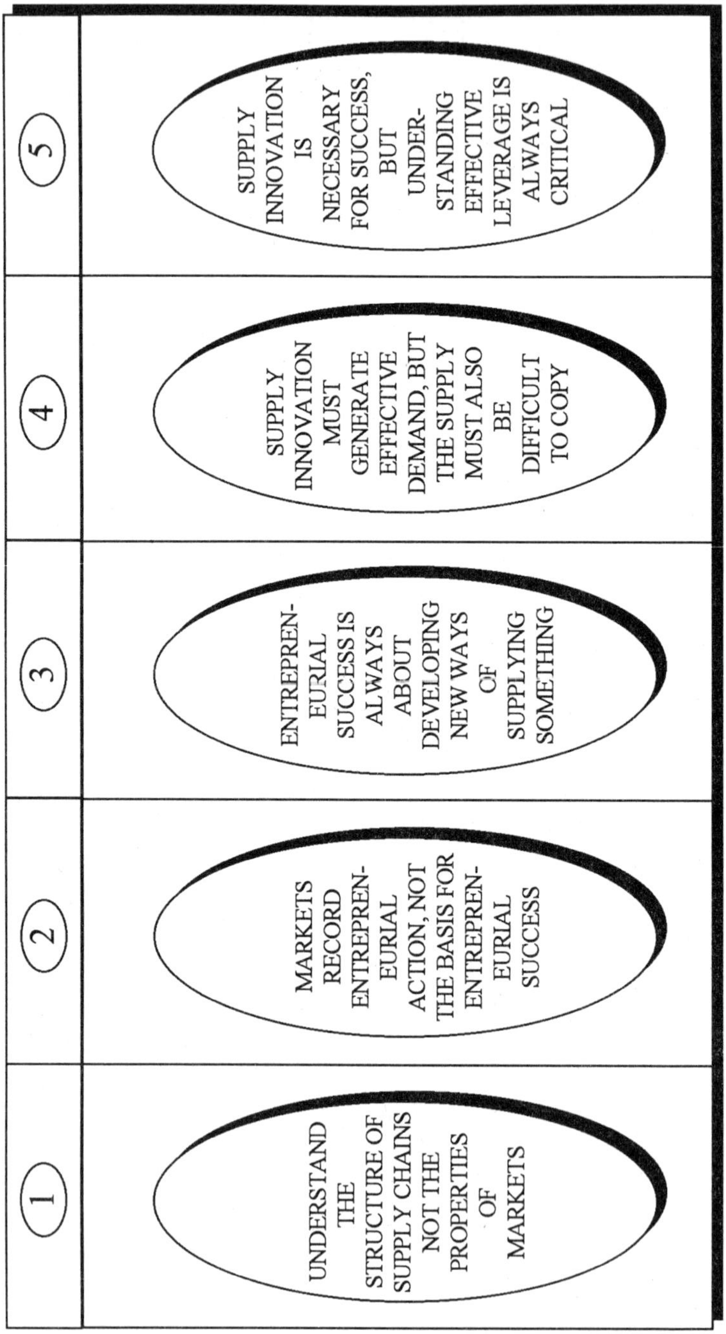

①	②	③	④	⑤
UNDERSTAND THE STRUCTURE OF SUPPLY CHAINS NOT THE PROPERTIES OF MARKETS	MARKETS RECORD ENTREPRENEURIAL ACTION, NOT THE BASIS FOR ENTREPRENEURIAL SUCCESS	ENTREPRENEURIAL SUCCESS IS ALWAYS ABOUT DEVELOPING NEW WAYS OF SUPPLYING SOMETHING	SUPPLY INNOVATION MUST GENERATE EFFECTIVE DEMAND, BUT THE SUPPLY MUST ALSO BE DIFFICULT TO COPY	SUPPLY INNOVATION IS NECESSARY FOR SUCCESS, BUT UNDERSTANDING EFFECTIVE LEVERAGE IS ALWAYS CRITICAL

control over a distinct set of resources (human, financial, technological, manufacturing, marketing etc.), which cannot be replicated by other companies, that competitive success is achievable. (Montgomery, 1995; Kay, 1996)

This approach, which recognises the attributes which particular resources can bring to companies, and the unique ways in which companies can order their resource base to attain business success, is a powerful antidote to those simplistic generalisations which assume that there is only one approach to business success. There seems little doubt that the *resource-based school* is on to something, because it recognises the contingent nature of business success, as well as the need for companies to be different to one another if they are to be successful. Unfortunately, as we argued in relation to the work of Kay earlier, while the *resource-based school* has correctly defined the contingent nature of the resources available to companies, it has not provided us with a proper theory of the resources that are most appropriate for business success, and under which circumstances. The *resource-based school* has stopped half-way, because it focuses primarily on the **existing** *internal resources* which the organisation possesses, and starts from a competitive market rather than a supply chain focus.

> *The resource-based school recognises that companies must develop unique and distinctive capabilities, but it does not explain how companies should think about what will be important in the future to make them unique and distinctive within supply chains.*

To develop a more holistic and inclusive view of business success, it is necessary to recognise that a company must take account of the fact that the resources it currently controls, or manages, are part of complex supply chains. Furthermore these supply chains are in a constant state of flux. Business strategy and operational practices should not, therefore, be focused on describing the resources which companies have internalised to be successful in the past (the *core competence* and *resource-based* approaches). On the contrary, they should be directed towards developing a methodology that will allow companies to understand which resources, within the supply chains in which they are currently involved, or in which they could be involved, are of critical importance to business success.

It is self-evident, therefore, that specifying what companies ought to focus on in the future cannot be determined from a post-hoc explanation of what happened in the past. A pro-active approach requires the development of a methodology which theoretically explains the reasons why firms exist, how they survive and prosper, and which strategies and operational practices are most appropriate for them under given circumstances. It follows, therefore, that while there can never be one type of strategy or operational practice which is always appropriate for all companies, *there may be a single theoretical and methodological approach which can be used under all circumstances as a way of thinking about what is appropriate.* The principles of this *way of thinking* can be summarised as follows:

Figure 56: *Three Principles for Appropriate Ways of Thinking*

- *Describing what was the basis of individual or corporate uniqueness and distinctiveness in the past can never provide a guide to purposive action in the future.*

- *A practical guide to purposive action requires the development of a way of thinking, which allows one to understand why what an individual or a company did in the past was the critical thing to do for that individual or company, under those unique contingent circumstances.*

- *Focusing on those properties and characteristics of supply and value chains, which provide opportunities for permanent or temporary monopoly, rather than on the conditions of markets, is likely to be the most fruitful way in which a practical guide for purposive action will be developed.*

If this logic is followed then it is clear that, in the future, the test of a good manager will not be whether they have the right strategy or operational practice under today's circumstances. Rather, the proper test of managerial competence must be whether they possess the type of thinking, and a way of looking at the world, which will allow them to recognise the full range of potential solutions which are available to them, and the likely consequences if any of these potential solutions are implemented under given circumstances. The test of academic rigour in this context, therefore, is not whether new concepts or ideas can be developed, but whether a theoretical and methodological approach can be constructed, which can predictively and descriptively explain the causes of business success in all circumstances, and can also stand the test of continuous empirical verification.

The remainder of this chapter is devoted to a brief exposition of an approach, which is being developed in line with the arguments outlined earlier about the superiority of *abstractive reasoning.* This approach will be used to develop ways of thinking, typologies of action and operational guides to business strategy and operational practice under given, but constantly changing, supply chain and market circumstances.

Asset Criticality and the Properties of Supply Chains

It was argued earlier that one of the major problems facing the *resource-based school* of business strategy was the fact that it tended to focus on the internal resources which companies currently possess, rather than on the relative value of the resources which exist in totality within existing supply chains (or which could be reordered to create completely new supply chains). It was also argued that one of the major problems for companies is the fact that the potential resources which might have a relationship with value in any existing supply chain are in a constant state of flux. This is because the world is contingent. The theoretical approach to be outlined in what follows is based on the recognition of this insight about *the dynamic characteristic of supply chain resources.* This line of thinking appears to be under-developed in the current business strategy and operational practice literature.

This dynamic flux within supply chains is caused by the fact that, within any primary supply chain, some of the resources which are necessary to deliver an end-product (or service) to a consumer are relatively more important than others, given the current state of market competition and technological innovation. These key resources, which shape and determine the allocation of value within a supply chain, can be defined, conceptually, as *critical assets.* These resources are of central importance to *the appropriation and accumulation of value in a supply chain* and, as such, are the *key supply chain resources*

Figure 57: Critical Supply Chain Assets

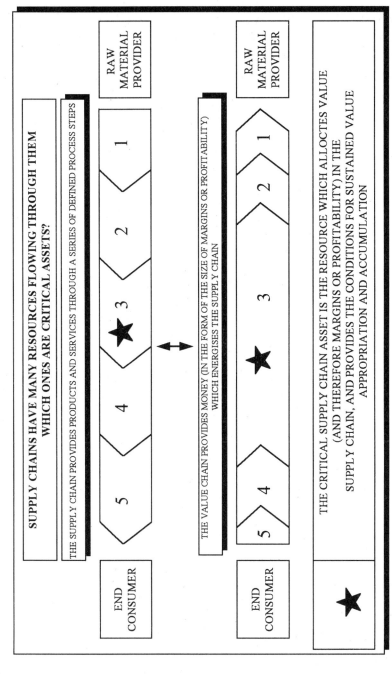

SUPPLY CHAINS HAVE MANY RESOURCES FLOWING THROUGH THEM WHICH ONES ARE CRITICAL ASSETS?

THE SUPPLY CHAIN PROVIDES PRODUCTS AND SERVICES THROUGH A SERIES OF DEFINED PROCESS STEPS

THE VALUE CHAIN PROVIDES MONEY (IN THE FORM OF THE SIZE OF MARGINS OR PROFITABILITY) WHICH ENERGISES THE SUPPLY CHAIN

THE CRITICAL SUPPLY CHAIN ASSET IS THE RESOURCE WHICH ALLOCTES VALUE (AND THEREFORE MARGINS OR PROFITABILITY) IN THE SUPPLY CHAIN, AND PROVIDES THE CONDITIONS FOR SUSTAINED VALUE APPROPRIATION AND ACCUMULATION

RAW MATERIAL PROVIDER

END CONSUMER

which companies must control and leverage if they are to achieve sustainable business success. See Figure 57 for a graphical presentation of the process which is summarised below.

> *A critical asset is that supply chain resource (or combination of resources), which is of such importance to the process of value appropriation and accumulation, that the possession of it gives its owner or controller the power to define and allocate value throughout the supply chain. There can, however, be more than one critical asset in a supply chain.*

It follows from this line of argument that what individuals and companies must possess now, and in the future, if they seek business success, is an ability to understand what transforms any supply chain resource into a potentially *critical asset*. To understand what makes any supply chain resource critical will necessitate an understanding of two phenomena. The first phenomenon is *the scope for purposive action* by individuals or companies seeking to own and control supply chain resources, so as to turn them into *critical assets.* The second phenomenon is *the characteristic of the supply chain,* which allows for particular resources to become *critical assets.*

As Figure 58 indicates, when explaining business success, it is essential to recognise that the key to the process is the ability of an entrepreneur (individual or company) to take ownership or control of all, or just one, of the major resources which the supply chain requires for the delivery of a valued product or service to an end consumer. If the entrepreneur can take control of any of these resources, which everyone else in the

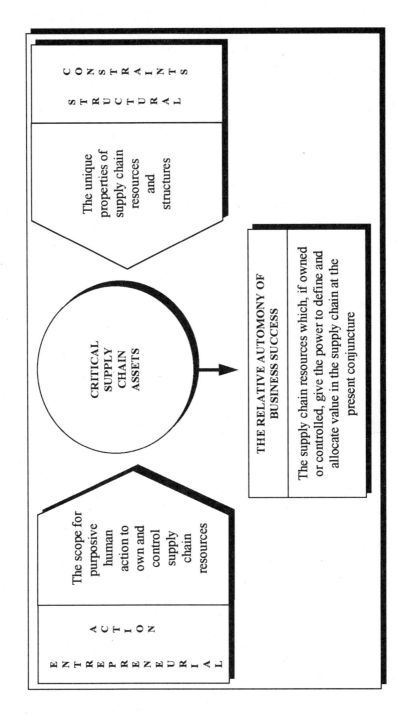

Figure 58: The Relative Autonomy of Entrepreneurial Action

supply chain must buy, then the scope for continuous value appropriation and accumulation will be assured.

It follows, therefore, that if supply chain resources can be owned or controlled in this way they will become ***critical assets,*** which will allow their owner or controller to define and allocate value in the supply chain. At the time of writing, in the PC information processing supply chain, Microsoft (with the industry standard for operating software—MSDOS) and Intel (with a relatively superior competence in the development and sale of microprocessor technology) each possess a ***critical asset***, which allows them to appropriate, accumulate and allocate value throughout the total PC information processing supply chain.

The essential point to recognise here is that the business success that Microsoft and Intel have experienced is not based on possessing the same resource, nor is it based on their being different as such.

> ***The basis of their business success is actually based on both companies being able to do the same thing but in different ways.***

What is it that they have both achieved? First, they have both achieved ownership and control over a specific supply chain resource which has a very high level of effective demand, because it is required by many different participants in a globally expanding supply chain. Second, and most important of all, they have turned this resource ownership and/or control into a ***critical asset,*** because they have been able to achieve a situation of *relative monopoly*.

It was argued earlier that the key to business success must be the capacity to create the conditions of permanent or temporary monopoly. There is little doubt that, although Microsoft and Intel have not in anyway sought to use illegal means to create monopoly, their current competencies are such that they possess a relative, if not an absolute, monopoly control over vital supply chain resources. This does not mean that they will be able to maintain this relative monopoly permanently, only that they have been able to create a situation of relative monopoly under the conjuncture of circumstances which currently exist.

As Figure 58 demonstrates, the ability of Microsoft and Intel to sustain their relative monopoly (competitive advantage) will depend on the conjuncture of two major forces. On the one hand, there is *the scope for purposive entrepreneurial action* by other human beings, which may create new ways of thinking and acting. These new ways of thinking will lead to innovation that may challenge the current ownership and control of supply chain resources, and may provide new opportunities to satisfy existing customers. On the other hand, this new *way of thinking* may assist in the development of completely new supply chains which challenge, or completely destroy, the existing supply chain.

The second dynamic is *the structural property of the supply chain* itself. All supply chains, although inherently complex, have unique and distinct properties. Some supply chains are based on regular and frequent transactions. These can be referred to as *process-based supply chains*, because there is a relatively permanent and regular process of supply chain relationships, delivering standardised products or services.

Other supply chains are characterised by irregular transactions. These are normally referred to as *project-based supply chains*, because there is no regular and standardised process. The end- product or service of such a supply chain is often unique, being created in a bespoke, ad-hoc way, in a process which is not permanently in place.

- ***Process-based supply chains have a process of
  regular transactions, delivering standardised products
  or services, through a relatively permanent structure.***

- ***Project-based supply chains have a process of
  irregular and infrequent transactions, delivering non-
  standardised products or services, through a relatively
  ad-hoc structure.***

Clearly, the structural properties of supply chains will shape
the ability of human beings to own and control the resources
that flow through them. The supply chain structure will
determine the circumstances within which it is possible for
human beings to act purposively to own and control resources,
through permanent or temporary superior competence, so that
they can become *critical assets*. This is another way of saying
that human beings can only achieve what it is possible for them
to achieve, and that they should understand what it is that is
appropriate for them to do under given circumstances.

It is obvious that, whether Bill Gates understood it or not at
the time, Microsoft's success was almost wholly linked to the
fact that the PC consumer was waiting for an industry standard
operating system. The reason why was because, in a newly
emerging process-based supply chain, for a product and service
that would be an essential component of the operating systems
of a company, nobody wanted to buy the wrong system. In
truth, everyone was waiting for the IBM-standard system,
because the real costs of ownership were not the buy-in cost of
the software or hardware in the PC, but the sunk and switching
costs related to the training of the people in the new way of
managing and processing information.

Once this new competence base was sunk in the personnel of the company, the costs of switching would, in the short to medium-term, far outweigh the superior relative benefits that any future operating and software systems might offer. In this supply chain the relative dominance of the industry standard was all. First mover advantages, as Apple and others eventually discovered to their cost, were not the most important long-term determinants of success. The majority of consumers, whether individual or corporate, wanted to buy the industry standard and, even though they were well behind the competition in this supply chain, most consumers assumed that the industry standard would be defined by IBM.

The fact that people were in fact buying Microsoft's standard operating system when they bought IBM compatible systems was, of course, the foundation of Microsoft's success, and, conversely, one of the major reasons for IBM's relative failure in this market-place. Was this success due to the purposive actions of Bill Gates and his colleagues? Obviously it was. Was it also due to the relative incompetence of IBM in understanding and managing what were the important supply chain resources *(critical assets)*? Of course it was. But the real explanation for the success of Microsoft, and the relative failure of IBM, cannot be constructed solely on the basis of an analysis of the relative competence of either of their staff.

A proper explanation must also take account of the fact that it was Microsoft's relative monopoly possession of the *critical supply chain asset*—in this case the dominant operating standard in the supply chain—which explains the company's success and IBM's relative failure. Microsoft not only has possession of the supply chain standard, but IBM also allowed them to sell it to their direct competitors in the PC business. The subsequent growth in the size of the PC supply chain on a global basis provided Microsoft with an opportunity to make money, not just from IBM, but from everyone in the PC supply chain.

IBM, unfortunately, had chosen the wrong supply chain resources to control and own, and ended up in a contested market, which it had little chance of monopolising. Microsoft, on the other hand, has a relative monopoly of one of the essential resources in a global, process-based supply chain. Bill Gates may or may not be a superior human being, but it is perfectly understandable why he is one of the richest men in the world. The company in which he is a major shareholder, *currently* owns and controls a ***global critical supply chain asset***.

The same line of argument can be developed in relation to the relative success of Intel in the same supply chain. To argue that Microsoft controls one supply chain resource as a ***critical asset***, does not mean that other actors in the same supply chain cannot do the same thing. It simply means that they are unlikely to be able to appropriate and accumulate value in the same way as Microsoft, unless they can find a way to usurp the control of that specific supply chain resource which Microsoft owns. Intel have clearly created a ***critical asset*** for themselves in the PC information processing supply chain. They have done it, however, not by competing with Microsoft head-on, but by providing a complementary resource to the supply chain.

Like Microsoft, however, Intel's success is based on their ability to own and control a specific supply chain resource in such a way that they are relative monopolists. It is this characteristic—*their ability to create either a permanent or a temporary monopoly*—that is the defining feature of a ***critical asset***, not the specific resource (the microprocessor or the software system) which is the current object of that relative monopoly control.

> ***Microsoft and Intel are both successful because they own and control valuable supply chain resources as critical assets.***

Intel's business success is, therefore, founded differently than Microsoft's in practical terms, but the source of its ability to appropriate and accumulate wealth in a sustained way is based on the same logical principles. Intel's success is based on having *a relatively superior competence* in the research, development, production and marketing of microprocessor technology. One does not need to have any knowledge of how this is created to know that it is not what Intel does, but the relative superiority of the way in which the company does it, that enables Intel to be successful. Intel, temporarily at least, has a *relatively superior competence* to its actual, or potential, competitors in the supply chain, and has, thereby, created a position of relative monopoly.

> *Intel's critical asset is its possession of a relatively superior competence in producing and marketing potentially imitable microprocessor technology.*

This is an interesting conclusion because, for Microsoft it is not *relatively superior competence* which is the basis of its success. For Microsoft, it is the possession of a supply chain standard which is extremely difficult to replace that is the key to its success. Microsoft's success comes not from being technically better than the competition, but from the fact that, having once standardised on a system, most consumers are unlikely to buy another system, however technically superior it may be. This means that Microsoft's success derives primarily from *the possession of an inimitable supply chain resource*. The strategic problem facing Intel, therefore, is always likely to be more challenging than that facing Microsoft. The reason is that Intel are trying to control a supply chain resource that is inherently much easier to copy and replace than Microsoft's supply chain resource.

> *Microsoft's critical asset is its possession of a relatively inimitable supply chain operating standard.*

The conclusion that one might draw from this is that, while there is always one strategic goal (to be a temporary or permanent monopolist) the ways in which this can be achieved will vary. This variation will not, however, be random, nor will it be simply the result of the genius of individuals. Clearly, in the context of business, genius resides in the ability of individuals to understand what are the properties of supply chains. Having understood this, it follows logically that real business acumen is then having the ability to understand what are the appropriate things to do, so that one or more supply chain resource can be owned and/or controlled in a relatively monopolistic way. This means that what it is appropriate for Intel to do in the future, and how the company should do these things, will not necessarily be the same as what was appropriate for them or anybody else in the past—although it could be. It all depends on which supply chain resources any individual or company is attempting to monopolise, and the contingent circumstances which face them. This leads to two general conclusions:

> *Business success, as the Microsoft and Intel examples demonstrate, is knowing which supply chain resources can be owned and/or controlled in a relatively monopolistic way, and how this can be achieved.*

> *Sometimes people achieve ownership and/or control over immensely valuable supply chain resources (critical assets) by accident rather than by design, and then claim prescience about their intent, when they did not actually have any in the first place. Such people are the inadvertent beneficiaries of contingent circumstances.*

This *way of thinking* takes the argument back to the nature versus nurture debate which was presented earlier. Clearly, business success will always reflect the symbiosis between purposive human action and the constraints on autonomous human action which are exerted by the structural properties of the environment. This is another way of saying that human beings only have a *relative autonomy* to change things; they must do what is appropriate under given circumstances. This is an extremely important point, because, despite the success that Microsoft and Intel have experienced in recent years, there is no guarantee that these companies will be able to sustain this success indefinitely. The reason for this is that there is always a conflict taking place between the structure of supply chains as they exist today, and the purposive entrepreneurial actions of human beings. This means that to sustain success people must act purposively at all times, but within the structure of the supply chain realities which face them.

If it is recognised that human beings are involved in a relentless war to control scarcity, through the ownership and control of the supply chain resources which are the basis for value appropriation and accumulation, it is inevitable that things will change. The reason is that, at any historic moment (or *conjuncture*) there will be a continuing and unremitting entrepreneurial attempts by those current, and potential, companies and individuals in a supply chain who do not possess *critical assets,* to find ways of breaking the dominance of those who do. This *war of movement* will take the form either of government regulation, or by people copying and adapting, or by people seeking—through technological innovation, or new organisational practices—to find more cost effective, or more functional products or services to satisfy supply chain demand.

This perspective leads one to argue further, however, that, while those who own and control *critical supply chain assets* will be able to dominate the process of value accumulation and appropriation in the short-term, they must constantly be on their guard against their possible loss of control over these assets. This loss of ownership and/or control could arise as a result of either, the practices of more entrepreneurial competitors operating within the existing supply chain, or due to technological innovations which provide the opportunity for entrepreneurs to create new product or services, or completely new supply chains. The development of either of these scenarios could dynamically reconfigure the existing relationships between supply chain resources, so that a formerly complementary, or residual, resource could become a *critical asset.* This dynamic transformation of supply chain resources would, thereby, destroy the value of existing *critical supply chain assets* and, potentially, create new ones.

It follows from this, of course, that if companies and individuals should be aware of the relative importance of particular resources within new and emerging product and service supply chains, then there must also be a relationship between the types of supply chains which exist and the importance of particular types of resources to these supply chains. Only some resources have the potential to become critical in supply chains, others do not. For example, the research, design, production and assembly of microprocessor technology is currently a *critical asset* owned by Intel in the PC supply chain. However, the plastic extrusion of PC monitor frames is not, and is unlikely ever to be so given its easy imitability. In the car assembly supply chain, the possession of customer-focused distribution networks, efficient assembly/production systems, superior in-house design and specification systems, and unique supplier development programmes are *critical assets,* while the manufacture of particular components is merely a complementary resource within the supply chain.

Only by understanding in this way, from first principles, *what are the dynamics of supply chains in relation to **the power** which particular actors have over the resources which flow through these chains,* will it be possible to develop an effective theory of the firm. Having achieved this, it will then be possible to provide the theoretical and empirical grounding for successful generalisations about what particular companies should do under specific circumstances. Once this has been achieved, it will be possible to delineate (through a proactive taxonomy) those operational *best practices* which will most satisfactorily support and assist the total business strategy of a firm.

This follows because, if a firm is to understand the resources it should manage for business success in the future, it must constantly review its understanding of the dynamic forces at play within supply chains (the competitive forces, the state of technology, the regulatory rules etc.). Only by understanding the impact of these factors on the relative value of the resources which, in combination, pass from raw material to end consumer, is it possible for the firm to understand which resources are capable of becoming *critical assets*. The *critical assets* will be those things which are so important to the supply chain that they must be insourced (owned and controlled through internal contracts and incentives). Anything which is not defined as a *critical asset* can normally be safely outsourced, through external contracts and supply relationship management techniques.

It is towards the development of such a theory of the firm that business management research should be directed, because it is only by focusing on the ***criticality of assets*** in supply chains that a truly entrepreneurial view of the firm can be developed. Having such a perspective will allow companies to understand which supply chain resources are key to their success, knowing this will then allow companies to understand which internal skills and capabilities (competencies) they must own and control internally and externally. It will also allow companies to be able to predict the ideal size, shape and scope of their organisations in relation to the supply chain resources which determine value appropriation and accumulation.

This will be achieved, not on the basis of describing what has happened in the past, but by developing a *way of thinking* which is grounded in an understanding of the contingent relationships between resources, assets and value in specific supply chains under defined, but dynamically changing, circumstances. In the final section of this chapter, the outlines of an entrepreneurial theory of the firm, which is based on this abstractive *way of thinking* is presented.

The Asset Criticality Theory of the Firm

Since much of what passes for business research appears to take place within a theoretical void in this section an entrepreneurial theory of the firm is outlined. The theory is based on the abstractive *way of thinking* recommended in this volume. This approach is directed, consciously, towards the rectification of the problem of theoretical myopia and provides the basis for an empirical verification of the author's theory of sustainable business success within supply chains. This general theory is outlined below.

A THEORY OF THE FIRM AND SUSTAINABLE BUSINESS SUCCESS

Sustainable business success is achieved, for individuals or corporations, by the flexible ownership and/or control of critical supply chain assets, which cannot be replicated or replaced by existing or potential competitors. This, rather than competitive positioning, is the essence of entrepreneurial activity.

A DEFINITION OF BUSINESS STRATEGY

Business strategy, properly understood, is the process by which individuals or corporations seek ways of owning, controlling and leveraging critical assets within existing or newly emerging supply chains, so as to appropriate and accumulate value from customers, suppliers, employees and competitors.

This theory of business strategy and business success in supply chains is based on ten key strategic propositions and ten key operational propositions. The ten key strategic propositions are linked to the general theory outlined above and are as follows:

STRATEGIC PROPOSITIONS

Strategic Proposition 1:

Individuals and companies are in business to accumulate and appropriate value for themselves, or for their owners, and for no other primary purpose.

Strategic Proposition 2:

Sustainable success in business, for individuals and for companies, comes from the possession of critical assets which can be owned and/or controlled, preferably in the absence of market competition. If market competition occurs then a secondary strategy of competitive positioning should replace an asset based strategy.

Strategic Proposition 3:

Critical assets are those resources which a company or an individual may own and/or control within a supply chain, but which are both in scarce supply and not easily replicable by others.

Strategic Proposition 4:

It is the ownership and/or control of critical assets which allows individuals and companies to appropriate and accumulate value from particular supply chains, and to dictate the allocation of value to other participants in those supply chains.

Strategic Proposition 5:

Business strategy is, therefore, a continuous entrepreneurial war of movement between individuals and companies to own, control and leverage critical assets in specific supply chains.

Strategic Proposition 6:

Knowing which supply chain resources can be owned and/or controlled effectively, within existing skills, capabilities and financial constraints, is a key attribute of strategic focus and alignment.

Strategic Proposition 7:

All supply chains have distinctive and unique properties but they can all be defined generically, as the complex delivery mechanism by which raw materials are transformed into purchasable products and services for end consumers. But only some resources (human, financial, technological, physical, locational, organisational or marketing) have the potential to become critical assets within any specific supply chain.

Strategic Proposition 8:

The distinctive and unique properties of the supply chain for any specific good or service will shape the potential of particular resources within the supply chain to become critical assets. To achieve sustainable business success, companies must align their corporate strategy with the effective ownership and/or control of those resources which have the potential to be monopolised on a temporary or permanent basis within the supply chain.

Strategic Proposition 9:

Supply chains are complex, and the products and services which flow through them, as well as the supply chains themselves, experience regular stages of emergence, growth, maturity and decline. In each of these stages the asset criticality (scope for monopoly) of particular resources will change. The strategies which individuals and companies must use to achieve sustainable value accumulation and appropriation will vary accordingly.

Strategic Proposition 10:

Sustainable business success is more likely to be achievable through a strategy which focuses on the continuous discovery, or creation, of supply chains in which it is possible for the individual or the company to own and or control resources which are irreplaceable or inimitable, rather than through a strategy which concentrates exclusively on the defence, by means of competitive supply chain positioning, of those critical assets which the company currently owns.

Linked to these ten strategic propositions are ten further operational propositions. These are focused directly on the way in which individuals or companies should manage *the boundary of the firm*, once they have determined those resources with a potential for criticality (which they should own and control) within particular supply chains.

OPERATIONAL PROPOSITIONS

Operational Proposition 1:

Companies which are successful in the long-term normally own and/or control, within the boundary of the firm, those resources in a supply chain which have the capability of being turned into critical assets. The make/buy decision is, therefore, the key strategic and operational decision for all companies.

Operational Proposition 2:

Successful companies only retain resources and activities which are non-critical within the existing boundary of the firm, if they can produce the required inputs in a more economical way than potential external suppliers. If this is the case, then the goal of the company must be to develop and leverage this competence (skill and capability) into an additional business within the supply chains in which it is critical.

Operational Proposition 3:

Internally, the corporate focus of activity for successful companies should always be on the creation of a relatively superior competence in owning, controlling, managing and leveraging critical supply chain assets than that which actual or potential competitors can achieve.

Operational Proposition 4:

Internal strategic alignment arises in successful companies as a result of a complete understanding, at all operational levels, of the need for a focus on the effective leverage of critical supply chain assets and the development of a superior competence to that of competitors.

Operational Proposition 5:

Strategically aligned and successful companies will not normally have a functional or silo management approach to internal management, but will focus instead on efficient operational processes which link effective demand management with effective supply management.

Operational Proposition 6:

In successful companies, the need to use tools and techniques to ensure the effective management of external demand, and of external supply, is recognised as being of equal importance to internal operational process management.

Operational Proposition 7:

Successful companies use external resource management of demand and supply as an effective technique for reducing transaction costs, improving quality, and stimulating innovation, so as to maximise value appropriation and accumulation.

Operational Proposition 8:

Successful companies recognise that there is no single way to manage external resources, on either the demand or the supply side of their business, but they do have a sophisticated understanding of, and operational methodologies to implement, the full range of external resource leverage techniques which are available.

Operational Proposition 9:

Successful companies use all of the appropriate external relationship leverage and contracting techniques which are available to them, from joint ventures, strategic alliances, sole sourcing, single sourcing, and preferred suppliers to arms-length multiple sourcing, and do not tie themselves to any one approach.

Operational Proposition 10:

Successful companies understand when certain types of external relationship leverage and contracting approaches are 'fit for purpose' and when they are not. They also recognise that all relationships are contingent. As supply chain circumstances change, and some resources become more or less critical to value appropriation and accumulation, then the external relationships in which the company is involved may have to change, as may the internal and external boundaries of the firm.

Conclusions

The fact that these propositions have been derived from a prior theorisation of the raison d'être of the firm, from experience, and from an analysis of historical cases of business success in market-based economies, does not imply that they are correct. For them to be proven, they must first be empirically tested to see if, under all circumstances, they are validated, or if, under all circumstances they are false. The benefit of this approach should, however, be self-evident. Although it will take some time to know whether the theory and its related propositions are proven it does, nonetheless allow us to develop a very clear framework for empirical research.

In order to undertake this research, it will, first, be necessary to:

- *Create a typology of supply chains—something which has never been undertaken systematically in business thinking.*

- *Develop a typology of resources within supply chains.*

Only then can we begin the process of empirical testing, to discover which supply chain resources have the potential to become *critical assets,* and whether or not the possession of these types of resources determines business success. Figure 59 demonstrates graphically how this research agenda might begin to be operationalised.

What is also evident is that the development of this type of methodology will allow us to determine whether there is one type of resource which becomes a *critical asset* in all circumstances, or, as one might suspect, whether only some resources are critical in some supply chains at particular moments in time. If, as one supposes, theoretically, it is the unique *conjuncture of forces* at play within a supply chain that determines which resources will become *critical assets*, then it

Figure 59: Segmenting Supply Chains by Structure, Resources and the Scope for Imitability

		TYPES OF SUPPLY CHAIN RESOURCES					
		RELATIVELY DIFFICULT TO IMITATE OR REPLACE			RELATIVELY EASY TO IMITATE OR REPLACE		
		SITE SPECIFIC	HUMAN	TECHNICAL	DEDICATED	SITE SPECIFIC	HUMAN	TECHNICAL	DEDICATED
SUPPLY CHAIN STRUCTURE	PROCESS-BASED (Regular transactions/ standardised products or services)							
	PROJECT-BASED (Irregular transactions/ non-standard products or services)							

will be possible to begin the complex process of mapping out which resources should be owned and/or controlled, and in what ways, to achieve sustainable business success under particular circumstances. This will provide the proper methodological and theoretical grounding for the specification of operational *best practices* under given conditions, within specific types of supply chains. This will be a major achievement, because compared with what companies need to know about *best practice*, and what academics and consultants claim they know, the state of knowledge about strategy and operations in supply chain management is still rudimentary.

There are a number of additional benefits which this theoretical and methodological approach will bring if it is successfully implemented. There is the obvious benefit of developing a new theory of business strategy, as well as a new *way of thinking* about the nature of supply chains, and about the most appropriate operational practices for companies in supply management. This approach will also allow us to understand more fully the effective boundary of the firm, and its strategic importance to business success. (Cox, 1996a, 1996b and 1996c) More importantly, perhaps, is the possibility that this line of thinking may challenge the myopia evident amongst both business management academics and practitioners in relation to what constitutes *best practice*. It may also help us to know whether or not a particular operational intervention by a firm is strategically appropriate or not under specific circumstances.

More importantly still it may contribute to the development of a new *way of thinking* within business management by both academics and practitioners alike. This *new way* will be based on the view that an argument in favour of a particular approach to business strategy, or operational practice, is not proven simply on the grounds that one, or even several, successful companies have pursued it in the past.

Rather, the appropriateness of a particular strategy, or operational practice, will be deemed to be validated if it supports and reinforces a theoretical perspective about causality. Any such theory should help us to understand why a particular strategic focus, or operational practice, was *fit for purpose* for a specific company or individual at a particular moment in time. If we can achieve this, then we may well have begun a process which leads to the sort of paradigm shift, or qualitative change in the nature of our perception of the world, which Kuhn referred to as a *scientific revolution.* (Kuhn, 1962)

If we adopt this *way of thinking,* it becomes obvious that what is ultimately necessary are two things. First, we need to reject the latest 'fads' to success emanating from the pens of consultants and academics using empiricist methodologies. Then we need to develop a comprehensive understanding of the full range of operational tools and techniques for the effective leverage of value within supply chains, which are available to all businesses. Having achieved this, it then becomes imperative that a second task is completed. This is the development of a theory, or theories, which explains why certain tools and techniques are more appropriate than others for particular companies operating under defined circumstances. Until we have such theories, it is debatable whether business management can become a properly grounded and robust discipline within the social sciences.

In this, and the preceding chapters, the reasons why this new *way of thinking* is necessary have been outlined. An alternative and contingent way of looking at business strategy and operational practice has also been introduced. This approach emphasises the importance of companies adopting a supply chain rather than a market-driven focus. By way of conclusion, in the final chapter, an indication is given of how this *way of thinking* can be operationalised by practitioners.

SECTION D

A STRATEGIC AND OPERATIONAL WAY FORWARD

7

On Business Praxis and Operational Implementation

In the last chapter the theoretical significance of *critical supply chain assets* was explained. The pivotal role of the entrepreneurial action in business success, in relation to intellectual property about innovation, was also outlined. These two insights laid the foundation for the development of an explicit, and empirically testable, theory of asset criticality. The chapter concluded, therefore, that the scientific study of business success requires the development of an epistemological approach to enquiry, which is based on *abstractive reasoning*. Only in this way, it was argued, will it be possible to develop codified knowledge of the causal factors behind business success in particular supply chain contexts. If this *way of thinking* is accepted it should be clear that this opens up a significant and new research agenda for the academic community to pursue in the future.

The problem is, however, that while this line of argument provides the academic community with a research agenda, it leaves practitioners in something of a quandary. When the author has discussed these ideas with practitioners, the response has nearly always been the same. Practitioners ask what it is that they can do, while they wait for the academic community to undertake the research which will codify the causal factors behind business success in any type of supply chain. The author has always been somewhat disappointed by this response, for two major reasons.

- *First, it demonstrates that the author is clearly having difficulty in getting his ideas, about the significance of entrepreneurial action in relation to intellectual property, across to the practitioner.*

- *Second, it also indicates that the practitioner has not fully grasped that the early codification of the causal factors in supply chains has, in itself, the potentiality to create a critical asset for those individuals (or for those companies) who actively participate in the discovery of these essential truths.*

What this problem demonstrates is that the practitioner is still operating within the mind-set of *the practitioner's dilemma*, which was outlined in a previous chapter. The practitioner still wants certainty about outcomes before operationalising any new ideas. As a result, they do not see that it is only by taking a chance on intellectual ideas, which are not yet fully formed, that permanent or temporary monopoly control over a new way of doing something can be achieved. The message which follows as a result of this insight, and which informs the thinking in this volume, should by now be axiomatic.

Sustainable business success requires that individuals take risks with uncertainty

What then should practitioners be looking for, and what should they do? The answer is straight forward enough.

> - *Practitioners should not look for operational guides to success which are already well documented, and which demonstrably lead to known outcomes.*
>
> - *They should look for individuals who have a unique way of thinking; individuals whose ideas, if they can be operationalised, will allow the practitioner to obtain permanent or temporary ownership and/or control of supply chain resources, in such a way that they can be turned into critical assets.*

Only in this way, by closing markets temporarily or permanently, can sustainable business success and advantage be achieved. This requires, in this author's view, the development of a new *business praxis*.

> *Business praxis, as used here, refers to that process by which properly grounded and robust theoretical insights about causality are operationalised within specific business contexts. It is, in this way of thinking, the fusion of scientific theory with operational practice in specific supply chain contexts.*

In this final chapter, an insight is given into how this *way of thinking* can be operationalised by practitioners.   This introduction to a new **business praxis** is developed in three stages.   In the first stage, some of the weaknesses in existing business thinking about operational practice are outlined.   In the second stage, the problem of **managing dualism** is introduced.   In the third stage a more appropriate *way of thinking* about **business praxis** and operational implementation is briefly introduced.   This *way of thinking* is based on an understanding of **the four dimensions of supply**.

The Tyranny of Descriptive Operational Methodologies

In a seminal article published in 1983, Peter Kraljic developed a descriptive methodology, based on a four box matrix, for the codification of different types of purchasing activity. (Kraljic, 1983) This *way of thinking*, which is now commonly known as *purchasing portfolio analysis* by procurement practitioners, has subsequently become the dominant approach to what the profession regards as operational professionalism.   The way in which the *purchasing portfolio analysis* framework categorises purchasing spend, and provides guidance for operational action, is presented in Figure 60.

As the Figure demonstrates, *purchasing portfolio analysis* is an operational methodology which correlates the level of purchasing spend with the degree of market difficulty in the supply markets in which a company or individual is operating. This is a way of segmenting the total level of spend within a company, as well as a guide for practitioners as to how they should manage the spend in each segment of the box matrix to obtain maximum effectiveness for the business. Generally

Figure 60: Purchasing Portfolio Analysis

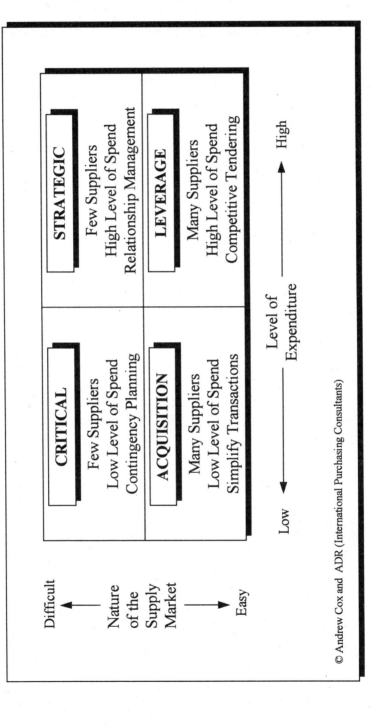

© Andrew Cox and ADR (International Purchasing Consultants)

speaking, this operational tool suggests the following guides to action:

Acquisition:

In this box of the matrix, the supply market is characterised by a large number of suppliers, each of whom is mutually inter-changeable, and the level of spend in the buying company is low.   The general operational guide to action which the methodology suggests, is that practitioners should simplify transactions by reducing the number of suppliers with whom they deal. Since the expenditure is defined as non-critical to the business, and because there are many alternative options if a supplier fails to meet the level of service quality required, then costs can be reduced by standardising with one or two existing suppliers. The overall benefit to the company is the fact that the costs associated with organising competitive bidding for contracts are reduced.

Leverage:

In this box of the matrix, the supply market is again characterised by a large number of suppliers, each of whom is mutually inter-changeable, but the level of spend in the buying company is high. The general guide to operational action which the methodology suggests, is that practitioners should use the size of their buying power to leverage the supply market aggressively. Since suppliers are, likely to be very willing to supply the buying company, and value its business highly, the guide suggests that aggressive negotiation for significant improvements in cost or quality is possible. The overall benefit to the business of this approach flows from the leverage on cost and quality that sheer volume provides for the buyer.

Critical:

In this box of the matrix, the supply market is characterised either by one supplier, or by only a very small number of suppliers. None of these suppliers are easily replaceable, and the level of spend for the buying company is relatively low. The general guide to operational action which the methodology suggests, is that, as a result of the buyer's relative dependency on the supplier, it is necessary for the buyer to develop contingency plans, in case the supply of what may be essential products or services is disrupted. The overall benefit to the business of this approach is that the dependency is recognised, and an appropriate counter-veiling strategy is put in place.

Strategic:

In this box of the matrix, the supply market is characterised either by one supplier, or by only a small number of suppliers. None of these suppliers are easily replaceable, and the level of spend is very high. This means that the products or services bought are of strategic importance to the business. This is a situation of high dependency for the buyer, and the general guide to operational action which the methodology suggests is that purchases with these characteristics are of such strategic importance to the business that close and collaborative relationships must be developed with the supplier. By developing these close and collaborative relationships, it is hoped that the supplier will give 'most favoured' status to the buying company, so that it can undertake its business successfully in the future.

It should be obvious from a cursory introduction to this *way of thinking* about operational practice, that it provides many benefits for those companies which have never thought logically and systematically about how to organise their existing purchasing spend. The methodology helps the practitioner to see what could, and perhaps should, be done for different types of spend under particular supply market conditions. There is little doubt, therefore, that for those companies which have never thought systematically about their procurement expenditure, this is a useful, first order, operational tool. On reflection, however, if we adopt the *way of thinking* recommended in this volume, we can see that, while it has some real strengths, it also has some serious weaknesses. These weaknesses can be defined as an over-reliance on a *descriptive, reactive and market-based way of thinking*.

The major weakness of the purchasing portfolio approach is that it is essentially a description of what *the current state of power* is between buyers and suppliers, within the supply chain in which the company is operating. The methodology suffers from the fact that, while it satisfactorily describes what *is*, it does not provide us with any pro-active thinking about what can, or should, be done *to change the existing reality of power* in the various supply chains in which we are involved. The *way of thinking* in this operational tool is reactive. It describes what a buyer must do, given the situation of relative power dependence in which he or she currently resides. As a result, it reacts to the prevailing structure of power in the market and completely fails to take us beyond a *knowledge* of what *is*.

In order to develop a really useful operational guide to action, we need a methodology which enables us to *understand* what it is that we can, and should, do *to create a new structure of power* within a supply chain. This new structure will be one which allows us to eradicate those existing market-based conditions, which are inimical to our ability to maximise the appropriation of value. The insight which flows from this *way of thinking* can be summarised simply enough.

> ***Purchasing portfolio analysis is a poor guide to operational action, because it fails to recognise that sustainable business success is, ultimately, about creating the conditions for the effective and flexible leverage of any, and all, supply chain resources, under as many conditions and circumstances as possible.***

This insight leads us to conclude that practitioners need operational tools which do more than describe what is the current reality of power within supply chains, and in the markets which form around them. What they really need is *ways of thinking* which allow them to understand how to break the dependency relationships which they may experience in these relationships. This, the author would contend, is the only appropriate way to think entrepreneurially about **business praxis**.

If we do not understand what business is really about, and if we refuse to acknowledge the critical role of **the four principles of effective leverage** in sustaining value appropriation and accumulation, then it is unlikely that we can do other than provide operational tools (such as purchasing portfolio analysis, SWOT and BPR) which merely describe what *is*. What is clearly needed to resolve this dilemma is a theoretically grounded *analytic way of thinking*, which provides a pro-active **business praxis** as a guide to operational implementation.

This penchant for *descriptive ways of thinking* is rife in the current literature on business and supply chain management. It should be clear, by now, to readers who have come this far, that the author's views on the meaning of effective supply chain management are somewhat different to the current mainstream. These views are founded on a belief that supply chain thinking should provide the basis for a proper understanding of, and a focus for, strategic action.

> *In this way of thinking, strategy should not be seen as a recognition of the need to compete with others, but as the development of operational methodologies, throughout the business, which provide opportunities for employees to eradicate, or to limit, competition within supply chains.*

This is not, however, how most writers conceive of the effective strategic and operational management of supply chains. In a recent article, Fisher has demonstrated both the strengths and weaknesses of current supply chain thinking within the dominant paradigm. (Fisher, 1997) His basic arguments are presented in Figure 61.

As we can see from Figure 61, Fisher contends that the appropriate way to think about business success is to start from a description of existing products or services, and then to link these with the current demand structure in the supply chain. This leads him to conclude that there are two types of demand. These two types are *functional demand* (regular and stable), and *innovative demand* (unstable and short-term). Fisher's thinking is that, based on these two types of demand, there must be only two types of products—functional and innovative ones. Fisher then argues that, in his experience, those companies which recognise this fact, and build supply chains and operational practices which are aligned in accordance with these two principle distinctions, will be the ones which are most likely to be successful.

Figure 61: Fisher's View of Effective Supply Chain Strategy

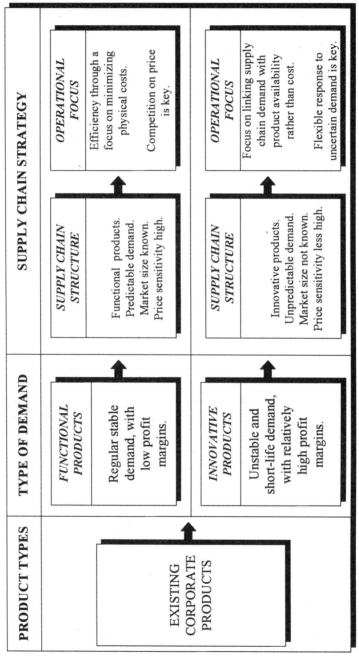

Based on Fisher (1997)

At one level this *way of thinking* makes eminent sense. There clearly is a need for companies to align their operational practices with the types of supply chains in which they are operating. This is in order that they will be able to deliver products and services to their existing and potential customers in the most appropriate way. Fisher is absolutely correct about this. Despite this, it is debatable whether Fisher's ***bare-foot empiricist*** approach leads him to fully understand that which he is attempting to analyse.

The first problem with Fisher's analysis is that he starts from the assumption that business success is about servicing existing products, and meeting existing demand. This, it was argued earlier, is not necessarily the right way to think about the conditions for sustainable business success. If all business success ultimately comes from the ability to be innovative in terms of supply offerings, so that ***critical supply chain assets*** can be owned and controlled, then it is obvious that Fisher's perspective is strategically and operationally reactive to, and descriptive of, the current power structure within supply chains.

This does not mean that Fisher is wrong to say that existing products should be aligned operationally with the structure of the supply chain. Clearly, significant operational and competitive improvements could be made by poorly managed companies if they adopted this *way of thinking*. The problem is that Fisher fails to recognise that this approach can only ever provide a temporary benefit to companies. The reason for this is that product and supply chain alignment only allows companies to do what is already self-evident and well known to those who understand operational alignment. Furthermore, while this alignment may provide focus, it can easily be copied by everyone. It does not, in itself, as a result, tell us how to reduce costs, or how to improve supply responsiveness more effectively than others.

It can be argued, therefore, that in order to be successful in reducing costs, or in developing supply chain responsiveness, it is not sufficient to *know* that this must be done. On the contrary, it is also necessary to understand *how* these specific business requirements can be achieved operationally. The view taken here, is that what ultimately must be done to achieve any operational improvement, is always linked to understanding how to bring about, pro-actively, the realignment of the existing structure of power within the supply chain. This is achieved through the development of innovative ways of *effectively leveraging* existing (or new) supply chain resources, not by describing the current nature of products, or the existing operational structure of the supply chain.

The fundamental problem with Fisher's approach, therefore, is that he is starting at the wrong end of the equation. Instead of focusing on demand for current products within existing market structures, and using logistics thinking to align the supply chain, he should be starting from an understanding of the fundamental characteristics of power within the chains which link supply and demand. If Fisher started from this perspective he would quickly realise that:

> *The keys to business success are not to be found in aligning products with supply chains, but in understanding those functional characteristics of supply chains which allow innovations in products and services to be leveraged effectively, so as to close markets to existing or potential competitors.*

We will return to this discussion about the seminal importance for *business praxis* of an understanding of both the structure of power in supply chains, and of the nature of functionality in supply, when we consider *the four dimensions of supply* in detail. Before continuing with this discussion, however, it is important, to dwell on one of the key dilemmas facing all practitioners when they confront operational reality. This is the problem of the need to manage dualism.

Managing Dualism: The Problem of Operationalising Fit and Innovation

In the previous discussion, it was argued that the approaches of Kraljic and Fisher can be criticised for their failure to assist practitioners in understanding what could, or should, be possible. Their focus was seen to be excessively reactive and descriptive. The reason for this is that many practitioners, academics and consultants do not think about the conditions for business success from *first principles*. In fact, what most business thinkers concentrate on, is how to help companies to improve their current operational practices. This is why business thinking is primarily about *management* (the fine-tuning of what is), rather than about *entrepreneurship* (the creation of what could be).

The real problem for companies (and for individual entrepreneurs), however, is that they cannot choose to do just one of these things; they must do both at the same time. Managing this dualism, of fine-tuning what is and trying to create what could be, is the essential dilemma of strategy and operational practice in achieving business success. Companies must manage what is, because they must survive in the supply chains in which they are currently operating, and in the markets which have grown up around them, if they are to stay in business. This means that they must *fit* and align themselves efficiently to provide the products and services which are currently in demand, and which existing supply chains can provide. On the other hand, they must also develop the ability to *innovate*. The critical importance of innovation, as a basis for the creation of the conditions of permanent or temporary monopoly, was explained earlier. There seems little doubt, however, that managing innovation is the single most important requirement for any individual or for any company.

This means that, although individuals and companies need to be efficient at what they are currently doing, they must also be able to find new ways of doing things. These new ways of acting will require two things:

- *An ability to find innovative ways to leverage existing supply chain resources more efficiently than their direct competitors, so as to provide themselves with a permanent or temporary relatively superior competence.*

- *A capaccity to see opportunities, before others, to create completely new supply chains, which have the potential to deliver innovative products and services, in a way that makes any invention difficult for others to replicate.*

The problem for companies, however, is that many practitioners simply do not understand that this is what business is all about. Many practitioners do not understand at all that success in business is about entrepreneurial activity, and, as a result, they confuse the management of existing processes, delivering already known products and services, with business thinking. The real challenge for companies is to put in place operational practices and ways of thinking that provide the basis by which employees will be able to understand what they should focus on. Clearly, if the arguments, presented in this volume have been accepted, this focus should be on *ways of thinking about the effective leverage of supply chain resources*, not on the copying of what is already known.

Obviously, it goes without saying that, if companies are not doing what is already known, then they must 'catch-up' by copying from others. This does not, however, invalidate the more important general point that, for sustainable business success to be achieved, companies should focus on the more effective leverage of what is already known. This means that success is ultimately about doing what is new, and this must be based on a willingness to take risks with uncertainty through a process of continuous innovation.

The problem for companies however, is that most people join companies because they are not risk-takers. They join companies, because they want to be well rewarded for not taking risks. This, presumably, is why the largest and most successful companies are inundated with applications for jobs. Human beings are, at one level, rational actors, who believe that there is a correlation between their own chances of material success, and the past and current performance of the companies with which they seek to work.

The problem for well-established companies, however, is that when they employ such people, they end up with relatively risk-averse employees. Risk-averse people normally do not innovate, but seek to rise through the hierarchical layers of the company by astutely playing the game of intra-organisational politics. As all companies are nothing more than a microcosm of the larger society within which they operate, the company mirrors the conditions of absolute and relative scarcity outside its boundaries. It is because the top jobs are in scarce supply, and because there are, potentially, an infinite number of people who would like to have these positions of power, status and authority, that all companies develop political processes through which scarce resources are allocated. People within companies, therefore, fight one another for the absolutely and relatively scarce resources which are available to them.

It should come as no surprise, therefore, that major companies do not stay at the top for very long, unless they have a permanent, or a near permanent, monopoly control over a particular supply chain resource. The reason is that the company will only rarely be a focused and collaborative body of individuals, pursuing a common agenda. Obviously, in some cultures the prevailing systems of deference and obligation will ensure that there is a higher propensity for collaboration to occur. Similarly, in companies that are privately-owned, and in which the power structure is transparent, this problem will be somewhat reduced. Nevertheless, in many companies, particularly those operating in liberal, Anglo-Saxon style individualistic cultures, the pursuit of individual rather than corporate interest will be very high on the agenda indeed.

In these types of companies, the problem of managing the dualism of fit and innovation will be most obvious. The reason for this is that in these companies the need for innovation is most likely to be challenged by the standard operating practices, which arise to defend the status quo of managing what *is*. These standard operating practices are often inimical to the imperative need to take risks with uncertainty. The reason why such standard operating practices exist is because, a large number of the practitioners in such companies do not really understand business. Furthermore, it is likely that many of those who are risk-averse, will also be the most astute at playing the political game within the company. These people will be the ones who rise to the top. Since their rise to pre-eminence is often based on not taking chances, and only on delivering what *is*, the whole culture of a company can come to be focused on incremental improvements in what is currently known, and on the direct copying of what demonstrably has not failed elsewhere.

Ironically, at many of the lower levels in companies, there may very well be intelligent individuals who, in a practical way, understand better than their senior managers many of the operational, and in some cases the strategic, problems and opportunities which confront the company.

> *The problem is that companies consistently appear to be unable to develop ways of ensuring that their senior staff know what is commonly understood at lower levels of the organisation.*

The author has come across this phenomenon many times, in conducting consultancy and training workshops for public and private sector organisations alike. As a result of this phenomenon, a common criticism is often levelled against consultants by practitioners working at lower levels in the company.

> *Consultants simply borrow your watch, only to tell you the time.*

My standard answer to this criticism is straightforward.

> *If you have a watch, but you have no way of telling the time, then you need someone, to whom you are prepared to listen, who has.*

What these two aphorisms indicate, is that both the practitioner and the author have a point. First, the practitioner is often correct in his or her assumption that consultants do not know as much about the business as the practitioners working within it. Relatedly, there are always a number of practitioners in the company, at lower levels of operational practice, who understand many of the key strategic and operational problems in the business. Second, the consultant can provide a valuable service. This service comes from asking the right questions about what is important, in order to draw out from practitioners what are their key strategic and operational problems. In doing this, because (having employed them) senior management are usually prepared to listen to what they say, consultants can provide the necessary conduit between the top and the bottom of an organisation.

Having said this, it is clear that practitioners who criticise the excessive use of consultants are correct. If senior management actually understood what was important, and could engineer systems of open dialogue and innovation within their companies, they would not need consultants in the first place. The problem is, however, that, because the company itself is a mechanism for the allocation of absolute and relative scarcity, innovation of this type is extremely difficult to achieve. Following this line of reasoning, it becomes obvious why ***empowerment*** has failed in most companies, and why Scott Adams' book, *The Dilbert Principle* (1996), has been a phenomenal best seller.

The reason why ***empowerment*** has a tendency to fail in practice, is because it has been proffered as a solution to business problems by enthusiasts who clearly do not understand the concept of power under conditions of absolute and relative scarcity. Senior and middle level managers control the scarce resources within the company, and they have only risen to the top of their company by understanding how to operate effectively within existing standard operating procedures. While innovation is clearly desirable, it should be recognised that it is also a threat to the current power structure within an organisation. It is probable, therefore, that, in this environment, senior and middle-level managers will only support those new initiatives which provide them with a reasonable opportunity to claim the rewards of success, and which also provide them with the opportunity to displace the consequences of failure on to others. This, it can be argued, is what most human beings will do in situations of scarcity.

As a result, it is clear that the concept of *empowerment* can have at least two meanings.

- *The first is that senior managers actually share their control over scarce resources within the company with their colleagues and employees, and take risks with uncertainty with them.*

- *The second is that senior managers offer employees and colleagues the opportunity to take risks with uncertainty, but fail to provide any real incentives to encourage risk-takers to innovate, while providing very clear penalties for those who take risks and fail.*

In this author's experience, most claims to have introduced *empowerment* are based on the introduction of something defined in the second rather than the first way. This is because it is hardly realistic to expect those who have climbed to the top of the 'greasy pole' of business competition within a company, to share their hard-earned positions of eminence with their juniors. This being the case, it is hardly surprising that the approach does not work. The reason for this conclusion is that it cannot be made to work, because senior managers cannot expect junior managers to take risks, without also providing them with clear incentives.

This also explains why *The Dilbert Principle* has been so successful. Scott Adams provides, in a highly readable and humorous form, a critique of business management 'fads'. In his amusing way, Adams is demonstrating quite forcefully, and with some sophistication, what many practitioners already know. This is the fact that few people in business really have a focus on what they should be doing, and that all too often business practice is simply about managing existing products and services in existing supply chains and markets, within a reactive and risk-averse power structure.

It is this author's view, however, that **empowerment** can be made to work, but only if we understand what it means logically from *first principles*. A *first principles* understanding of empowerment would force us to arrive at a third meaning for the concept, based on the recognition of a number of simple logical premises.

THE FOUR PRINCIPLES OF EMPOWERMENT

- *The company is, and always will be, a device for the effective ownership and control of scarce supply chain resources.*

- *The company, unless it is comprised of a collection of partners, will always be a hierarchical structure, which allocates and manages scarcity within its own boundaries*

- *By definition, the internal corporate power structure should be directed towards the appropriation and accumulation of supply chain value. If it is not, then the company will fail.*

- *Effective management of the power structure in a company, requires that all of the staff within it are empowered by their understanding of the opportunities for, and the potentialities of, effective supply chain leverage.*

This *way of thinking* leads to the conclusion that much of the existing thinking on **empowerment** is misguided. It is wrongly focused on ideas of collaboration and participatory democracy, rather than upon what is essential for business success. This third *way of thinking* about the concept leads to a simple conclusion.

What is critical for business success is the ability of companies to educate (empower) their staff, so that they have the theoretical knowledge of the mechanisms of leverage, as well as a practical understanding of the real opportunities which exist for their effective use in supply chains, so that they can take appropriate risks with uncertainty.

The way in which this *way of thinking* about **business praxis** can be operationalised is discussed in the next section.

Business Praxis and the Four Dimensions of Supply

In the previous section, the weakness of a primary focus on the effective management of current products and services, in the context of supply chain alignment, was outlined. In this discussion, it was argued that there is a need to develop a *way of thinking about effective leverage,* which focuses both on the management of what is, and what should or could be. Business success, it was argued, must ultimately be about managing this dualism, because companies must survive today, as well as be able to seek out the opportunities for sustained value appropriation and accumulation in the future. The problem, however, is that this is not easy to achieve, particularly when many practitioners do not really understand the entrepreneurial basis of business success.

As the author has argued throughout this volume, the basis for business success is not fundamentally different for existing and for new supply chain products or services, whatever practitioners may believe. Although practitioners appear to believe that there is a difference between what is required for business success in the management of existing products and services and for completely new ones, this can be shown to be a false assumption. Business success for all types of products and services must ultimately be based on the ability of practitioners to do two things.

- **To know and understand the four principles of effective supply chain leverage.**

- **To be prepared to take chances on uncertainty by innovating in the ways in which existing or new products or services are be supplied.**

Knowing these two important things is not, however, enough on its own. Practitioners must also understand that sustainable business success comes from leveraging supply chain resources, in such a way that they become *critical assets*. A *critical asset* is defined in terms of the ownership and/or control of a supply chain resource, so that it provides the basis for relative degrees of permanent or temporary monopoly. In other words, the ownership and/or control of this resource provides the basis for the individual or company to determine the allocation of value in the supply chain, through a process of market closure. It follows, therefore, that practitioners must also understand the bases on which supply chain markets can be closed. Figure 62 provides a summary of the ways in which supply chain markets can be closed.

As we can see, there are four primary mechanisms of monopolistic market closure and a fifth, oligopoly, which provides the basis for a more limited, but still highly beneficial, route to the determination of value allocation within supply chains. The first of the four monopolistic mechanisms of market closure is *legal regulation*. Under this mechanism, it is the granting of a monopoly right to an individual or to a company by a government agency, that has the legitimacy and authority to make such decisions within a given territorial area, which provides the basis for the control or ownership of supply chain resources, so that they can become *critical assets*. In the UK,

Figure 62: Forms of Supply Chain Market Closure

TYPES OF SUPPLY CHAIN MARKET CLOSURE	FORMS OF SUPPLY CHAIN MARKET CLOSURE
1 *LEGAL REGULATION*	The market is restricted by the granting of a legal right to monopoly to an individual or a company by government authority.
2 *NATURAL MONOPOLY*	The structure of the supply chain allows for only one supplier of a product or service on a permanent basis.
3 *RELATIVE SUPERIOR COMPETENCE*	A monopoly achieved by the ability to perform knowable, but difficult to replicate ways of doing things. This eradicates the competition temporarily.
4 *OWNERSHIP OF AN INDUSTRY STANDARD*	The buyers of a product or service consciously or unconsciously decide to create an industry standard by purchasing from only one supplier.
5 *COMPETITIVE OLIGOPOLY*	A collusive cartel, on a formal or informal basis, between horizontal competitors which agrees to restrict competition in order to maintain profit margins.

the awarding of oil drilling licenses in the North Sea would be a classic example of this practice. Once the drilling rights in any section of the North Sea have been granted to one company, then they are not available to any other company for the duration of the license. History is replete with examples of this type of practice. The examples, given earlier, of the British Crown granting trading rights to the Merchant Adventurer companies in the seventeenth century testify to this practice.

In essence the establishment of artificial barriers to trade, which governments create to restrict competition from overseas individuals and companies, is also an example of this practice. This is so, because restrictions on trade are nothing more than an mechanism designed to allow indigenous suppliers to control potentially valuable supply chain resources within national territorial areas. This is clearly a form of protection of a particular supplier's control over supply chain resources, which only exists as a result of the politically induced legal regulation.

Interestingly enough, even privatisation can be seen as the creation of a form of monopoly or oligopoly, if it is not also accompanied by liberalisation. Privatisation, particularly when it involves the sale of supply chain resources which are limited in supply, is nothing more than a legal intervention by the government of a country to pass ownership and control of valuable supply chain resources to private individuals. The ownership and control of these resources, may then allow these individuals to mange them as ***critical supply chain assets.***

The second form of market closure is that which flows from *natural monopoly*. By natural monopoly we mean two things. First, it refers to a situation in which only one supplier is necessary for the effective delivery of a particular product or service. In other words, it makes no sense for some things to be provided by more than one supplier. In the case of a sewage system or a coastal lighthouse, there would be no benefit for an individual or company to compete with the existing supplier over the provision of a similar product or service. The natural monopoly arises as a result of the costs of provision, and the improbability that the costs incurred could ever be recouped satisfactorily if competition took place.

The second form of natural monopoly, resides in the unique talents or abilities of particular human beings. Great artists and performers, like Pavarotti, Picasso, Van Gough, Jack Nicklaus, Michael Jordan, or Pele, have a natural ability which is unique to them and cannot be replicated. It is worth stressing, however, that the possession of talent does not guarantee its owner a reward. Only if the possessor of the talent has the intelligence or the good fortune, to find the appropriate supply chains in which to leverage their talent will value appropriation and accumulation be possible. It is, therefore, not just knowledge or talent which is the key to business success, it is also understanding how to leverage it effectively.

The same message can also be applied to the owners of natural monopolies. Presumably, there must be effective ways in which to leverage and manage natural monopolies to appropriate and accumulate the maximum value from them, as well as less effective ways of doing this. The possession of the natural monopoly, even if it is regulated, will obviously guarantee some minimum levels of value appropriation and accumulation, but mere possession does not guarantee that the owners will automatically reap the full benefits of possession. This will, arguably, depend on their relative competence in managing and leveraging the resources which are available to them.

The role of competence in management is of critical importance in understanding business success. The reason is that there are relatively few opportunities for companies to obtain legal or natural monopolies. In other words, the structures of supply chains do not provide a large number of opportunities for individuals or companies to own and/or control resources which have the structural potential to be unique. The reason for this is that most natural monopolies are either site-specific or human-specific. By site-specific we mean that the natural monopoly resides in the locational properties of the supply chain (as in the case of the construction of the sewage system, or the fact that we do not need two railways systems running alongside one another, or the fact that we are unlikely to build more than one tunnel across the English Channel). The human-specific nature of natural monopoly should be clear from the earlier discussion of individual talent and ability.

In both cases it is clear that, while we can know what it is that provides the relative monopoly for the individual or for the company, it is not possible (or only with very great difficulty) for us to replicate and compete against the monopoly. These conditions for market closure are, in fact, structurally quite distinct and are not the basis on which most business success is founded. This is because most things which individuals and companies compete over to produce and supply are knowable and, eventually, imitable. The reason for this is that it is very difficult for individuals to control intellectual property. As soon as a *first mover* innovates, then the new product or service is eventually known by everyone else in the industry. Copying and competitive adaptation by all other interested parties is then bound to follow. A contested market will inevitably emerge if there are no significant barriers to market entry.

This is why the most important mechanism for effective market closure, under most conditions, is likely to be that which resides in a *relatively superior competence*. This concept was explained earlier, but it is worth summarising its characteristics again here. By a *relatively superior competence* we mean the ability to build into the standard operating practices of the organisation an understanding of the need to constantly innovate, rather than to rely on the copying or adaptation of what others are doing. This strategic focus will either be directed to finding new operational ways of doing existing things, or of finding completely new products or services to produce and/or supply chains in which to operate. The importance of this focus is that it recognises that individuals and companies need to be constantly aware that sustainable success comes, in the absence of permanent forms of monopoly, from the creation of temporary situations of relative monopoly. In each case, however, the opportunity to appropriate and accumulate value from the supply chain arises from an ability to close markets, and to stop them being contested for as long as possible. IBM's historic and continuing dominance of the mainframe computing supply chain, and Intel's ability to do the same for microprocessors more recently, are good examples of this practice.

There are two other forms of monopoly, or near monopoly, which can be engineered by the conscious actions of individuals and companies operating within the same supply chains. The first of these is the monopoly which arises from the conscious decision by buyers within a supply chain to seek an industry standard. This type of relative monopoly through *ownership of an industry standard* is evident in the way in which Microsoft has built its success. While there are clearly competing products and services in the supply chain, the Microsoft operating system has, through the uncoordinated and unwitting decisions of a multitude of individual buyers, taken on the features of an industry standard.

It is also possible, however, that the creation of an industry standard may result from the conscious actions of a number of buyers. In the North Sea oil industry the major oil exploration companies have, in recent years, worked together to create common industry standards for many of the components which they commonly buy. The rationale here is that by reducing the number of types of components, and by choosing only one of each type, they will be able to force the supply industry to accept one standard. Obviously this could, if the buyers do not continue to coordinate their actions, lead to one supply company, with a *relatively superior competence*, owning and controlling the new industry standard.

The final form of market closure is not a monopoly as such, but a hybrid of it. This is the market structure known as *oligopoly*. Under oligopoly, the continuous pursuit of aggressive competition in a contested market results in a recognition by the major players who control a substantial share of the market, that there is little to be gained from zero-sum conflict. The reason for this is that the competitors find it difficult to create a *relatively superior competence*, and, as a result, have to pass more and more of the value in the supply chain to the customer.

This being the case, the major players in the market informally (or in some cases formally through cartels) agree not to compete, but instead to rig the market so that they can all retain an acceptable profit margin. There is evidence that this practice is rife in many areas of business, and that it is the natural tendency in particular types of supply chains. These are those supply chains in which there is little scope for the development of innovative intellectual property, and where the contested markets which have formed have become increasingly concentrated, with high barriers to market entry and expensive sunk costs in production and logistical delivery.

The problem for the practitioner who seeks business success, however, is that knowing the bases on which markets can be closed is not sufficient. While it is a necessary part of the development of business competence, on its own it is of little value. For a knowledge of the mechanisms of market closure to be truly useful it must also be linked, as Figure 63 indicates, to a knowledge of *the four principles of effective leverage* which were discussed in the previous chapter.

Unfortunately, knowing both of these things is not sufficient for the achievement of sustainable business success. To achieve business success a knowledge of the capabilities of market closure and effective leverage is necessary, but practitioners

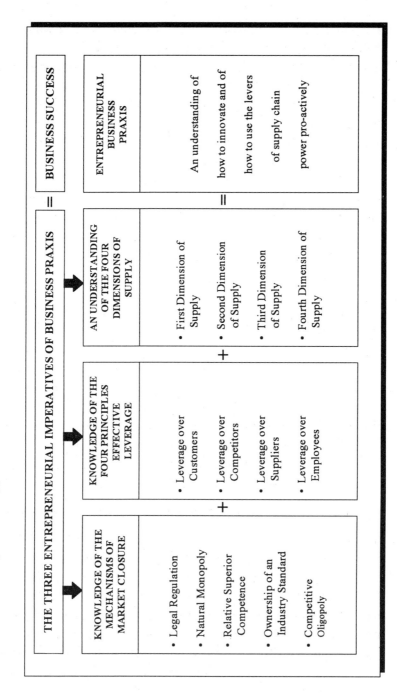

Figure 63: An Entrepreneurial Approach to Business Praxis

must also focus these two capabilities on specific supply chain realities and opportunities. What practitioners must understand, therefore, is how to think pro-actively about the dynamic nature of supply chain management under dynamic circumstances. How can this pro-active *way of thinking* be operationalised?

Figure 64 provides an overview of how this pro-active *way of thinking* can be operationalised. It provides a summary of **the four dimensions of supply**. It is important to know that there are four ways of thinking about supply, because much of the current thinking in business management fails to recognise that there are different ways in which supply chains can be characterised. As the discussion below will demonstrate, a pro-active approach to business success is only really achievable if we recognise two things.

- *It is necessary to understand the four dimensions of supply, and to develop guides to strategic and operational practice which incorporate all of them.*

- *It is also necessary to recognise that an entrepreneurial approach can only be achieved if we start from an understanding of the fourth rather than from the first dimension of supply.*

This sounds complicated, but it is, in fact, not as difficult to grasp operationally as it may at first appear. The best way to understand each of these insights is to define what each of *the four dimensions of supply* means, and to explain the ways in which each one of them is important, and how having a knowledge of each of them can contribute to business success.

In most of the literature written about purchasing and supply

Figure 64: The Four Dimensions of Supply

THE DIMENSIONS OF SUPPLY	FOCUS OF ENQUIRY	INTELLECTUAL AND EPISTEMOLOGICAL FOCUS	KEY OPERATIONAL QUESTIONS	POWER AND BOUNDARY OF THE FIRM FOCUS
① THE FIRST DIMENSION OF SUPPLY	Existing organisational products and/ or services	Descriptive and reactive to existing supply chain and market offerings	• How can existing suppliers be leveraged? • How can existing products be aligned with supply chains appropriately? • How can margins be improved for existing products?	• The existing observable power structure is taken for granted • Leverage is focused on bargaining and negotiation • The existing boundaries of the firm are fixed
② THE SECOND DIMENSION OF SUPPLY	The total structure of the supply chain, incorporating and co-ordinating the network of suppliers in the chain	Descriptive but also prescriptive in relation to existing supply chain and market offerings	• How can value be delivered to the customer more effectively? • How can trust and collaboration be built? • How can virtual organisations be maintained?	• The existing observable power structure is taken for granted but modification is attempted • Leverage is focused on collaboration • The existing boundaries of the firm may become relatively porous and flexible
③ THE THIRD DIMENSION OF SUPPLY	The existing structure of power in the total supply and value chain, and the contested supply chain markets	Descriptive but with an analytic focus on the structure of power in the existing ownership and control of supply chain resources	• Who has power over supply chain resources and value? • Which supply chain resources are critical assets? • What are the current levels of margins and monopoly in the supply chain?	• The existing observable power structure and structural properties of supply related to value appropriation and accumulation are the focus for analysis • Leverage is not an issue • The existing boundaries of the firm are accepted
④ THE FOURTH DIMENSION OF SUPPLY	The potentiality for re-ordering supply chain resources in such a way to provide greater functionality to customers, while changing the existing configuration of power in the chain through a critical asset focus	Analytic and prescriptive focus on the importance of understanding which supply chain resources provide the basis for innovation over functionality and supply chain power	• How can existing supply chain power be reconfigured? • What is the functionality which the supply chain delivers? • Which innovative supply chain resources will allow us to create critical supply chain assets in the future?	• The existing power structure is the subject of strategic innovation and realignment • The boundaries of the firm are contingent and will be determined by entrepreneurial action using the four principles of effective leverage

management, or logistics, the primary focus of enquiry is on the description of the current products or services which the individual or the company buys. The key operational questions are about how the existing supply base can be more effectively managed, through the proper alignment of existing management procedures and operational tools and techniques. This is the *way of thinking* which was criticised earlier in this chapter, when we discussed *purchasing portfolio analysis* and the work of Fisher on product and supply chain alignment.

This is not to argue, however, that properly segmenting what is currently bought, or describing the existing supply market systematically, cannot have significant benefits for companies. Indeed, one could go further and argue that, in the majority of companies of which the author has had experience, the general level of competence of the personnel, and the general level of sophistication of corporate operational tools and techniques, is extremely low. The tools and techniques which are commonly used to describe the existing structures of supply chains, and to segment the existing purchasing spend, are either rudimentary or, in many cases, completely lacking.

Thus, it is not surprising that *purchasing portfolio analysis* and Fisher's product and supply chain alignment techniques appear to many practitioners to be revolutionary. Since they are operating without a proper understanding of what is a professional approach to external resource management, any tool or technique which appears to offer a way of thinking logically will be picked upon as if it were the answer to all of their problems. The difficulty is that most practitioners do not appear to know what a professional tool-kit for buying, or for managing external resources effectively, should look like.

This criticism is not just directed at the procurement and purchasing departments in companies, but is also directed at those senior and middle managers in functional departments which have significant levels of external spend. It is also directed at those senior and middle managers whose departments act as specifiers for those functional departments which must eventually buy goods and services operationally. It is also directed at the most senior managers who undertake strategic make-buy decisions, or who outsource existing skills and capabilities, without understanding the structure of existing supply markets, To assist those who do not know what a professional approach to external resource management should entail, Figure 65 provides a list of ten of the key operational tools in buying and external resource management, which all competent companies should have in place throughout the business.

Figure 65: *Ten Professional Tools and Techniques for Buying and External Resource Management.*

- Purchasing Portfolio Analysis
- Product and Supply Chain Alignment Analysis
- Quotation Analysis
- Competition and Enquiry Analysis
- Purchase Price and Cost Analysis
- Negotiation Planning and Conditioning Analysis
- Purchase Price Forecasting Analysis
- Collaboration Analysis
- Relational Competence Analysis
- Effective Leverage Analysis

Each of these tools and techniques is valuable. Each one can provide ways of thinking and check-lists for action which, if internalised and operationalised, will assist practitioners in managing external resources more effectively. This is both the strength and the weakness of this *first dimensional way of thinking* about supply.

> • *The first dimension of supply provides a clear descriptive focus on the existing products and services which are purchased, given the current boundary of the firm within the supply market. This way of thinking is, however, essentially reactive to the existing structure of power within the supply chain.*
>
> • *As a result, it provides no basis for an holistic approach to strategy and operational practice, other than through the more effective leverage of the existing products and services offered by current suppliers in supply chain markets.*

If this is both the strength and the weakness of the *first dimension of supply,* what does the *second dimension of supply* offer which the first does not? It is apparent that in recent writings, particularly those associated with the work of Womack and Jones (1990 & 1996) on *lean enterprise* and of Lamming (1993) on *lean supply,* an attempt has been made to demonstrate the utility for business success of conceiving of supply in a more comprehensive manner. This *way of thinking* argues that the key to business success is to recognise the importance of the totality of the supply chain, from the end consumer to the initial raw material supplier.

In this conception, the supply chain is seen as the mechanism by which value is added to the end customer, and business success is achieved through the ability of a network of companies to recognise their coincidence of interest. It is argued that, by recognising this coincidence of interest, and by collaborating together to take waste out of the system, a more efficient total supply chain can be constructed. The key to success in this *way of thinking*, is, then, the ability of the network of companies (a virtual company) to construct a more efficient supply chain then their direct competitors, in order to win a larger share of volume in the market.

This is an interesting approach to supply chain thinking, and one which goes further than **the first dimension of supply** in developing our understanding of business success, but it can be criticised on a number of grounds. The first criticism is that it is still a descriptive way of looking at supply chains, which fundamentally fails to challenge the existing structure of power within them. This means that it cannot be regarded as a properly *entrepreneurial way of thinking* about business success. The reason is that the current boundaries of the firm are taken for granted.

The basic task of business management in this approach, therefore, is simply for network partners to recognise their existing positions of relative dependence or domination, and to commit themselves to the maintenance of these positions. This raises the interesting question of who in the supply chain will act as the engine of innovation? If waste is to be taken out of the chain to delight the end consumer, then somebody's profit margins must be eradicated, or at least severly squeezed. This is because, logically, supply chain waste must surely be some other company's profitability.

This is not to argue, however, that this approach is necessarily wrong. Rather, it is to argue that this can be a highly appropriate way of leveraging suppliers, customers and competitors under the right conditions. What this *way of thinking* demonstrates is that it is possible to describe the existing structure of relationships in the supply chain and, by adopting a collaborative approach, encourage a network of players in the chain to recognise their coincidence of interest, in such a way that the network begins to leverage the supply chain pro-actively. This can be a powerful mechanism for value delivery to customers, particularly if it operates within high volume, low variety process supply chains, in which there is regular spend on relatively standard items. As was argued in the last chapter, however, this is not what the structure of all supply chains looks like, and this approach cannot be a satisfactory basis for thinking entrepreneurially in all supply chains.

- *__The second dimension of supply__ provides a clear focus on the description of the total supply chain. It also provides a pro-active and collaborative approach to the realignment of wasteful supply chain relationships and practices, amongst a network of existing suppliers of products and services.*

- *This way of thinking is still, however, reactive to the existing structure of power and the current products and services in the supply chain. It, therefore, fails the test of a properly holistic approach to the entrepreneurial management of effective leverage in all supply chains. This is because it tends to work best in process-based supply chains, with a dominant player shaping and leading innovation.*

What stands out in both the first and the second dimensions, is their descriptive rather than analytical methodological approach. Clearly, both approaches do not fully explain or analyse the power structures which run through supply chains. The first dimension is only concerned with the relative power of the buyer in relation to the existing supply market. The second dimension goes beyond this, and focuses on the totality of the network of relationships within which any supply offering has to be made. Nevertheless, even the second dimension still takes the existing power structure as given, and merely attempts to create a collaborative approach to leverage, presumably against those who are the weakest in the chain.

This myopia about *the dynamics of power within supply relationships* is the most telling criticism which can be levelled at both the first and second dimensions of supply. If the arguments presented in this volume have been accepted, then it should be clear that, business success must ultimately be about *changing the existing balance of forces* within a supply chain in favour of the entrepreneurial company. To change the balance of forces means that entrepreneurial individuals and companies must understand what is the current structure of power in a supply chain. This structure of power, moreover, will not simply be a statement about the relationships of dominance and dependence which exist between any company and its suppliers.

On the contrary, to understand the existing structure of power within a supply chain, it is necessary to describe the relative power of companies as they are involved in reciprocal buying and supplying relationships, as well as the other three aspects of power which flow from **the four principles of effective leverage**. To include all four principles one would, therefore, need to consider supplier power, as well as the relationships which each company has with its own customers, its relative power in the market with horizontal competitors, and its own relationships with its employees. Only by understanding each of these types of relationships, is it possible to fully comprehend the structure of power within companies and within the supply chains in which they are embeded.

The reason for this is that when one talks about power in supply chain, one is really describing the ability of individuals or companies to create for themselves situations in which the ownership and/or control of particular supply chain resources can be achieved. If individuals or companies are able to own and/or control supply chain resources in such a way that they have a high degree of monopoly control over them, then, by definition, they will have supply chain power. This power will be demonstrated by their ability to determine the flow and allocation of value in the chain, and by their ability to maintain a continuous basis for value appropriation and accumulation in the form of sustainably high profit margins.

The ***third dimension of supply*** provides an analysis of the structure of power within the value chain which operates in parallel with the physical supply chain. It is a way of analysing, as well as a way of describing, *who gets what, where, how and when* in the scramble for allocative scarcity within the existing supply chain.

- ***The third dimension of supply*** *provides a clear descriptive and analytical focus on the power structures which exist in existing supply and value chains.*

- *This descriptive approach also provides a mechanism which allows us to understand, analytically, what is the fundamental basis for individual and corporate profitability.*

- *This way of thinking leads one to the conclusion that relatively high profit margins for individuals and companies will always be based on the ability of supply chain participants to own and/or control supply chain resources, through the use of the four principles of effective leverage, in such a way that they can be turned into critical assets.*

The third dimension provides a *way of thinking* about supply chains which lifts the veil of power, by focusing on the reality of the structures of dominance and dependence in business relationships. Despite this analytical strength, it is still primarily a descriptive way of looking at current power structures in existing supply chains and markets, and, as a result, cannot provide the pro-active approach to supply management which business strategy requires. By analysing what the existing structure of power is in the supply and value chain, however, it provides an important *under-labour* for what becomes possible when **supply chain functionality** has been understood.

In order to properly develop a pro-active and analytical approach to entrepreneurial business management, it is necessary to understand, from first principles, what supply and value chains provide. In this light, it is important to recognise the significance of *the functionality* which supply chains provide to customers. While supply chains obviously do deliver products and services to the customer, this is not what they fundamentally provide. In the abstract, it can be argued that what supply chains really provide is *functionality*. By *functionality*, one simply means that supply chains provide the capacity to satisfy particular human needs (essential things which are necessary for survival) or wants (things which are not necessary for survival, but which are valued because they have a utility, or are scarce, or both).

The important thing to understand about *functionality*, however, is that while the basis on which the *functionality* of things is founded (i.e. *the capacity to deliver a particular valued outcome*) does not change very much over time, the specific products or services which can be provided to satisfy this need do change as a result of innovations in technology. People buy things, therefore, to satisfy their desire for *functionality*—this does not change. But the ways in which this *functionality* can be delivered to the consumer do change as technology and supply chain configurations are realigned.

Generally speaking, therefore, human beings will have a high propensity to buy those things which provide the *functionality* they require, especially if the *functionality* can be provided either at lower cost, or with improved quality for the same price, or, preferably, at a lower price with an improved quality.

If we adopt this *way of thinking,* it is possible to argue that the basis for sustainable business success is relatively easy to understand. All that practitioners must understand is that the basis for all business success is the capacity to satisfy **supply chain functionality** more effectively than competitors. If practitioners can discover new ways of satisfying the existing requirements for a particular level of functional quality in a cheaper way, or if they can provide a more efficient and cheaper way of delivering the existing *functionality*, then they will be successful. A simple example will explain this insight.

Before IBM discovered that it was possible to process information in a complex and sophisticated way using mainframe technology, the same information had still been processed, but by other means. IBM did not change the functionality of supply. On the contrary, there had always been a demand for information processing. IBM merely found a more efficient way of delivering this service to the consumer, and, presumably, at a higher level of quality and a lower cost than before. If it had not been able to do this, then it is debatable whether it would have been able to make a profit and remove the majority of its competitors who were still using the old technology, from the supply chain.

What IBM achieved was the effective closure of the market to other potential suppliers, by developing a **relatively superior competence** in the delivery of corporate information processing. IBM was able to stop, in most cases at least, a contested market operating and, as a result, it became a relative monopolist and one of the most successful companies in the history of the world. Interestingly enough, despite its recent corporate crises over the failure to achieve the same monopoly control in the PC market, IBM has survived, largely as a result of the perpetuation of this relative monopoly in the mainframe supply chain, and by leveraging off this by diversifying into the business solutions business. There is an interesting lesson here, for those interested in sustainable business success. The lesson is clear.

- *The essential key to business success is the capacity to understand supply chain functionality, and then to devise a corporate strategy which will allow the individual, or the company, to eradicate competition.*

- *This market closure is achieved by focusing on improvements in the cost and quality of a particular functionality, in order that, given the current state of intellectual knowledge about the delivery of any given functionality, a relative or absolute monopoly position can be engineered in a supply chain.*

- *This is the perspective which is adopted when the way of thinking which is associated with <u>the fourth dimension of supply</u> is understood.*

This leads to a general conclusion about how business success is achieved entrepreneurially:

> *Entrepreneurial business success is, essentially, based on an analytic way of thinking about functionality, which allows the individual, or the company, to create new supply chains, or to pro-actively restructure the current configuration of power within an existing supply chain, through the effective leverage of innovations in intellectual property.*

It should be obvious to those who have come this far, that this fourth dimensional *way of thinking* about supply provides the basis for the operationalisation of *the four principles of effective leverage*. This *way of thinking* focuses on the need to conceive of strategy as the development of a process by which individuals understand how to innovate with supply chain functionality. Operational practice is then the process by which a strategic vision about functional innovation is implemented, within the existing structure of power which is embedded in a particular supply chain. The goal of operational implementation is, therefore, to completely reconfigure power relationships in the supply chain through the use of the *four principles of effective leverage*, in such a way that the individual or the company becomes a permanent or a temporary monopolist of *critical supply chain assets*.

There is one final point to make here, however, which is of great significance for those who seek to align strategic and operational practices for business success through an innovative and entrepreneurial focus on supply chain resources. It is absolutely essential for practitioners to differentiate between *product innovation, process innovation and supply chain innovation* when operationalising business praxis. These three different types of innovation can be defined easily enough.

PRODUCT INNOVATION

Refers to that process by which, through the invention of new products (or services) to satisfy an existing supply functionality, the current structure of power (value allocation) within a supply chain can be reconfigured, in favour of the owner or controller of the new product (or service), by the use of the four principles of effective leverage to create a new critical supply chain asset.

PROCESS INNOVATION

Refers to that mechanism by which, through the invention of new ways of organising the systems and patterns of working with existing products and services, a more efficient way of delivering the existing functionality in the supply chain is devised. Those who possess, or have access to, the knowledge about this way of working will be able to reconfigure the current structure of power (value allocation) within an existing supply chain, by the use of the four principles of effective leverage to create a new critical supply chain asset.

SUPPLY CHAIN INNOVATION

This can take two forms:

Supply Chain Replacement

The first form refers to that process by which the invention of a completely new way of delivering an existing supply functionality creates the opportunity to deliver the desired functionality in such a significantly radical way that a completely new supply chain can be created. In this process, the new product or process invention has such an major impact on the costs and quality, by which the functionality of supply to customers is delivered, that the existing supply chain is almost wholly, or completely, eradicated. The power structure is not so much reconfigured as destroyed by the creation of a completely new structure of power (value allocation). A new power structure is created based on a new set of critical supply chain assets, which can be used to appropriate and accumulate value from the new supply chain, using the four principles of effective leverage.

Supply Chain Invention

The second form refers to that process by which, in the natural development of society, opportunities arise for entrepreneurial individuals and companies to create completely new supply chain functionalities. Through the natural and entrepreneurially dynamic process by which existing supply functionalities are delivered—by changes in products and processes and supply chains—opportunities for the creation of new supply functionalities arise. These will be created by entrepreneurs seeing things which others cannot, and by there willingness to take risks with uncertainty. If such an entrepreneurially created new supply functionality generates a sufficient level of demand when it is offered to potential customers, then it is likely that a new way of appropriating and accumulating value will have been invented. This outcome creates a new supply chain, which will have a prevailing power structure (system of value allocation) based on the effective leverage of the current ownership and/or control of the critical supply chain assets.

This fourfold differentiation of forms of innovation is a simple enough point to make, but it is important nonetheless. The reason for this is because many practitioners do not appear to understand that, as a source of sustainable business success, a focus on *product* or *process innovation* is often far less valuable than *supply chain innovation*. This is not to argue that *product innovation* and *process innovation* within an existing supply chain cannot lead to success. Rather, it is to argue that practitioners often ignore the significant improvements to value accumulation which can flow from *supply chain innovation*.

A few examples will make this point clear. In the Britain in the early nineteenth century the followers of Ned Ludd (the Luddites)—who were hand-loom weavers—smashed the power-looms which, at that time, were being introduced into factories to weave cloth. The reason why they did this was obvious: the new product (the power-loom) destroyed the basis by which the hand-loom weavers appropriated and accumulated value from the supply chain. The new invention made their skills uneconomic and largely redundant. The Luddites smashed machines in the forlorn hope that they could continue to appropriate material wealth from the supply chain as they had always done so in the past.

They failed because, in a society predicated on the private ownership of property rights, and pursuing a policy of support for unbridled competition and the maximum individual appropriation of value, the coercive monopoly of violence (which resides within the State) was ranged against the Luddites. Their attempt to destroy the deleterious consequences of *product* and *process innovation* in their supply chain led to the introduction of new laws, which could impose imprisonment and, in some cases, execution for the smashing of machines. It also led, between 1812 and the early 1820s, to the armed forces being used to quell recurrent outbreaks of Luddism in Britain.

There can be little doubt, however, that it was the innovation in the means of production that the power-loom and the factory system instituted, which fundamentally changed the balance of power within the cloth weaving supply chain. The small, home-based hand-loom weavers could no longer compete against the new, products (power-looms) and large-scale production processes (factory systems). However, it is worth making the point that this competitive conflict between groups attempting to claim a right to appropriate value in the supply chain did not change the functionality of supply. There had always been a need for woven material for clothing; the power-loom and the factory system simply provided the basis for a new and more efficient way of supplying what had traditionally been required in an existing supply chain. This is, then, an historic example of *product and process innovation within an existing supply chain functionality*.

Product and *process innovation* around an existing supply functionality can, therefore, have a profound effect on the balance of power over the allocation of value within an existing supply chain. It is clear, also, that this effect will only ever occur if someone takes a risk with uncertainty, within the existing supply chain, and innovates to create new processes and products. As important as this *product* and *process innovation* may have been in the case of the Luddites, and as it continues to be for millions of people around the world today, it is, arguably, less significant as a mechanism for sustainable business success than supply chain innovation. As Figure 66 indicates supply chain innovation can, potentially, be more valuable than *product* or *process innovation*.

As the Figure demonstrates there are two forms which supply chain innovation can take. It can take the form of *supply chain replacement* or *supply chain invention*. *Supply chain replacement* refers to that process by which a completely new way of supplying an existing supply chain functionality is created. In doing so the existing structure of power within the current supply chain is destroyed and replaced by a new power structure. In the new power structure the appropriation, accumulation and allocation of value is now determined by the new owners and/or controllers of the **critical supply chain**

Figure 66: The Life-Cycle of Product, Process and Supply Chain Innovation

TYPES OF INNOVATION	THE LIFE-CYCLE OF INNOVATION		
	EMERGENCE	GROWTH AND MATURITY	DECLINE
PRODUCT INNOVATION	A new product destroys the existing balance of value allocation in the supply chain. A temporary monopoly for one, or a few, suppliers is provided.	A frenzy of imitation by competitors reduces the monopoly control of critical supply chain assets by one, or a few, suppliers.	A new product, process or supply chain begins to destroy the existing balance of power over value in the supply chain.
PROCESS INNOVATION	New products and ways of working destroy the existing balance of value allocation in the supply chain. A temporary monopoly for one, or a few, suppliers is provided.	A frenzy of imitation by competitors reduces the monopoly control of critical supply chain assets by one, or a few, suppliers.	A new process, product or supply chain begins to destroy the existing balance of power over value in the supply chain.
SUPPLY CHAIN REPLACEMENT	A series of product or process innovations creates an opportunity to completely reconfigure the way in which an existing functionality is provided	The new supply chain destroys the old supply chain, and gives first movers the chance to monopolise critical assets. Competition based on imitation and adaptation will ensue if it is possible.	New product or process innovation may modify the power in the value chain. The real threat comes from the emergence of a new supply chain.
SUPPLY CHAIN INVENTION	A new functionality emerges out of entrepreneurial risk taking. A completely new supply chain is created.	First movers have the chance to monopolise scarce supply chain resources as critical assets before a contested market forms.	New product or process innovation may modify the power in the value chain. The real threat comes from the emergence of a new supply chain.

assets. These may be very different supply chain resources than those which they have replaced. The replacement of the inland waterways, as a means of delivering a supply functionality associated with the movement of goods and people, by the railway system in the middle of nineteenth century in Britain is a classic example of this process at work.

Supply chain invention refers to that process by which, through the dynamic interaction of innovations in products and processes in existing supply chains, entrepreneurial individuals see opportunities to create completely new supply functionalities. In this process the individual sees the scope for value appropriation and accumulation from the creation of a completely new supply offering to potential consumers. Having made this offering, and having discovered that an effective level of demand exists, a new supply chain can be created. The development of the travel agency business by Thomas Cook, which was mentioned earlier, is a classic example of this phenomenon.

Thomas Cook saw that the development of a leisured class of individuals, with high levels of accumulated and disposable wealth, would require alternative forms of diversion. The opening-up of the Continent of Europe by the steam-packet ship and the railway provided the technological means for Cook to see the possibilities for a new supply functionality, which could be serviced by a completely new physical supply chain. Cook invented the supply functionality and its physical chain. He was not, however, able to monopolise it and competitors quickly created a contested market, as they imitated and adapted his original idea.

Clearly, although Thomas Cook was not able to do so, in such a new supply chain the possibilities for individuals and companies to seize first mover advantages, and to control and own *critical supply chain assets* as monopolists, will be more readily available than in supply chains where a contested market is already in place. This is because, in an emerging supply chain the significance of any new supply offering to other potential, or actual, competitors will not be so readily apparent as it would be in an existing supply chain, which was merely experiencing *product* or *process innovation*. In such a supply chain there is, on the other hand, a much greater likelihood for a *frenzy of imitation* to occur, whenever a new *product* or *process innovation* is introduced. The reason for this is because, particularly in the growth and maturity stages of the *product* or *process innovation* life-cycle, it is much more likely that a contested market will already have developed.

It follows, therefore, that practitioners must be aware of the importance of the criticality of supply chains assets, and of the principles of effective leverage and entreprepreneurial action. But, they must also be aware of the properties of supply chains, and the way in which *product, process* and *supply chain innovation* can significantly constrain, or open-up opportunities, for value appropriation. Whichever of the four approaches to innovation a practitioner decides to focus upon, it is important that they also recognise the need to develop strategic and operational methodologies, which allow them to understand the processes through which products, processes and supply chains emerge, grow, mature and decline.

Only by understanding, in this way, the innovative life-cycle of products, and of supply chains, will practitioners be able to develop an appropriate understanding of the the possibilities for the monopoly control and ownership of supply chain resources. By being able to understand the life-cycles of products, processes and supply chains it will also be possible for practitioners to focus their operational practices appropriately on the *four principles of effective leverage*. If they can achieve this then it will be easier for them to become relative monopolists of those **critical supply chain assets** which they have the skills, capabilities and financial resources to own and control.

Having this knowledge and understanding ought to provide practitioners with the necessary skills and capabilities to allow them to develop the ***nous*** to be able to compete successfully for a share of absolute and relative material scarcity. Unfortunately, because scarcity exists, not everyone who competes can expect to achieve business success. Only those who have ***relatively superior competence***, or who are able to own or control ***structural supply chain assets***, will be assured of winning a significant share of the material wealth (value) which is allocated through competition and the pursuit of individual self-interest.

The only mechanism by which these forces of monopoly can be controlled is, of course, through the effective regulation of private action, within specific territorial areas of the world. This, of course, requires a capacity for collective political action and an ability to arrive at a consensus over the allocation of absolute and relative scarcity. This has never been achieved satisfactorily by human beings. It seems inevitable, therefore, that, in the absence of this consensus, control over the allocation of material scarcity will remain a primarily private rather than public phenomenon. This being the case, it can be argued that those who have a knowledge and an understanding of the conditions under which business success can be achieved will have an advantage over other human beings in the constant material war of each against all. The only way of avoiding this state of nature is to decide, either to opt out of the contest and to be satisfied with spiritual rather than material rewards, or to pursue the political solution which has, so far, eluded mankind.

Conclusions: The Way Forward for Strategy and Operational Practice

It follows from everything that has been said above, that many practitioners (and the companies for which they work) do not really understand what are the ways in which business success is achieved. Similarly, because of the epistemological and theoretical myopia which characterises much of the academic community's analysis of business issues, the failure by practitioners to be able to think about what is appropriate under specific supply chain circumstances, is compounded. This being the case it is necessary to spell out what might be done to rectify this malaise.

The most important thing that can be done is to encourage practitioners and academics alike to focus more effectively on supply chain and leverage *ways of thinking*. Only in this way will it be possible for us to understand what it is that needs to be done to provide the conditions for sustainable business success. Relatedly, as was outlined at the outset, it is necessary for people to begin to recognise their own ignorance (or, if you prefer, their lack of enlightenment). Only through a willingness to recognise one's own ignorance, is it possible to begin the process of developing knowledge and understanding.

This being the case, and because the author believes that there will be sufficient practitioners and academics who understand that the possession of a better *way of thinking* about causality will provide them with a competitive advantage, it is proposed that the best way to demonstrate how the ideas introduced in this volume can be operationalised is through a series of **Ways of Thinking Workshops**. Those interested in learning more about these workshops, or the ideas in this volume, should contact the author at the address over the page for more information:

Professor Andrew Cox,
CSPM,
Birmingham Research Park,
University of Birmingham,
Birmingham, B15 2SQ, UK.

Email: a.w.cox@bham.ac.uk

or,

Email: andrewcox.associates@btinternet.com

or,

on the Internet at:

http://www.btinternet.com/~business.success
http://www.btinternet.com/~andrewcox.associates

Bibliography

Adams, S. (1996), *The Dilbert Principle: A Cubicle's Eye View of Bosses, Meetings, Management Fads and Other Workplace Afflictions*, New York, Harper Collins.

Ansoff, H.I. (1965), 'The Firm of the Future', *Harvard Business Review*, (September /October), pp. 162-78.

Ansoff, H.I. (1988), *Corporate Strategy*, Harmondsworth: Penguin.

Aristotle. (1983), *The Politics*, Harmondsworth: Penguin.

Brandenburger, A.M. and Nalebuff, B.J. (1996), *Co-opetition*, New York: Doubleday.

Carlisle J. and Parker R. (1989), *Beyond Negotiation: Redeeming Customer-Supplier Relationships*, Chichester: J.Wiley & Sons.

Coase, R.H. (1937), 'The Nature of the Firm', *Economica* (N.S.), 4 386-405 (November).

Cox, A. (1996a), 'Relational Competence and Strategic Procurement Management: Towards an Entrepreneurial and Contractual Theory of the Firm', *European Journal of Purchasing and Supply Management*, 2(1), pp.57-70

Cox, A. (ed.), (1996b), *Innovations in Procurement Management*, Boston, UK: Earlsgate Press.

Cox, A. (1996c), 'The Strategic Options Facing the Firm in the 1990s: Competing on Efficient Operations, Core Competencies, Lean Enterprise or Relational Competence', *Proceedings of the Institute of Operations Management Conference: The Way Forward Through Operations Management*, (NEC, Birmingham, 5th/6th June 1996), Coventry: The Institute of Operations Management., pp.149-166.

Cox, A., Furlong, P. and Page, E. (1986), *Power in Capitalist Society: Theory Explanations and Cases*, Brighton: Wheatsheaf Books.

Cox, A & Hines, P. (eds.),(1997) *Advanced Supply Management: The Best Practice Debate*, Boston, UK: Earlsgate Press.

Fisher, M.L.(1997), 'What is the Right Supply Chain for Your Product?', *Harvard Business Review*, pp.105-116. (March/April).

Hannah, L, (1997 forthcoming), 'Marshall's Trees and the Global 'Forest': Were Giant Redwoods Different?', in Lamoureux, N., Raff. D & Temin, P (eds.), Title Unknown , Chicago: Chicago University Press.

Hamel, G and Prahalad, C.K. (1990), 'The Core Competence of the Corporation', *Harvard Business Review* (May-June), pp.79-91.

Hamel, G and Prahalad, C.K. (1993), 'Strategy as Stretch and Leverage', *Harvard Business Review*, (March/April), pp.75-84.

Hamel, G and Prahalad, C.K. (1994), *Competing for the Future*, Cambridge Mass.: Harvard Business School Press.

Hammer , M. (1996), *Beyond Re-engineering*, London: Harper-Collins.

Hammer, M. & Champy, J. (1993), *Re-engineering the Corporation: A Manifesto for Business Revolution,* London: Nicholas Brealey.

Hayek, F.A.,von (1948), *Individualism and Economic Order*, Chicago: Chicago University Press.

Hayek, F.A., von, (1978), *New Studies in Philosophy, Politics and Economics*, London: Routledge & Kegan Paul.

Hines, P. (1994), *Creating World Class Suppliers*, London: Financial Times/ Pitmans.

Kay, J. (1994), *Foundations of Corporate Success*, Oxford: Oxford University Press.

Kay, J. (1996), *The Business of Economics*, Oxford: Oxford University Press.

Kirzner, I.M. (1973), *Competition and Entrepreneurship*, Chicago: Chicago University Press.

Kirzner, I.M. (1985) *Discovery and the Capitalist Process*, Chicago: Chicago University Press.

Kraljic, P. (1993), 'Purchasing must become Supply Management', *Harvard Business Review,* pp.109-117 (September-October).

Kuhn, T.S. (1962), *The Structure of Scientific Revolutions*, Chicago: Chicago University Press.

Lamming R. (1993), *Beyond Partnership: Strategies for Innovation and Lean Supply.* New Jersey: Prentice Hall.

Lamming R and Cox, A. (eds.), (1995), *Strategic Procurement Management in the 1990s: Concepts and Cases.* Boston, UK: Earlsgate Press.

Lewis, J.D. (1990), *Partnerships for Profit,* New York: Free Press.

Lewis, J.D.(1995), *The Connected Corporation: How Leading Companies Win Through Customer-Supplier Alliances,* New York: Free Press.

Lukes, S. (1977), *Power: A Radical View*, London; Macmillan.

Macbeth, D. and Ferguson, N. (1994), *Partnership Sourcing: An Integrated Supply Chain Approach,* London: Financial Times/Pitman.

Machiavelli, N. (1532), *The Prince,* New York: Mentor Books (1953 edition).

Marx.,K. (1970), *The Communist Manifesto*, Harmondsworth: Penguin.

Marx. K (1984), *Capital: A Critical Analysis of Capitalist Production*, London: Lawrence & Wishart.

Mintzberg, H and Quinn, J.B. (1996), *The Strategy Process: Concepts, Contexts and Cases.* New Jersey: Prentice Hall.

Mises, L. Von, (1949), *Human Action: A Treatiste on Economics*, New Haven: Yale University Press.

Montgomery, C.A. (ed.), (1995), *Resource-Based and Evolutionary Theories of the Firm*, A.H. Dordrecht: Kluwer Academic Publishers.

Moore, J.F. (1996), *The Death of Competition: Leadership and Strategy in the Age of Business EcoSystems*, New York: Harper Business Books.

Olson, M. (1965), *The Logic of Collective Action*, Cambridge, Mass: Harvard University Press.

Penrose, E. (1959), *The Theory of the Growth of the Firm*, Oxford: Oxford University Press.

Peteraf, M.A. (1993), 'The Cornerstones of Competitive Advantage: A Resource Based View', *Strategic Management Journal*, 12: pp.95-117.

Peters, T.J. and Waterman, R.H. (1982), *In Search of Excellence*, New York: Harper & Row.

Porter, M.E. (1979), 'How Competitive Forces Shape Strategy', *Harvard Business Review*, pp.137-145 (March-April).

Porter, M.E. (1980), *Competitive Advantage: Creating and Sustaining Superior Performance*, New York: Free Press.

Porter, M.E. (1985), *Competitive Strategy: Techniques for Analyzing Industries and Competitors*, New York: Free Press.

Porter, M.E. (1996), 'What is Strategy?', *Harvard Business Review*, pp.61-79 (November-December).

Ricardo, D. (1971), *Principles of Political Economy and Taxation*, Harmondsworth: Penguin.

Schumpeter, J.A. (1934), *The Theory of Economic Development*, Cambridge, Mass: Harvard University Press.

Schumpeter. J.A. (1939), Business Cycles, New York: McGraw Hill.

Schumpeter, J.A. (1950), *Capitalism, Socialism and Democracy*, London: Allen & Unwin.

Schumpeter, J.A. (1954), *History of Economic Analysis*, London: Oxford University Press.

Smith A. (1776), *The Wealth of Nations*, Harmondsworth: Penguin, (1985 edition).

Taylor, F.W. (1911), *Principles of Strategic Management*, New York: Harper & Row.

Williamson, O.E. (1975), *Markets and Hierarchies: Analysis and Antitrust Implications*, New York: Free Press.

Williamson, O.E. (1985), *The Economic Institutions of Capitalism: Firms, Markets, Relational Contracting*, New York: Free Press.

Willer, D. and Willer, J. (1973), *Systematic Empiricism: A Critique of a Pseudo-Science*, New Jersey: Prentice Hall.

Womack, J, Jones, D. and Roos, D. (1990), *The Machine That Changed the World*, New York: Rawson Associates.

Womack, J. and Jones, D. (1996), *Lean Thinking: Banish Waste and Create Wealth in Your Organisation,* New York: Simon Schuster.

Advanced Supply Manangement: The Best Practice Debate
edited by Andrew Cox and Peter Hines
(ISBN 1-873439-51-2), 1997, 285 pages.

Strategic Procurement Management in the 1990s: Concepts and Cases
edited by Richard Lamming and Andrew Cox
(ISBN.1-873439-41-5), 1996, 215 pages.

Innovations in Procurement Management
edited by Andrew Cox
(ISBN 1-873439-46-6), 1996, 349 pages.

The European Union at the Crossroads : Problems in Implementing the Single Market Project
edited by Paul Furlong and Andrew Cox
(ISBN 1-873439-16-4), 1995, 227 pages.

Public Procurement in the European Community:
(Series ISBN 1-873439-30-X)

Volume 1: The Single Market Rules and the Enforcement Regime After 1992
by Andrew Cox (ISBN 1-873439-00-8), 1993, 302 pages
Volume 2: A Guide to the Procurement Cases of the Court of Justice
by Sue Arrowsmith (ISBN 1-873439-05-9), 1992, 261 pages
Volume 3: The Texts of the Community Directives
by Andrew Cox and Frances Lamont (ISBN 1-873439-40-7), 1993, 262 pages
Volume 4: Remedies for Enforcing the Public Procurement Rules
by Sue Arrowsmith (ISBN 1-873439-45-8), 1994, 449 pages

Outsourcing: *A Business Guide to Risk Management Tools and Techniques*

by Christopher Lonsdale and Andrew Cox (ISBN 1-873439-61-X), July 1997

The Management of Outsourcing Risk: The Lessons of Experience

by Andrew Cox and Christopher Lonsdale (ISBN 1-873439-66-0), December 1997

ORDERING EARLSGATE BOOKS

To order existing or forthcoming books from Earlsgate Press contact:

Direct at:
> **Earlsgate Press,**
> **The Plantation,**
> **Rowdyke Lane,**
> **Wyberton,**
> **Boston, Lincolnshire,**
> **PE21 7AQ, UK.**
> *Tel:*   *(UK): 01205 350764*
> *Fax:*   *(UK): 01205 359459*
> *Email:*   *earlsgate.press@btinternet.com*
> *Internet:*   *http://www.btinternet.com/~earlsgate.press*

Indirect at:
> All good bookshops in all major countries or through the internet.